City and Islington College

D0308814

331.8809 LVTL
3WEEKS
£7.95

CITY AND ISLINGTON
SIXTH FORM COLLEGE
283-309 GOSWELL ROAD
LONDON EC1V 7LA
TEL 020 7520 0652

British Trade Unionism

c. 1770-1990

A READER IN HISTORY

British Trade Unionism

Unionism

c. 1770–1990

A READER IN HISTORY

Keith Laybourn

Senior Lecturer and Head of the Division of History,
The Polytechnic, Queensgate, Huddersfield

ALAN SUTTON

First Published in the United Kingdom in 1991 by
Alan Sutton Publishing Limited
Phoenix Mill · Far Thrupp · Stroud · Gloucestershire

First Published in the United States of America in 1991 by
Alan Sutton Publishing Inc
Wolfeboro Falls · NH · 03896–0848

Copyright © Keith Laybourn 1991

All rights reserved. No part of this publication may be reproduced,
stored in a retrieval system, or transmitted, in any form, or by any
means, electronic, mechanical, photocopying, recording or otherwise,
without the prior permission of the publishers and copyright holders.

British Library Cataloguing in Publication Data
Laybourn, Keith
British trade unionism c. 1800–1990: a reader in history.
1. Great Britain. Trade unions, history
I. Title
331.880941

ISBN 0–86299–784–4

Library of Congress Cataloging in Publication data applied for

Cover illustration: THE BOSSES' BOGEY Agricultural labourer (to
his mate): 'Beant us a pair of daaft old crows, to be skeered away from
the Union and they good things by that old guy?'
The Daily Herald, 13 March 1914
(courtesy of the Trades Union Congress Library).

Typeset in 10/12 Ehrhardt.
Typesetting and origination by
Alan Sutton Publishing Limited.
Printed and bound in Great Britain by
The Guernsey Press Co. Ltd, Guernsey, Channel Islands.

CONTENTS

PREFACE

The purpose of this collection of documents is to provide the reader with a comprehensive coverage of the main events and developments in trade-union history over the last two and a half centuries. Inevitably, this entails the inclusion of national material, trade-union legislation, Trades Union Congress material, and the like – some of which will obviously have appeared in other publications. Important national events, such as the case of the 'Tolpuddle Martyrs' of 1834, will also have been covered extensively in other forms. Nevertheless, this book offers new sources, as in the case of the Saddleworth weavers, the Glass Bottle Makers of Yorkshire, material on the Clydeside dispute, and the Liverpool material on the General Strike, and much else, which has not been generally available before. It is also the first widely-available document book to attempt to cover such a large period of trade-union history. Most books confine themselves to a swathe of one hundred years, or less, or to a particular theme. The larger stage of this book, by way of contrast, means that students, academics and general readers should have an easy access to the full range of British trade-union history.

In drawing up this collection, several considerations have had to be kept in mind. In the first place, national events and trade-union legislation have had to be included because of their immense importance to the whole history of the trade-union movement. Secondly, an attempt has been made to achieve regional diversity in the material used to enable readers to focus upon the relevant material for their own area. Thirdly, great efforts have been made to ensure that there is industrial diversity in the range of material used – although, obviously, some industries have been more effectively unionized than others throughout their history.

Ultimately, the purpose of this Reader has been to produce a relatively inexpensive publication which offers a comprehensive coverage of British trade-union history, and which illustrates its diversity of approach, industry, region and experience.

NOTE

The documentary material in this Reader is divided into sections which focus on particular periods of British trade-union history. There is a brief introduction to historiography, debates and sources for the study of trade-union history. Thereafter, each chapter is prefaced by a commentary which provides a background to the extracts, with numbers in brackets referring to the documents which follow.

ABBREVIATIONS

AEU	Amalgamated Engineering Union
EETPU	Electrical, Electronic Communication and Plumbing Union
LRC	Labour Representation Committee
NGA	National Graphical Society
NUM	National Union of Mineworkers
OMS	Organization for the Maintenance of Supplies
SOGAT	Society of Graphical and Allied Trades
TUC	Trades Union Congress

INTRODUCTION

The emergence of the trade-union movement has been one of the most significant events in recent British history, not least because for almost three centuries unions have normally been rejected, both formally and informally, by the state and employers who have seen them as dangerous organizations which threaten the free operation of the market and prevent much needed technological change. In recent years unions have been considered to be a major reason for the 'British disease' of industrial decline and stagnation. Perhaps only during the First World War, the Second World War and the years between 1945 and the early 1970s have there been any major honeymoon periods between trade unions, employers and government – even though many unions have enjoyed good long-standing relations with their employers through established negotiating arrangements. At the present time, the consensus gone, they are once again seen as being in conflict with the aims of the state – a situation which has led to the imposition of restrictions on their freedom of action and to a substantial decline in membership.

The structure of trade unions has, of course, changed substantially over time. In the eighteenth century trade unions were small, often insecure, societies of skilled or semi-skilled workers. Many quite clearly emerged to deal with a particular dispute and disappeared once the issue was reconciled. By the mid- and late nineteenth century, unions had widened their base as their legal right to exist became accepted and their membership broadened out to include many of the unskilled. Local societies of skilled workers came together to form national organizations – both of a federal and centralized nature. The emergence of the Trades Union Congress in the 1860s also added impetus to the movement and enabled it to campaign for improvements in trade-union rights. Nevertheless, the trade-union movement still had many deficiencies. In the first place, the number of workers organized within unions was never more than a small proportion of the total workforce and they represented an exclusive body of workers, even though they were not by any means a skilled aristocracy of labour. Secondly, the number of female trade unionists, except in cotton textiles, was always small. Women, indeed, as evidenced in the documents included here on the Victorian and Edwardian clerks, were seen as a potential weakness to the trade-union movement – accepting low wages and having no life-long commitment to their work. Not surprisingly, then, trade unions frequently ran campaigns to get women out of the industry, most obviously in the textile industry where mothers were encouraged to stay at home.

During the twentieth century the weaknesses of nineteenth-century trade unions have been reduced. In the first place, there has been an enormous widening of the trade union base in most industries to a situation where, by the late 1970s, about half the workforce were members of unions – although that proportion declined in the 1980s. The increasing move towards amalgamations has also greatly strengthened the movement to such an extent that while in 1917 266 trade unions represented just over four and a half million workers affiliated to the TUC, there were only 83 unions affiliated in 1988, with just over nine million members. The twentieth century has also seen the increased involvement of women in trade unionism, although the union structure is still overwhelmingly dominated by men.

The move from exclusivity to openness has meant that the involvement and place of the individual within unions has changed. Until the mid-nineteenth century the majority of workers in any union would have participated directly in the affairs of the local branch. From the late nineteenth century onwards, however, when mass unionism became more common, the move was, increasingly, to hire and pay for professional organizers. This was a major feature adopted by the Gasworkers' and General Labourers' Union and by the other large 'new unions' of the late 1880s and early 1890s. The problem, of course, is that the officials often lose touch with their members, as was evidenced on Clydeside during the First World War and in the Hull dockers' dispute in 1954. Unofficial strike action by trade unionists is often a reflection of this type of situation.

As the history of the trade-union movement has developed there have been many debates and issues which have fascinated historians. For the early history of British trade unionism there has been much discussion about the extent to which trade unions existed prior to the Industrial Revolution. Whereas it was often suggested that trade unions only really emerged in a permanent form at the beginning of the Industrial Revolution, an increasing amount of evidence now suggests that Britain was a far more industrialized society in the seventeenth century than is often supposed, or was indicated by Gregory King's survey, and that there were many small industrial disputes by bodies of workmen who, if the brevity of their association can be ignored, might be regarded to have been members of trade unions.[1]

Another debate has focused upon the importance and effectiveness of the Combination Acts of 1799 and 1800 in restricting trade unionism. It has been argued that the Acts were a new attempt by the state to oppress the working classes.[2] Yet others have argued that there was nothing new in the legislation and that it was a rather ineffective instrument of oppression. More recently, it has been asserted that the Acts, as well as extending old restrictions, also introduced new penalties for actions that were purely industrial and would not have been, by themselves, acted upon by other eighteenth-century legislation directed against combinations.[3] There may well have been a class dimension to the Acts.[4] Connected with this tends to be a third debate associated with the repeal of the Combination Acts in 1824 and 1825. Why did the repeal take place? Was it the product of the lobbying of Francis Place or did other factors come into play?

For the decades of the 1830s and 1840s the most controverted debate concerns the extent to which trade unionism can be seen as part of the wider political Labour movement. In other words – the question goes – were trade unions deeply involved in the radical, republican and chartist periods of the 1830s and 1840s or did they remain aloof from such activities? In the early 1970s John Foster wrote that trade unionism was very closely associated with the political consciousness of the working classes.[5] This view was countered by that of A. E. Musson who denied the connection.[6] However, recent evidence does tend to suggest a connection and involvement in type.[7]

For the period of the mid-Victorian prosperity, from 1850 to 1875, the main concern of historians has been to determine the extent to which trade unions came to an accommodation with capitalism. There is presented, on the one hand, the image of fobwatched and top-hatted trade union leaders hobnobbing with the chief industrialists and employers of the day, a situation reflected in the relationship between Alexander MacDonald, the miners' leader, and Lord Elcho, who had extensive coal interests. Left-wing writers have particularly pressed this view forward, cultivating an impression of respectability presented by the trade union Junta and the interpretation of the Webbs of events in this period.[8] Yet other historians have questioned the extent to which there could be such an accommodation and suggest that in reality the interests between labour and capital were antagonistic and could not be easily reconciled.

For the late nineteenth century the focus changes once again, in an attempt to measure the political impact of 'new unionism'. This has led to a plethora of questions. Were the Webbs correct in their estimation of 'new unionism'? What was new and distinctive about the new unions? In general there is less of a debate here and more a consensus that new unionism refers to both the formation of new unions among the unskilled, semi-skilled and skilled, and the opening up of existing unions to new members. Many of the 'new unionists' were committed to the eight-hour day and state intervention but, it is argued, one should not expect all the new unions to be general in form nor particularly socialist in intent.

By the early twentieth century, the trade-union movement was expanding gradually. There was an amalgamation movement, more officials were involved, and trade unions were becoming increasingly associated with the Labour Party, the independent political party of the working class. The characteristics of these trends have been closely scrutinized. Nevertheless, there remains the underlying feeling among some writers that the revival of the pre-First World War trade-union movement had a lot to do with the emergence of the industrial syndicalist movement led by Tom Mann.[9] Yet, although Bob Holton may argue that British syndicalism was tremendously important in this period, it is clear that the evidence for this is all rather limited. There appear to have been few syndicalists and their influence upon the pattern of trade unionism appears to have been rather slim.[10] They were not directly associated with many of the major industrial conflicts of this period, the vast majority of strikes had no intention of threatening and overthrowing society and the views of syndicalists were clearly not widespread.

The First World War saw the rapid increase in trade union membership and, despite the contrary impression given by the events on Clydeside, the vast majority of trade unions clearly did well out of the war and supported the war effort. In the post-war years, however, the movement fell back and the major focus of attention has been placed upon the General Strike. Numerous questions have been asked about this event. What were the causes of the General Strike? Was it the culmination of the rise of militancy since 1910? How effective was it? Why did it fail? What were the consequences of the end of the dispute? Genuine debate still divides historians on many of these questions. Nevertheless, the issue which divides most concerns the extent to which the General Strike can be seen as a watershed in British industrial relations. Some Marxist writers certainly see it in this light, as do other writers of a right-wing perspective.[11] They, of course, differ as to the real meaning of that defeat. On the other hand, a body of opinion, represented by Gordon Phillips, maintains that the General Strike did little to alter the pattern of industrial relations and did not force the TUC to change direction.[12] This view is further reflected in the work of Professor H.A. Clegg who has recently suggested that, in any case, the General Strike should not be seen as a defeat for it actually checked employers, made them think about industrial action, and actually slowed down the pace of wage reductions.[13]

Since the Second World War, trade unions have assumed an increasingly important part in the British economy. Herein lies their strength and their weakness. Because of their heightened presence and role they have been drawn more closely into decision making, into the National Economic Development Council and similar bodies. At the same time, their greater importance has made them a target for those who see many of Britain's industrial ills in terms of the restrictive attitudes of trade unions. Hence, the 'Thatcherite' attack upon trade unions throughout the 1980s can be seen as an attack upon the restrictive nature of trade unionism. Yet, although there are many issues, there have been few major debates about the history of trade unionism during the last forty-five years – except perhaps on the issues of consensus and the extent to which trade unions have contributed to the 'British Disease': ' Was there a political consensus in the post-war years?' and 'Are trade unions responsible for Britain's industrial decline?' The majority opinion on the first question appears to be that there was a political consensus, although Professor Ben Pimlott begs to differ. On the second question there are still marked differences between Conservative writers and politicians, although even they prefer to attack the burden of the welfare state rather than trade unions as the principal cause of Britain's industrial decline. On the other hand, writers such as Alan Sked have stressed that while the 1979 'Winter of Discontent' did much damage to the image of trade unions, there is little to suggest that trade unions added considerably to Britain's economic problems and decline which, in any case, have been evident for more than a century.[14]

The sources and focus of trade-union history have changed dramatically over time and vary according to the period which is being examined. For the seventeenth and eighteenth centuries, the evidence of trade-union activities is often indirect – arising from government legislation, newspaper reports and Home Office papers – rather than from the trade unions themselves. This is, perhaps, not surprising given the restrictions which were imposed upon trade-union activity but it does tend to colour perspectives. And even in areas where there was a tradition of trade-union activity, albeit under the surface, that means that trade-union documents as such are rare. For instance, in the records of the Calderdale Archives at Halifax, where there is a vast amount of trade-union material on the engineering and textile trades, the earliest document which refers to trade unions, and then in the form of an 'Odious Document' disassociating workers from the unions, does not appear until 1834. It is reproduced, in part, in this collection.

Clearly, trade-union records were kept but the secret nature of many organizations, and the loss of records as they were passed from secretary to secretary, has meant that there is little of a substantial nature available until the mid-nineteenth century when more open and permanent bodies began to emerge. Thereafter, there is a plethora of trade-union material available – trade-union collections containing minute books, insurance records, membership lists and a miscellany of other material. The formation of many trades councils, particularly in the 1860s and 1890s, also adds enormously to the body of available evidence and provides a different perspective on trade unionism. The

London Trades Council, some documents from which appear in this collection, reflects upon the fact that trade unions and trades councils often emerged from industrial disputes and that the purpose of these bodies was often to secure industrial peace.

Many libraries and trade-union organizations have kept trade-union collections. The National Union of Mineworkers' headquarters at Barnsley contains, for instance, a superb collection of trade union documents, government reports relating to mining and an extensive collection of newspaper cuttings. The Calderdale Archives at Halifax must also contain one of the most impressive collections of trade-union archives, particularly on engineering. In addition, many prominent libraries have built up collections based upon the activities of one man, such as Francis Place and George Howell (which incidentally are available on microfilm). The most impressive of these collections must be that of the British Library of Political and Economic Science which, at the centre of its trade-union records, has the Webb Collection. This collection of rule books, annual reports, pamphlets and written notes must surely rank as one of the most important bodies of British trade-union material available. Gathered together by the Webbs in the late-1880s and early-1890s, it forms the base of the British Library collection which also includes trade-union newspapers and journals.

From the 1950s, then, the perspective of trade unionism has changed. Instead of documents looking at the movement from above, the view switched to one from below. As trade unions became more numerous and important in the twentieth century this view has been complemented by other focuses – most obviously the emergence of a rank and file and shopfloor dimension to history which has not always been picked up by the official trade-union documents. The first evidence of this appears with the Shopstewards' movement on Clydeside. Though technically not part of this collection, autobiographical accounts and surveys of work practice are beginning to appear.[15]

Finally, one should not ignore the vast amount of government material produced on combinations and trade unions. Apart from Home Office material and government legislation there were many royal commission reports on trade unions and labour, most obviously the ones conducted between 1867 and 1869, during the early 1890s, and the Donovan Commission of the 1960s, all of which are referred to in this Reader. But beyond this there is a vast amount of regular and routine information produced by government departments. From the late 1880s the Labour Department of the Board of Trade provided details of strikes and details of trade unions. In addition, there is an enormous collection of relevant material deposited by government departments in the Public Record Office.

In a more commercial form, both Harvester Microform of Brighton and EP Microform of Wakefield have produced collections of documents on aspects of trade-union and labour history. Indeed, EP Microform began producing microfilm records of some trades councils in the 1880s, most notably the records of the Bradford District Trades and Labour Council. Other similar material has been published by smaller companies. And one must not ignore the primary material published by the *Bulletin of the Society of Labour History*, now retitled *Labour History Review*, which occasionally produced pamphlets on the primary material of Labour history as well as publishing such material in its main journal.

The dramatic decline of the British trade-union movement in the 1980s has been the cause of much revived interest in the history of the movement – partly in the hope by some that such investigations might provide clues to the possible reasons for decline and suggestions for its future revival. The 'new realism' of the movement has already dictated that it will have to recognize its diminishing importance and influence within the Labour Party and any future Labour government, and that it must come to terms with the 'Thatcherite' legislation of the 1980s.

This Reader attempts to provide the broad perspectives of British trade-union history and documentary evidence on some of the major events that have occurred. There will never be an ideal balance between nationally prominent events and more local and parochial activities but this Reader does at least attempt to provide evidence for most regions and focus upon the major events in the different periods identified. Nevertheless, the increasing availability of trade-union documents may, in future, begin to change the focus from the trade union to the shopfloor and plant activities. Any Reader can, therefore, never be more than an interim report, a sampling of the available evidence aimed at enriching current debates.

NOTES

1. P.H. Lindert, 'English occupations, 1670–1811', *Jn. Econ. Hist.*, XL, No. 4 (1980), pp. 685–712.
2. E.P. Thompson, *The Making of the English Working Class* (Penguin, 1968), p. 546 and J. Foster, *Class Struggle and the Industrial Revolution: early industrial capitalism in three English towns* (Unwin, 1977), pp. 38, 49–50.
3. J. Moher, 'From Suppression to Containment: Roots of Trade Union Law to 1825', in *British Trade Unionism 1750–1850* (Longman, 1988), ed. by J. Rule, pp. 74–97.
4. J.V. Orth, 'The legal status of English trade unions, 1799–1871' in *Law-Making and Law-Makers in British History* (1980), ed. by A. Harding (Royal Historical Society, 1980). pp. 195–207.
5. Foster, *op. cit.*
6. A.E. Musson, 'Class Struggle and the labour aristocracy, 1830–1860', *Social History*, 3 (1976), pp. 340–3.
7. I. J. Prothero, 'London Chartism and the trades', *Econ. Hist. Rev.*, xxiv, no. 2 (1971), pp. 202–18; R. Fyson, 'Unionism, Class and Community in the 1830s: Aspects of the National Union of Operative Potters', *British Trade Unionism 1750–1850* (Longman, 1988), ed. by J. Rule, pp. 200–19.
8. S. and B. Webb, *The History of Trade Unionism* (1894); T. Lane, *The Union Makes Us Strong* (Arrow books, 1971), and also supported by the views of J. Foster, *op. cit.*, and the various writings of R.C. Challinor on mining.
9. Bob Holton, *British Syndicalism 1900–1914* (Pluto, 1976).
10. H.A. Clegg, *A History of British Trade Unions since 1889: Vol II, 1911–1933* (Clarendon Press, Oxford, 1985), chapter 2.
11. J. Foster, 'British Imperialism and the Labour Aristocracy', *1926: The General Strike* (Lawrence and Wishart, 1976), ed. by J. Skelley, pp. 3–57.
12. G.A. Phillips, *The General Strike: The Politics of Industrial Conflict* (London, Weidenfeld and Nicolson, 1976), chapter 13, particularly pp. 293–5.
13. Clegg, *op. cit.*, chapters 11 and 13.
14. A. Sked, *Britain's Decline* (Historical Ass., 1987).
15. A. Exall. 'Morris Motors in the 1930s: Part I', *History Workshop*, 6, Autumn 1978.

EARLY TRADE UNIONISM c. 1770–1850

The organization of workers into groups which would now be recognized as trade unions, began well before the occurrence of the Industrial Revolution. In the seventeenth century groups of artisans organized themselves on a permanent and temporary basis and by the eighteenth century industrial conflict and threatening behaviour (2, 5) were not unusual features of British industrial life, a fact testified to by the large body of legislation, of a general and a trade nature, which emerged throughout the eighteenth century (1). Employers were never very happy about the independent actions of their employees and often organized to use the law to ensure that the workers remained dutiful and obedient to their wishes (3, 4) The law, in any case, was generally hostile to trade organization – although the forty or so acts which existed to forbid workers' combinations were clearly not effectively or consistently applied. Trade unions and workers' combinations were obviously more clearly established and widespread in the seventeenth and eighteenth centuries than is commonly supposed, although one must always reflect that trade-union membership up to the 1850s was essentially confined to the few and to the skilled.

Historians have focused much of their attention on the Combination Acts of 1799 and 1800 and their repeal in 1824 and 1825. It used to be argued that the 1799 and 1800 acts were unusually repressive to workers and that they favoured the employers. Equally, it was maintained that the legislation was simply the introduction of more of the same type of legislation that had been introduced in the eighteenth century. Neither of these views would hold up well today. In the first instance, trade union activity, for wage demands and against the introduction of new machinery, continued (7 to 16), and was occasionally of a violent nature. The London unions seemed to be thriving and there was plenty of evidence of similar growth and activity throughout the country, particularly in Lancashire, Yorkshire and South Wales. Secondly (6), it is clear that the 1799 and 1800 Acts introduced specific penalties for the simple act of combination, whereas previous legislation was often concerned with assault and the destruction of property, actions which would have been felonies in any legal context.

The repeal of the Combination Acts was the work of many individuals although it was Francis Place who came to be identified with its success. As he indicates (18), he began his work in that direction in 1814, motivated by the belief that if trade unions were made legal they would quickly come to accept that they could do little to buck the market and would accept the 'Iron Law of Wages'. Maintaining that the Combination Acts were ineffective he secured the Appointment of a Committee on Enquiry in 1824, which was packed with his sympathizers, who heard much evidence of the need for repeal. The Combination Acts were repealed, in the wake of this report, but the outburst of industrial action which followed led to the formation of a fresh Committee of Investigation and the introduction of a new law in 1825 (19). This permitted trade unions to combine to peacefully campaign for wage increases but limited their ability to combine to regulate the mode of production by the use of violence. The problem of the legal rights of trade unions has remained ever since. Picketing had its limits, as it has today. One should also remember that a Master and Servant Act, shortly before the repeal, ensured employers a stronger position in law than that enjoyed by their workmen.

Nevertheless, the repeal of the Combination Acts paved the way for the wider and more open organization and activity of trade unions, although balanced against this was the attempt of employers to restrict and undermine the new movement. Both developments are evident in the case of the Bradford Woolcombers' and Weavers' Strike of 1825 (20), where the employers attempted to deal with a demand for uniform wage rates throughout the district by forcing workers to sign a 'Form of Denial', in which they declared that they were not members of a trade union. Similar tactics were used by the Saddleworth employers although, as George Shaw's diary indicates, trade unionism was still a rather feeble and limited activity among the Saddleworth weavers (21).

Yet some significant, if short-lived, developments were achieved. John Doherty helped to set up the Grand General Union of all the Operative Spinners in the United Kingdom in December 1829, although this body was crippled by the strain of the Ashton strike at the end of 1830 (22). Doherty also organized the National Association for the Protection of Labour in 1830, which won some support from miners, potters, blacksmiths, and others, as well as textile workers. It enjoyed some success until 1832, running two newspapers and winning support in the Midlands, Lancashire and Yorkshire (23). The Swing Outrages of 1830 in agricultural Kent (24), the creation of the Committee of United Weavers (28) and the formation of the Operative Builders' Union (25) all added to the general atmosphere of industrial unrest and industrial assertion. The last of these organizations also became involved in the extension of Owenite principles and in September 1833 the 'Builders' Parliament' of 500 delegates was persuaded to set up a 'Builders' Guild', which was to start cooperative building schemes. Similar moves were also made by Robert Owen who, in 1833, planned the formation of a General Union of Productive Classes, which came to fruition as the Grand National Consolidated Trades Union in February 1834. A body of men of mixed views – some wanting Owen's peaceful evolution of society on cooperative lines through the Unions, others wanting immediate workers's control and expecting conflict. Owen, and John Doherty, were also involved in the activities of the short-lived National Regeneration Society (27), which demanded the eight-hour day.

Most of the activities of the above organization were brought to a halt by the collapse of strikes, the intervention of the authorities and the divided nature of the trade-union movement. They also collapsed in the wake of the unjust treatment of the 'Tolpuddle Martyrs' (29). The story is well known and essentially revolves around the decision of George Loveless to form a Friendly Society of Agricultural Labourers at Tolpuddle in Dorsetshire on the occasion of which he made use of an Initiation Ceremony. The magistrates, hearing of this, posted placards threatening members of the union with transportation and arrested Loveless and five of his companions. They were subjected to an unfair trial, sentenced under the Act of 1797 forbidding 'unlawful' oaths and transported to Tasmania, or Van Dieman's Land, until they were granted a free pardon and returned to Britain in 1838 and 1839 – well after the major trade-union disturbances had ended.

These events, of course, temporarily welded the trade-union movement together and there were many protests in London and throughout the provinces, the most famous being the great meeting in Copenhagen Fields (31) and the disturbances in Oldham in April 1834 (30) when violence occurred, a man was shot, and large meetings were held. But thereafter, the Grand National Consolidated Trade Union and many of the other wider national organizations of the trade-union movement collapsed. In addition, employers began to force upon their employers the 'Odious Document', demanding that they be no longer a member of a trade union (32).

However, one must not suppose that trade unionism was much less effective. Obviously the movement to form national and general unions had failed but many unions continued to operate satisfactorily, if less ostentatiously, than before in an atmosphere in which attention was drawn more to the Anti-Poor Law Movement, the Factory Movement, Chartism and Owenism. Most of the major trades had a trade-union organization of some type – although many unions were small, particularly in the woollen and worsted textile industry and among skilled workers in the printing and engineering trades and industries. There were, however, some larger unions such as the Miners' Association of Great Britain, formed in the 1840s under the leadership of Martin Jude and represented, in court actions, by W. P. Roberts, the Chartist lawyer.

In many respects these small, skilled, and often fleeting trade unions were far from timid in their response to employers. Although the heyday of the national organizations might have passed and the case of the 'Tolpuddle Martyrs' might well have dissuaded many from joining or continuing with trade unions, it it clear that the surviving trade unions were willing to demand improved working arrangements and better wages. This was particularly evident in the case of the potters (34) whose union organizations emerged, collapsed and re-emerged with enviable resilience, which gave rise to the suggestion that they were 'Martinmass unions', unions which emerged at the time of the feast of St Martin's on the 11 November each year, when workers would come together, but then disappeared quickly. In this process of development, centralized unions became federal, new leaders and representatives of trade unions, such as George J. Holyoake (33) emerged and there were even further demands for the formation of general unions (35). Such steady and unspectacular growth was achieved in a period when economic fortunes were mixed and economic conditions were not propitious for trade-union growth. With the rapid improvement in the economic conditions in the 1850s the whole outlook for trade unionism improved dramatically.

1) *An Act to prevent unlawful combinations of workmen employed in the woollen manufactures, and for better payment of wages, 1726.*
(12 Geo. I c. 34.)
Whereas great numbers of weavers and others concerned in the woollen manufactures in several towns and parishes in this kingdom have lately formed themselves into unlawful clubs and societies, and have presumed, contrary to law, to enter into combinations, and to make by-laws or orders, by which they pretend to regulate the trade and the prices of their goods, and to advance their wages unreasonably... ; and whereas the said persons so unlawfully assembling and associating themselves have committed great violence and outrages upon many of his Majesty's good subjects ... ; and it is absolutely necessary that more effectual provision should be made against such unlawful combinations, and for preventing such violence and outrages for the future and for bringing all offenders in the premises to more speedy and exemplary justice: may it therefore ... be enacted .... That all contracts, covenants, or agreements, and all by-laws, ordinances, rules or orders, in such unlawful clubs and societies, heretofore made or entered into, or hereafter to be made or entered into, by or between any persons brought up in or professing, using or exercising the art and mystery of a woolcomber or weaver, or journeyman woolcomber or journeyman weaver, in any parish or place, within this kingdom, for regulating the said trade or mystery, or for regulating or settling the prices of goods, or of advancing their wages, or of lessening their usual hours of work, shall be and are hereby declared to be illegal, null and void to all intents and purposes; and further, that if any woolcomber or weaver, or journeyman woolcomber or journeyman weaver, or other person concerned in any of the woollen manufactures of this kingdom

shall ... be knowingly concerned in any contract, covenant or agreement, by law ordinance, rule or order of any club, society or combination by this act declared to be illegal ... every person so offending being thereof lawfully convicted upon the oath or oaths of one or more credible witnesses, before any two or more justices of the peace ... upon any information exhibited or prosecution within three calender months after the offence committed ... [shall be liable to three months' imprisonment].

2) *The Calico Printers of Lancashire in the Eighteenth Century, threatened with new printing machinery*
(Letter quoted in E. P. Thompson, 'The crime of anonymity', in D. Hay, P. Linebaugh and E.P. Thompson (eds), *Albion's Fatal Tree. Crime and Society in Eighteenth-Century England* (Penguin edition, 1977), p. 318.)
You must immediately give any more Mashen Work for we are determined there shall be no more of them made use of in the trade and it will be madness for you to contend with the Trade as we are combined by the Oath to fix prices we can afford to pay him [one of their number who had been imprisoned] a Guinea Week and not hurt the fund if you was to keep him there till Dumsday therefore mind you comply with the above or by God we will keep our Words with you we will make some rare Bunfires in this Countey and at your Peril shake in their Shoes we are determined to destroy all Sorts of Masheens for Printing in the Kingdom for there is more hands then is work for so no more from the ingerd Gurneman Rember we are a great number sworn nor you must not advertise the Men that you say run away from you when you il Usage was the Cause of their going we will punish you for that our Meetings are legal for we want nothing but what is honest and to work for selvs and families and you want to starve us but it is better for you and a few more which we have marked to die then such a Number of Pore Men and their families to be starved.

3) *Worsted Committee in Yorkshire*
(Worsted Committee: *Publication of Notices, 21 June 1779.* The
Records and Minute Books of the Worsted Committee, located in J. B.
Priestley Library, University of Bradford.)
Resolved that Hand Bills be presented and distributed by the Inspec-
tors amongst the Spinners Weavers & setting forth the substance of
the Clauses in the Act of the 17th Geo R making them subject to be
Committed to the House of Correction for neglecting to work up
Materials for the Space of 8 Days or suffering themselves to be
employed by any Master before they shall have wrought their former
work, also the Clause directing that the Work people in the Woollen
Manufactory shall be paid in Money & not in Goods, and that the
Inspectors after the 27th Day of April next will have the Orders to
prosecute for such offences. . . .

4) *The control of Combinations*
(i)   (West Riding Quarter Session Order Book, 31 July 1777)
        William Hartley of Bradford, Journeyman Woolcomber.
        John Greenhough of Bowling, Journeyman Woolcomber.
        Samuel Green of Bradford, Journeyman Woolcomber, . . . have
        been convicted upon the information and oath of John Thorn-
        ton . . . for keeping up, continuing, acting in, making, entering
        into, and being knowingly concerned together, at Bowling . . . in
        a contract agreement of Combination contrary to the form of
        the statute in that case made and provided to advance their
        wages as journeymen woolcombers and for presuming to put
        such contract agreement or Combination into execution and in
        consequence thereof refusing to work for reasonable and
        accustomed wages . . . that the three men be given three
        months' hard labour in the Wakefield House of Correction.
(ii)   (*The Leeds Intelligencer*, 4 October 1791)
        Whereas we whose several names or marks are hereto sub-
        scribed and set being hired servants of Messrs. Sidgwicks,
        Wood, and Co., to work in their cotton mill at this place, did on
        Thursday, the 22 inst., conspire and combine together, and did
        leave our said masters' work without any cause; and afterwards
        assembled in a riotous and tumultuous manner, refusing to
        return to our work and grossly insulting the different masters

16

and overlookers at the mill, and all other servants who refused to join in the combination.

And whereas our masters have, in consequence of our bad behaviour, commended prosecutions for the same, but on condition of our publicity asking pardon and making full submission, have humanely consented to desist from any further proceeding. Now we do hereby publicly acknowledge the great offence which we have committed, and humbly ask pardon of our said masters, and return then thanks for their lenienty in pardoning us, promising never to be guilty of the like offence in future; and hoping that this will be a warning to all other hired servants and deter then from entering similar combinations.

5) *Industrial Unrest in Liverpool, 1791*
(PRO, Home Office 42/20, taken from A. Aspinall, *The Early English Trade Union* (London, Batchworth Press, 1949), pp. 2–3)
Henry Blundell [Mayor of Liverpool] to Henry Dundas [Home Secretary]

Liverpool, 27 May, 1792

I was informed yesterday afternoon that the great body of carpenters intended to leave their work on Monday morning unless their wages were advanced. I immediately sent to three of them to call upon me, that I wished to speak to them. They came. And in conversation of some length they told me it was their intention to ask an advance of 4d. per day, but that they should request it civilly and obtain it peaceably or relinquish it; and I might depend upon it, they would give me no trouble: they would not disturb the peace of the town, and I verily believe they will not. Yet it may not be quite prudent to rely upon this assurance, and perhaps you will be so good, Sir, as to order one of the troops of Grays, which are now at Manchester, into Warrington. . . .

There seems too general an appearance of discontent amongst all the artificers and labourers, which must if possible be prevented spreading into tumult. Annexed is the copy of a note I have this moment received, which comes from a large body of men, and we must either comply with this demand or be guarded against the consequences. The other owners of collieries and flats [Flat bottomed boats used in river navigation] in this neighbourhood have received the like notice.

Liverpool, 26 May, 1792 (Copy)
The masters of the coal flats in your employ do hereby give notice that
they will not proceed in the said flats after the 9th day of June next
ensuing, under one shilling per ton per trip – which they hope you will
agree and consent to without any stop being put to the said business as
we are determined not to proceed under that price from that date.

6) *The Combination Acts of 1799 and 1800*
(Combination Act of 1800. (39 & 40 Geo III, *c.* 100)

WHEREAS it is expedient to explain and amend an Act, passed in
the thirty-ninth year of His present Majesty, intituled 'An Act to
prevent unlawful combinations of Workmen';

BE IT THEREFORE ENACTED that from and after the passing
of this Act all contracts, covenants and agreements whatsoever, in
writing, at any time or time entered into, by or between any journeyman manufacturers or other workmen within this kingdom for obtaining an advance of wages of them, or any of them . . . or for lessening or
altering their or any of their usual hours of time or working, or
decreasing the quantity of work (save except any contract made or to
be made . . .), or for preventing or hindering any person or persons
from employing whosoever he, or she, or they shall think proper to
employ . . . are hereby declared to be illegal . . . .

AND BE IT FURTHER ENACTED. . . ; and every journeyman and
workmen who, after the passing of this Act, shall be guilty of any of the
said offences, being thereof lawfully convicted, upon his own confession
or the oath or oaths of one or more credible witness or witnesses, before
any two Justices of the Peace for the county, riding, division, city, . . .
where such an offence shall be committed . . . within three calendar
months next after the offence shall have been committed, shall, by order
of such Justices, be committed to and confined in the Common Gaol
within his or their jurisdiction, for any time not exceeding three calendar
months, or at the discretion of such justices shall be committed to some
house of correction within the same jurisdiction, there to remain and be
kept to hard labour for any time not exceeding two calendar months.
[Similar penalties were imposed on those involved in persuading,
intimidating or threatening other workmen to do the same. The Act also
provided means by which disputes could be settled by arbitration and,
finally, by a Justice of the Peace.]

7) *The Gloucester Weavers, 1802: The destruction of their power*
(T. Exell, *A Brief History of the Weavers of the County of Gloucestershire*
(Stroud, 1838), pp. 6–7, 10–11)
[In 1802 the clothiers promoted] a bill to suspend the weavers'
protecting laws and after this the spoilers broke in upon the weavers'
rights and privilege – shop looms were introduced . . . and the
manufacturers became master weavers themselves. The system of
apprenticeship was done away with and things became dreadfully
confused – the clothiers looked upon the weavers as an army defeated
and taken prisoner. . . . There is no rule or order among the masters
themselves but they appear to be vieing with each other who shall bring
wages to the lowest point . . . if the government does not interfere I can
see nothing but destruction at our heels.

8) *The Caulkers of Deptford, 1802*
(PRO, HO 42/66, taken from Aspinall, *op. cit.*, p. 48)
John Harriott [Thames Police Court magistrate] to John King [Under-
Secretary of State]
Thames Police Office, 6 August 1802
[. . .] Notwithstanding the assurances given on Tuesday last by the
disaffected caulkers not to disturb or molest others, complaints have
been made before us of violent assaults made on those who are
disposed to work – some of which complaints are now in train to bring
the offending parties forward. At the same time we hear they have
retracted altogether their promise to leave this dispute to be settled by
arbitration.

Late last night Mr. Brent, while attending on these complaints said
he had heard a report that the caulkers at the King's Yard, Deptford,
had been driven from their work. Although I could not believe it true,
I thought it right to go down there this morning and am happy to say
all was quiet. But I was informed by the officers of the Yard that on
Wednesday night a strong party of men (supposed to be caulkers) went
down the river in three boats to meet some King's caulkers coming
from Chatham in a vessel to work at the merchants yards, and
compelled them to return. From the general spirit that seems to
pervade the whole (shipwrights, caulkers and sawyers) I fear that
nothing short of strong coercive measures will bring them to any
order.

9) *John Gast, the Shipwright, on the need for parliamentary interference, 1802*
(J. Gast, *Calumny Defeated: or, A Compleat Vindication of the Conduct of the Working Shipwrights, during the late Dispute with their Employers* (Deptford, 1802), p. 34)
The interference of Parliament has in many instances been deemed necessary; the better to terminate disputes, between artificers and their employers; and the laws promulgated, by which the price, as well as the time of labor, has been ascertained; so that no disputes thereon can ever exist, without an immediate and efficacious remedy to terminate them.

10) *The Lancashire Weavers' Turnout, 1808*
(HO papers, taken from Aspinall, *op. cit.*, pp. 95, 102–3)
(i)   *Letter from R. A. Farington, JP, to Lord Hawkesbury,* (HO 42/95)
Manchester, 24 May, 1808 6pm
[. . .] The rejection of the Weavers' Bill [to guarantee a minimum wage for weavers] is the avowed cause of the disturbance, and an increase of wages in that branch of the manufactory is called for. They profess a determination not to work longer at the present prices, and endeavour to prevent the well disposed from continuing at their looms. . . .
(ii)   *Mayor of Wigan to Lord Hawkesbury*
(HO 42/95)
Wigan, 15 June, 1808
[. . .] In this borough and the neighbourhood the principal employment of the people is in the cotton manufactures, and we have within the borough 3,000 weavers. The rejection of the Bill introduced into Parliament to fix a minimum of the wages to be paid to weavers in those manufactures immediately created universal discontent amongst them. And on Monday, 30 May, many of them from the adjacent villages entered the town in different parties and expeditiously collected as many shuttles from the weavers residing here as they could obtain, which they marked with the owners' names and locked up near the places from whence they were taken. Most of the owners of the shuttles were as ready to deliver them as the collectors were to receive them, but in some few cases the owners were intim-

idated to part with their shuttles by the number of the collectors and the general voice of the people that all the shuttles should be taken . . . . On the next day many weavers of this town began to collect shuttles at the extremities of the town in a similar manner, and I appointed and swore about 200 special constables and called out the volunteers, and we traversed the town and pursued the weavers . . . but they fled.

[. . .] I have committed one of the shuttle takers to Lancaster Castle for felony in taking two shuttles.

[. . .] In travelling the streets with the military and constables I was sorry to see so great and general ferment amongst the lower order of inhabitants. Their common cry was, 'Give us bred, we are starving!' [. . .] It must be admitted that the earnings of an industrious weaver are but small, and that provisions are high, and that such a man with a wife and two children can scarcely provide bread for himself and family. . . .

11) *London Dock Strike, 1810*
(*The Times*, 7 July 1810)
Yesterday the workmen employed at the London Docks struck for an increase of wages. They demanded an advance of from 18s. to a guinea per week. The number employed amounts to about 1,000, and such as were backward in approving the conduct adopted by the leaders were roughly treated. Constables were called in, and we are happy to say the malcontents did not betray any spirit of outrage other than that of persisting in the demand for an increase in wages.

12) *Thomas Large, a Leicester stocking weaver and the reaction of London trade unionists, 1812*
(*Records of the Borough of Nottingham 1800–1835 (1952)*, *VIII*, Thomas Large to Thos. Roper and the Framework-Knitters Committee, 24 April 1812)
[Large was part of a deputation to London in 1812 who were attempting to lobby MPs in support of a Bill to regulate conditions in the hosiery industry. In so doing he, and his colleagues, met with London trade unionists.]
We have had an opportunity of speaking to them on the subject, they thought we possessed a fund on a permanent principle to answer any

demand, at any time, and if that had been the case would have lent us two or three thousand pounds, (for there is £20,000 in the fund belonging to that Trade) but When they understood our Trade kept no regular fund to support itself, Instead of Lending us money Their noses underwent a Mechanical turn upwards, and each saluted the other with a significant stare, Ejaculating, Lord bless us!!! what fools!!! they richly deserve all they put! and ten times more!!!! We always thought stockeners a sett of poor creatures! Fellows as wanting of spirit, as their pockets are of money. What would our trade be, if we did not combine together? perhaps as poor as you are, at this day! Look at other Trades! they all combine, (the Spitalfield weavers excepted, and what a Miserable Conditions are they in). See the Tailors, Shoemakers, Bookbinders, Gold beaters, Printers, Bricklayers, Coatmakers, Hatters, Curriers, Masons, Whitesmiths, none of these trades Receive Less than 30/- a week and from that five guineas this is all done by Combination, without it their Trades would be as bad as yours. . . .

13) *The Luddites, 1812*

(i)   *Letter from James Hardy, Land Agent, to his employer, Walter Spencer-Stanhope*
(Spencer-Stanhope Collection, 2169)
Dated 25 March 1812
Place Horsforth
Honoured Sir,
[. . .] I am sorry to inform you there hath been a most desperate outrage committed here by the mob (or Luddites as they are called, supposed to be Croppers). On Tuesday morning about one o'clock they came to the mill at Wood Bottom, occupied by Messrs Thompsons, and demanded of the watch the keys of the gig mill, he not having them, they then attempted to force open the door, not being able to accomplish this, the General (so called) ordered the windows to be broke and to enter the mill which was immediately done, they broke the greatest part of the shears and cut in pieces some fine cloth that was in the machines. The General then called over the mob and ordered his men to dismiss, informing the watchman that if they continued working the mill in Rawdon Park by the gig they

would visit them in a few days. During the time they was committing the outrage, the watch was ordered to lay down with his face to the ground and a guard sat over him threatening him if he looked up they would fire upon him. . . .

Your Most Obedient & humble Servant.

James Hardy.

(ii)   *Case against the Yorkshire Luddites*
       (PRO, TS11/813/2676 21703)

The disturbances within the West Riding of the County caused by a set of People calling themselves Luddites, but who are now proclaimed to be a desperate gang of Discontented Croppers or Shear Men, had risen to so serious and alarming a height by the Month of April last, that strange as it may appear in a country like that in which we live the Civic power was no longer found effectual to afford protection to Individuals and their property, even in their houses, and in the bosom of their own families! – within which even Mills or Buildings a certain kind of Improved Machinery or finishing frames (used in the dressing and finishing of Woollen cloath) had been introduced, or was used, it had become necessary to introduce a Military Guard also for its protection.

Such was the case at Mr. William Cartwrights' of Rawfolds which is in the neighbourhood of Huddersfield. He had employed the whole of an extensive mill which was a water mill, in the working of this species of improved machinery and which mill it was publicly known to the Croppers or Shear Men would be defended by W. Cartwright and a Guard of Soldiers who he had placed therein at the hazard of existence, for they had constantly fought with him in the Mill for cause precious in the expectation of his long threatened attack. Hitherto the perpetrators of this Diabolical and Disgraceful attack had met with no resistance from the owners who used of such improved machinery.

And it is said, that at no less time, 10 important places where this kind of obnoxious Machinery had been used, it had been unlawfully and viciously destroyed by the Luddites, who flushed with so much success, and confident in their measures and discipline as they imagined, concentrated upon a ground attack on W. Cartwright and of giving the death blow to the use of this kind of machinery by the complete demolition of his mill which was known to be defended by a Military Guard. Of course it was expected that if this bold attempt upon a guarded mill should succeed it would strike such terror into all the other owners as to operate in the utter discontinuance of such machinery in future.

(iii)   *A letter sent to a Huddersfield Master, 1812*
(PRO, Home Office Papers 40/41)
Sir,

Information has just been given in, that you are a holder of those detestable Shearing Frames, and I was desired by many men to write to you, and give you fair warning to pull them down, and for that purpose I desire that you will understand I am now writing to you, you will take notice that if they are not taken down by the end of the next week, I shall detach one of my lieutenants with at least 200 men to destroy them, and further more take notice that if you give us the trouble of coming thus far, we will increase your misfortunes by burning your buildings down to ashes, and if you have the impudence to fire at any of my men, they have orders to murder you and burn all your Housing. You will have the goodness to go to your neighbours to inform them that the same Fate awaits them if their Frames are not taken down . . . I would have the Merchant Master Drapers, the Government and the Public know that the grievances of such a number of men is not made sport of for by the last returns there were 2782 sworn Heroes bound in the Bond of necessity either to redress their grievances or perish in the attempt, in the army of Huddersfield alone, nearly double sworn men in Leeds. . . .

        Signed by the General of the Army of Redresses,
                NED LUDD Clerk

14) *The Scissor Grinders of Sheffield, 1817*
(Letter from William Todd (Postmaster at Sheffield) to Francis
Freeling, 4 January 1817, HO 42/158, quoted in Allinson, *op. cit.*,
p. 227)
[. . .] For a long time, to the serious inconvenience of the trade and
prosperity of this town, a combination has existed among the workmen
belonging to the various branches. The fact of this combination has
been brought home to some of the parties, and the magistrates have
condemned them to three months' imprisonment, against which they
have appealed to Quarter Sessions. I was present at the examinations
held on this business. . . .

It is a complete system of Luddism, and an opportunity is now
offered to check its progress in this town, and at the same time, to
deter offenders in other places.

The magistrates, on passing sentence, recommended that the
master manufacturers should prosecute all the persons, INDI-
VIDUALLY, for a CONSPIRACY, in addition to the combination.
Now, the masters are afraid to do this, for fear that they may incur the
displeasure of the workmen and be injured in their persons or
property.

Should not the Attorney-General be ordered by Government to
prosecute these men for the conspiracy? . . .

15) *The Lancashire Weavers' Strike, 1818*
(Letter of J. Lloyd to Henry Hobhouse, Under-Secretary of State, HO
42/178, quoted in Allinson, *op. cit.*, p. 248)

Stockport, 19 July, 1818
[. . .] From the inquiries I have made I understand that the masters
cannot afford to raise the wages of the power loom weavers. Indeed,
they ought not to do so by apparent compulsion. It is most pernicious
for masters to yield to the intimidation of the ungrateful workmen. The
boys were getting 15s per week by the looms when they turned out, and
those who turn out have an idea that if they subdue Mr. Garside, the
master in general will be under the necessity of advancing to their
terms. His factory and workpeople are well watched, and shall receive
all the protection I can procure. His confidence is strengthened by the
attention which has been latterly paid. I believe he had good cause to
complain of the apathy and unwillingness of the respectable

inhabitants and of the constables themselves in the first instance, who dared to dispute the policy of his conduct. . . .

16) *The Blaenavon Miners Submit, 1822*
(Letter from Revd W. Powell to Henry Hobhouse, April [May] 18, 1822, HO 40/17/43, quoted in Aspinall, *op. cit.*, p. 357)
[. . .] A deputation of his [Mr Hill's of Blaenavon] colliers have just waited upon him to tender their unqualified submission, and to state to a man that they are ready to return to work on Monday without conditions. [. . .]

I have also just seen Mr. Homfray of Tredegar, whose master colliers have resumed their work, and I have little doubt that the rest will speedily follow the example of the Blaenavon men, as I have this day convicted and committed their chief speaker.

The triumph of the law is at this moment of unspeakable consequence, because if the men had been able to hold out for another month or six weeks, I fear the masters would have felt obliged to give way, the trade being certainly in an improving state, with the almost certain prospect of a rise in price next quarter day, which will enable the masters to give an advance of wages. . . .

17) *John Gast, London Shipwright, and the need for General Unionism* (*Trades' Newspaper*, 16 April 1826)
I have often told you, and I now repeat it, that the antidote is in your own hands. Throw away your sotting, . . . your jealousies and divisions, your over-reaching of each other, your underselling your labour – let all the useful and valuable members of every trade, who wish to appear respectable, unite with each other, and be in friendship with all other trades, and you will render yourselves worthy members of society, at once respectable and respected. You need not care for Blacks or Scabs, Jackdaws or Yellows. The industrious classes are the wealth and strength of the nations and nothing but their own conduct makes them poor and impotent.

18) *Francis Place and the Repeal of the Combination Acts*
(i)   (From Francis Place MSS, 27,798ff 12–14)
          In 1814, therefore, I began to work seriously to procure a repeal of the laws against combinations of workmen. . . . As

often as any dispute arose between masters and men ... I interfered, sometimes with the masters, sometimes with the men ... always pushing for the one purpose, the repeal of the laws.

I wrote a great many letters to trade societies in London, and as often as I heard any dispute respecting the Combination Laws in this country I wrote to some of the parties.... Few condescended to notice my application, and scarcely any furnished me with the information which I wished to have; but many of the country papers inserted the articles I sent to them....

(ii)   (From Place MSS 27,798ff 20–24)

On the 12th February [1824] Mr. Hume made his motion and obtained his Committee. It was with difficulty Mr. Hume could obtain the names of twenty-one members to compose the Committee; but when it had sat three days, and had become both popular and amusing, members contrived to be put upon it, and at length it consisted of forty-eight members.

[...] Mr. Hume wrote a circular letter announcing the appointment of the Committee, and inviting persons to come and give evidence. [...] Meetings were held in many places; and both masters and men sent up deputations to give evidence. The delegates from the working people had reference to me, and I opened my house to them. Thus I had all the town and country delegates under my care. I heard the story every one of these men had to tell. I examined and cross-examined them; took down the leading particulars of each case, and then arranged the matter as briefs for Mr. Hume; and, as a rule, for the guidance of the witnesses a copy was given to each ... Thus he was enabled to go on with considerable ease, and to anticipate or rebut objections.

The workmen were not easily managed. It required great pains and patience not to shock their prejudice ... They were filled with false notions, all attributing their distresses to wrong causes which I, in this state of business, dared not attempt to remove Taxes, machinery, laws against combinations, the will of the masters, the conduct of magistrates, these were the funda-mental causes of their sorrows and privations. All expected a great and sudden rise of wages, when the Combination Laws should be repealed; not one of them had any idea whatever of the connection between wages and population. [He spent three months preparing them for presenting evidence.]

19) *The Combination Acts of 1824 and 1825*
(i)   *The Combination Act of 1824*
         (Combination Act of 1824, 5 Geo IV, *c.* 95)
         An Act to repeal the Laws relative to Combination of Workmen; and for other purposes therein mentioned (21st June 1824).
         Whereas it is expedient that the laws relative to the combination of workmen and to fixing the wages of labour, should be repealed; and that certain combinations of masters and workmen should be exempted from punishment; and that the attempt to deter workmen from work should be punished in a summary manner; be it therefore enacted. . . .That from and after the passing of this Act [all attempts to combine to increase wages or change hours, etc.], shall be and the same are hereby repealed. . . .
         II And be it further enacted that journeymen, workmen or other persons who shall enter into any combination to obtain an advance or to fix the rate of wages, or to lessen or alter the hours of duration of the time of working, or to decrease the quantity of work, or to induce another to depart from his service before the end of the time . . . for which he is hired . . . shall not therefore be liable or subject to any indictment or prosecution for conspiracy. . . .
         V And be it further enacted, that if any person, by violence to the person or property, by threats or intimidation, shall wilfully or maliciously force another to depart from his hiring or work before the end of the time . . . he is hired [and other similar situations]; every person so offending, or causing, procuring, aiding, abetting, or assisting in such offences, being convicted thereof in manner hereafter mentioned, shall be imprisoned only, or imprisoned and kept to hard labour, for any time not exceeding two calendar months.
(ii)   *The Combination Act of 1825*
         (6 Geo IV, *c.* 129)
         III And be it further enacted, that from and after the passing

of this act, if any person shall by violence to the person or property, or by threats or intimidation, or by molesting or in any way obstructing another, force or endeavour to force any journeyman, manufacturer, workman or other person hired or employed in any manufacture, trade or business, to depart from his hiring, employment or work, or to return to his work before the same shall be finished, or prevent or endeavour to prevent, any journeyman, manufacturer, workman or other person, not being hired or employed, from, hiring himself to, or from accepting work or employment from any person or persons; [. . .]; every person so offending or aiding, abetting or assisting therein, being convinced thereof in manner hereinafter mentioned, shall be imprisoned only, or shall and may be imprisoned and kept for hard labour, for any time not exceeding three calendar months.

20) *The Bradford Woolcombers' and Weavers' Strike, June 1825*
(i) *John Tester's account*
     (John Tester, 'History of the Bradford Contest', MSS, Bradford branch of West Yorkshire Archives)
     The first branch of the Union Association was formed at Manningham on the 16th August 1824. The members of it were all journeymen weavers originally. . . . They had invited masters as well as weavers to join them; their only object being the equalisation of wages as near as could be found practical.

     A long discussion took place as to whether the children working for these firms against which it was proposed to strike were to leave their work but not many were for their being taken out of the factories.

     This committee considered that as the matter was now assuming a serious form it was necessary to increase their numbers. . . . They applied to the different tramping societies, which were six in number. . . . Afterwards the Irish were assembled together and requested to send one man as their representative.
(ii) *James' Account*
     (Extract from J. James, *History of Worsted Manufacture*, 1857, p. 402)
     As the demands were not acceded to at the Conference, the

combers next day (Tuesday, 7 June) struck against three firms in Bradford, Messrs John Wroe, Messrs Margerison and Peckover and Messrs Leach and Cousins. (These were the three firms which paid the lowest wages.)

Resolution of Master Manufacturers' Committee – 8th June

1. That as it appeared from evidence that the prices paid for combing are higher that they have been for the last ten years or so and that the present price of provisions is more reasonable than frequently during the period, the request made is unreasonable.
2. That the meeting views with concern the manner in which the above request has been made and feels it their duty by every means in their power to counteract a combination which if not suppressed would strike at the root of the prosperity of the town and neighbourhood. Under these circumstances, they pledge themselves as individuals and partnerships not to employ any comber who shall continue to be a member of the union.
3. That it is the opinion of the meeting that the demand for the weavers is unreasonable; being fully aware however of the depressed state of that branch for the last six to eight months, they will feel pleasure in giving an advance when the circumstances of the trade shall change so as to allow it, but looking upon the combination of weavers as equally dangerous to that of the combers, they pledge themselves to employ no weaver who is a member of the union.

Form of denial

We, the undersigned, in the employ of . . . hereby declare that we are not members of the union of combers and weavers nor will we contribute to its support either directly or indirectly, so long as we remain in your employ.

Minute of 29 June – of Master Manufacturers' Committee

Resolved that all the combers employed by any basketeer shall sign a declaration at the warehouse of the masters that they do not belong to the union before their principals shall be allowed to weigh out any more wool to such combers, and that combers refusing to sign shall return their combs immediately. [. . .]

Letter from John Carter to Master Manufacturers' Committee
Lightcliffe, Sept. 3rd 1825

Sirs,

In answer to the circular I have received from you, I would beg to say that the few workpeople I employ are chiefly elderly men and their families who have been employed under me nearly all their lives. I apprehend that they do not belong to nor are connected with any club or union, nor have they the least disposition for any advance of wages. Should such circumstances take place in the present situation of trade, I feel it is my duty to unite with the general body of manufacturers in resisting their demands.

I remain, Sir, your most obedient servant,

John Carter

If any of my men be in the union, I shall certainly discharge them.

(iii) *The Bradford Strike*

(Extract from the *Leeds Mercury*, May 1826)

The committee of the Bradford Union of Woolcombers and Stuffweavers have published a statement of their income and expenditure. From it, it appears that £14,091 12s. was disbursed during the strike to 2000 men, 213 women and 2923 children. The whole expenditure including all expenses is stated to be £15,826 6s. 9d. For the support of the turn out, the sum of £1843 2s. 6d. was received by the committee from Leeds, Huddersfield £1688 12s. 1d., London £1098, Loughborough £1193 4s., Bradford £594 1s., Halifax £392 11s. 10d., and a variety of smaller sums from other places.

Masters had claimed that the best workers were able to earn between 27s. and 23s. a week combing. *Leeds Mercury* thought that an average wage for 11 hours a day would be about 16s. to 17s. Some might earn more by working longer. There had already been some increase during the preceding 15 months. Not all masters had paid the increase.

Another consequence of this mischievous contest is that it will precipitate the use of machinery and instead of the power loom and the combing machine being brought gradually to the worsted business, which is the proper and beneficial mode of introducing such changes, the cost of the machine is sharpened and the impatience of the master manufacturer excited to supersede the necessity of manual labour by the general and sudden introduction of such machines.

Comparison of Costs of Hand and Power Loom Weaving (supplied by the Masters' Committee).

Power loom – weaving five pieces of cloth in *one* week; wages 11/3, power and room 1/6, Sizing, Loom winding and interest in capital 2/6 – Total 15/3d.

Hand Loom Wages paid in Bradford for weaving five pieces of cloth by hand £1 5s. Od. (Wages demanded by strikers said by Masters' Committee to be £1 10s. Od.

21) *The Saddleworth Union*
(i)   *Poster issued 1st December 1828*
        [Typed copy in hands of Dr K. Laybourn. Original was with the Saddleworth History Society, but seems to have been lost or mislaid.]
        To the Master Woollen Manufacturers, Ley-Preyers, and other Inhabitants.

        A Paper very numerously and respectably signed, having lately appeared and being addressed to the Saddleworth Weavers' Union, the Committee find themselves called on 'for purposes of conciliation, to publish an official notification of what are their general intentions, and what objects they confined their views'. The Committee therefore consider it their duty to comply with the request; and in the first place, they conceive that they cannot anyway better do this, than by republishing their *Declaration*, as prefixed to the general Rules of the Union. . . .

                          DECLARATION
'The design of the founders of this Union is, protection to Trade generally; by adopting such lawful means as they consider calculated to procure for the Labouring Class in the Woollen Business something like competent wages for their labour.'

'The First or preliminary design is to create a Fund of Money by collection of weekly contributions and donations; and in cases of emergency to crave the assistance of the neighbouring districts, and also lend assistance in return when circumstances and the State of the Fund will admit it.'

The first objects to which it is intended to direct the energies of the Union are, an equalization of wages throughout the Parish; and putting a stop to that ruinous and unlawful system of paying wages in goods; and also bringing into operation the provisions of the Arbitration Act, 'passed the reign of George the Fourth'.

These were the original intentions or views of the Founders of the Union; and though it has been expedient to remodel the institution, by engrafting in the original stock 'A Friendly Society' as a Branch from the neighbouring district; which is conducted on the principles exactly the same as all other Secret Benefit Societies, with provision for Funeral Expenses of deceased members and their wives; and also Relief of the Sick, for as many as choose to enter that department of the Institution; and also a System of Discipline, organized and confined exclusively to the objects of promoting Moral Improvement, the well regulating and governing the Society, – and enjoining peace and harmony, – and enjoining peace and harmony, and a strict obedience to the Laws of the Realm; ... [...]

We shall therefore conclude for the present, with expressing an ardent wish, that the Manufacturers of Saddleworth, who have DISCHARGED THEIR WORKMEN, merely on the ground of their being in the Union, would look at, – and consider well, – the NINE DISTINCT HEADS OF RECOMMENDATION IN THE ADDRESS before alluded to, – where it is recommended, to pay wages in Money, ... To balance accounts when required, – to ticket the price of work before delivery, ... To measure according to Act of Parliament, ... And we will add, pay WAGES such as will enable the Workmen TO LIVE, without applying to the Parish for assistance to make up the deficiency, ... : do these things, and we doubt not, the consequence will be, that the DISPUTES betwixt MASTERS and WORKMEN in SADDLEWORTH, will be rare as they have been common: remove the Cause and the Effect will cease.

By Order of the Committee

Saddleworth, December 1st 1828.

(ii)   *George Shaw's Diary, 14 February 1829 on the end of the Saddleworth Union*
(As reference (i))

Last night about (I cannot exactly tell what time) the redoubtable Saddleworth Weavers' Union gave up the ghost. The invincible, the everlasting Society of friendship and honour, which was to have lasted for ever was dissolved. The reason of it being given up at the present time seems to (people say) be the great falling off in their revenue occasioned by the desertion of some of the members who were distressed and out of employment. I was firmly convinced in my own mind that eventually this would be the case, but I never expected it so soon. Indeed, all the men quite hooted the idea of giving up a short time ago. They pretended that the Rochdale Committee regularly sent them £30 per week and the West of England Committee £39, and that as to some of their members falling off, it was all nothing, they were only a few of the worst description, who because they must not live entirely upon it have left in a passion – I am tempted to believe everything has not gone right, there being a strange waste of money somehow or other in it. It has the appearance of a whirlpool; whatever was put into it was greedily swallowed up in the vortex and never left any trace of itself behind. Its mouth has been as bad to satisfy as the carnivorous jaws of the grave. In my humble opinion the head men or people in office had no bad trade of it. They have laid up much good in store I think, or else, what has become of the money? There has been no expenditure equal to income. Its members, at least, few of them have been in little or any distress, everything has seemed in a very prosperous condition until the coalition of the masters against it, and to give up in the very first struggle shows plainly that the money has been decamped, and who can have taken it? I say 'Those through whose fingers it has passed'.

22) *The Grand General Union of Spinners, 1829*
(Resolutions of the Delegates from the Operative Cotton Spinners who met at the Isle of Man (December 1829), Home Office Papers, 40/27 [1829])

3. That one Grand General Union of all the Operative Spinners in the United Kingdom be now formed for the mutual support and protection of all.

4. That every member of this Association shall contribute the sum of one penny a week to the general fund, over and above the local levy, or expense of each District, and that all persons receiving benefit from either a local or the general fund, shall contribute the same sum.

6. That all male piecers capable of spinning be caused to pay one penny weekly, to the general fund as members of this association, and that in cases of strikes all such as remain out shall receive the same allowance as the spinner, and that Mr. Johnstone and Mr. Doherty be appointed to prepare an entrance ceremony for the admission of piecers as members.

7. That the sum of 10/- a week be paid to every member of this association when they are on strike against a reduction of wages.

8. That 10/- a week be paid to members when contending for an advance of wages the same as when resisting reductions, but that no district or part of a district be allowed to strike for an advance without first having obtained the consent and authority of the other districts.

9. That no person be allowed to turn out either for an advance or against a reduction of wages, without the consent and authority of the whole districts, and that no more be allowed at any time to come out than what can be supported with the stipulated sum on any consideration whatever.

18. That no person or persons be learned or allowed to spin after the 5th April 1830 except the son, brother or orphan nephew of spinners, and the poor relations of the proprietors of the mills, and those only when they have attained the full age of 15 years; . . .

19. That any person who may work as a spinner at any rate below what is considered a fair and legal price shall be fined £5 and continue a regular paying member of all fair dues and demands for one year before he be entitled to the benefits of the trade and any member causing one under his control to do so shall be fined in one half the sum and be exposed throughout the whole trade.

24. That female spinners be urged to become members of an association to be formed exclusively for themselves, ...

23) *The National Association for the Protection of Labour, 1830*
(Organized by Doherty as a General Union, this body ran two papers, *The United Trades Co-operative Journal* and *The Voice of the People.* This extract is taken from *The United Trades Co-operative Journal*, 10 July 1830)

NATIONAL ASSOCIATION
FOR THE PROTECTION OF LABOUR
Resolutions and Laws

Agreed to by the meeting of Delegates held in Manchester, on Monday, Tuesday and Wednesday, the 28th, 29th and 30th June, 1830.

Resolved, 1 That the miserable conditions to which, by repeated and unnecessary reductions of wages, the working people of the country are reduced, urged upon this meeting the imperative necessity of adopting some effectual means for preventing such reductions and securing to the industrious workman a just and adequate remuneration for his labour.

2. That to accomplish this necessary object a Society shall be formed consisting of the various organised Trades throughout the kingdom.

3. That this Society be called 'The National Association for the Protection of Labour'.

14. That the funds of the Society shall be applied only to prevent reductions of wages, but in no case to procure an advance. Any trade considering their wages too low may exert themselves to obtain such advance, as they may think necessary and can obtain it by their own entreaties.

24) *The Swing Outrages, 1830*
(Leaflet published by Henry Hetherington, Home Office Papers, 40/25 [1830])
[...] The Gentlemen and Farmers of Kent are in the greatest consternation on account of the organised system of conflagration, from which so many of them have suffered. Every man who has ever employed an Irishman is in constant dread of a visit. The insurgents go

about in bands of 150, and coolly demand the keys of the barns to destroy the thrashing-machines, and all idea of resistance is out of the question. Indeed when the gentlemen have applied to their servants to assist them in repelling the attack, they have met with a flat refusal. The signals are given by sky-rockets and as many as fourteen stack-yards have been in flames at the same time. There has long been a sullen discontent among the peasantry of England; may the Aristocracy take warning in time. [. . .]

25) *The Operative Builders, 1833: Manifesto of the Operative Builders' Union.*
(From R.W. Postgate, *Builders' History*, p. 463, from the Owen correspondence in the Co-operative Union Records, Manchester)
[. . .] Seeing no prospect of any improvement in our condition, being also conscious that our most valuable materials are ignorantly wasted by being senselessly scattered throughout the four quarters of the world and that our industry and skill and unlimited powers of invention are now most grossly misdirected; we without any hostile feelings to the Government or any class of persons, have been compelled to come to the conclusion that no party can or will relieve us from the tremendous evils which we suffer and still greater which are coming upon us, until we begin in earnest to act for ourselves and at once adopt the recommendation of Sir Robert Peel, 'to take our own affairs into our own hands'.

We have decided to follow this advice and with this view we have formed ourselves into a National Building Guild of Brothers, to enable us to erect buildings of every description upon the most extensive scale in England, Scotland and Ireland.

By the arrangement and organisation which we have adopted we shall accomplish the following important results.

1st – We shall be enabled to erect all manner of dwelling and other architectural designs for the public more expeditiously, substantially and economically than any Masters can build them under the individual system of competition.

2nd – We shall be enabled to withdraw all our Brethren of the National Builders' Guild and their families from being a burden upon the public, for they will be supported in old age, infancy, sickness or infirmity of any kind from the funds of the Guild.

3rd – None of the Brethren will be unemployed when they desire to work, for when the public do not require their services they will be employed by the Guild to erect superior dwellings and other buildings for themselves, under superior arrangements, that they, their wives and their children may live continuously surrounded by those virtuous external circumstances which alone can form an intelligent, prosperous, good and happy population.

4th – We shall be enabled to determine upon a just and equitable remuneration or wages for the services of the Brethren according to their skill and conduct when employed by the public.

5th – We shall also be placed in a position to decide upon the amount of work or service to be performed, each day, by the Brethren, in order that none may be oppressed by labour beyond the powers of their mind.

26) *The Grand National Consolidated Trade Union, 1833–4*

(i)   (Robert Owen, from a speech in *The Crisis*, 19 October 1833)
The members of this Union have discovered that competition in the sale of their productions is the chief and immediate cause of their poverty and degradation, and that they can never overcome either as long as they shall conduct their affairs individually, and in opposition to each other.

They are, therefore, about to form national companies of production; each trade or manufacture to constitute one grand company or association, comprising all the individuals in the business throughout Great Britain and Ireland; but each trade and manufacturer to be united to all others by a general bond of interest by which they will exchange their productions with each other upon the principle of equitable exchange of labour for a fair equal value of labour; and all articles, upon the principle of economy and general advantage, will be produced of the best quality only.

The next step in gradation will be the union of the master traders and manufacturers with the operatives and manual producers; and when these two parties shall fully understand the value of this union, the Government will not only feel the necessity of uniting with them, but it will also discover the advantage to the whole empire of this national bond of union.

(ii) (From the Rules of the Grand National Consolidated Trades Union, 1834. A copy in the Goldsmiths' Library, University of London and reproduced in G.D.H. Cole and A.W. Filson, *British Working Class Movements: Select Documents 1789–1875* London, Macmillan, 1967).
Rules and Regulations of the Grand National Consolidated Trade Union of Great Britain and Ireland, instituted for the purpose of the more effectively enabling the working classes to receive, protect and establish the rights of industry.

GENERAL PLAN AND GOVERNMENT

I. Each Trade in this Consolidated Union shall have its Grand Lodge in that town or city more eligible for it, such Grand Lodge to be governed internally by a Grand Master, Deputy Grand Masters, and Grand Secretary, and a Committee of Management.

27) *The National Regeneration Society, 1833–4*
(Resolutions of the Society for Promoting National Regeneration, 25 November 1833, from *The Pioneer*, p. 109)
It was unanimously resolved
1. That it is desirable that all who wish to see society improved and confusion avoided, should endeavour to assist the working classes to obtain 'for eight hours work the present full day's wages', such eight hours to be performed between the hours of six in the morning and six in the evening, and that this new regulation should commence on the 1st day of March next.
2. That, in order to carry the foregoing purposes into effect a society should be formed, to be called 'The Society for Promoting National Regeneration'.
15. That Messrs. Oastler, Wood, Bull, Sadler, and others, be urgently requested to desist from soliciting parliament for a ten-hour bill, and to use their utmost exertions in aid of the measures now adopted to carry into effect, on 1st of March next, the regulation of 'eight hours work for the present full day's wages'.

28) *Committee of United Weavers, 1833*
(Extract from the *Liberator*, a Glasgow paper, quoted in the *Voice of the West Riding*, 28 September 1833)
At a meeting of the Committee of United Weavers [. . .]
'Resolved – That it be recommended to the united weavers in England, Ireland, and Scotland, also the various united operatives of these realms, that they take into early consideration the propriety of fixing a day when the whole shall simultaneously suspend work for one month, or till the rights of labour and property are properly ascertained and adjusted, a certain provision of the real necessaries of life established for the truly industrious to the extent of our national resources, and till every sane and mature member of the community be invested with the elective franchise.'
This shows that a knowledge of the sullen, deep, dogged, and unsubduable power of *passive resistance* is rapidly gaining ground among those who form the foundations of society – . . .

29) *The Tolpuddle Martyrs, 1834*
(George Loveless, *The Victims of Whiggery being a statement of the Prosecution Experienced by the Dorchester Labourers in 1834*)
National Agricultural Labourers' Union, Blandford, 1875, being a reprint of the pamphlet produced in 1837, copy in the Webb Collection, British Library of Political and Economic Science (Coll E, B, cv, iii).
About the years 1831–2, when there was a general movement of the working classes for an increase of wages, the labouring men in the parish where I lived (Tolpuddle) gathered together, and met their employers, to ask them for an advance in wages, and they came to a mutual agreement, the masters of Tolpuddle promising to give the men as much for their labour as the other masters in the district. . . .
Shortly after we learnt that, in about every place around us, the masters were giving the men money, or money's worth, to the amount of ten shillings per week – we expected to be entitled to as much – but no – nine shillings must be our position. After some months it was reduced to eight shillings per week. This caused great dissatis-faction. . . . [Applied to the Magistrate for judgement on this action of the employers.] I was named to appear, and then we were told that we must work for what our employers thought fit to give us, as there was

no law to compel masters to give any fixed sum of money to their servants. In vain we remonstrated that an agreement was made. [. . .]

From this time we were reduced to seven shillings per week, and shortly after our employers told us they must lower us to six shilling per week. The labouring men consulted together what had better be done, as they knew it was impossible to live honestly on such scanty means. I had seen at different times accounts of Trade Societies; I told them of this, and they willingly consented to form a friendly society among the labourers, having sufficiently learnt that it would be in vain to seek redress of employers, magistrates or parsons. I enquired of a brother to get information how to proceed, and shortly after, two delegates from a Trade Society paid us a visit, formed a Friendly Society among the labourers, and gave us directions how to proceed. This was about the latter end of October 1833. On the 9th of December, 1833, in the evening, Edward Legg (a labourer), who was witness against us at the trial, came and desired to be admitted into the Society; by which means he was introduced there I cannot say; but well do I know that James Hammett, one of the six that he was sworn to, was not there.

Nothing particular occurred from this time to the 21st February, 1834, when placards were posted up in the most conspicuous places, purporting to be . . . from the magistrates, threatening to punish with seven years transportation any man who should join the Union. This was the first time that I heard of any law being in existence to forbid such societies. I met with a copy, read it, and put it in my pocket. February 24th, at day break, I arose to go to my usual labour and had just left my house, when Mr. James Brine, constable of the parish, met me and said 'I have a warrant for your arrest from the magistrates.' [The others were also arrested and sent to County Hall on 15 March to await trial.]

As to the trial, I need not mention but little; the cowardice and dastardly conduct throughout are better known by all that which were present than could be by any description that I can give it; suffice it to say the most unfair and unjust means were resorted to in order to frame the indictment against us; the grand jury appeared to ransack heaven and earth to get some claim against us, but in vain; our characters were investigated from our infancy to the then present moment . . . , and when nothing whatever could be raked together, the unjust and cruel judge, Williams, ordered us to be tried for mutiny, and conspiracy, under the act 37 Geo III, cap. 123, for the suppression of mutiny and conspiracy against the marines and seamen, a number of years ago at the Nore. The greater part of the evidence against us on our trial, was put into the mouths of witnesses by the judge; . . . I shall not soon forget the address of the judge to the jury, in summing up the evidence; among other things he told them, that if such Societies were allowed to exist, it would ruin masters, cause stagnation in trade, destroy property – and if they should not find us guilty, *he was certain that they would forfeit the opinion of the grand jury.* [They were found guilty.] I instantly formulated the following short defence, in writing, to him: 'My Lord, if we have violated any law, it was not done intentionally; we have injured no man's reputation, character, person, or property; we were uniting together to preserve ourselves, our wives, and our children from utter degradation and starvation. We challenge any man, or number of men, to prove that we have acted or intend to act, different from the above statement.

[He then described his harsh treatment, his transportation for seven years and the fact that, after a campaign in Britain to free him, he was informed that he and the other Dorchester labourers would be released on 20 January 1837. He left Hobart for Britain on 30 January and arrived in London on 13 June 1837.]

30) *The Disturbances at Oldham, April 1834*
(*Voice of the West Riding,* 19 April 1834)
Oldham, during the last week, has been the theatre of some very extraordinary scenes and acts – acts that will have a very great influence on society at large, and more particularly on one portion – the working class. The famous exploits of Exeter and Dorchester have been attempted at Oldham, and the men there have nobly and morally, firmly and quietly resented the aggressions. [. . .]

On Monday night last, three police officers (one of them in a state of beastly intoxication, and the other two as far removed from sobriety as you please) broke into one of the Trades' Lodges, apprehended two men and carried off a book containing the initiation cere-monies. . . . The house in which this lodge was held is situated within a few yards of a manufactory against which there had been a strike for some time; and the master of which, in consequence, employed a number of 'knobsticks', or 'black-uns'. These characters have made themselves particularly obnoxious in the town, not only from consenting to work at what the men formerly employed in their places considered 'under-wages' – but also from the violent and desperate nature of their conduct: they often sallying out of the mill armed with bludgeons, blunderbusses, pistols, and attacking the peaceable passers by. . . .

The news of the arrest of the two Unionists spread like wildfire; and it being reported that the prisoners would be marched off to Manchester, the people, instead of going to their daily labour on Tuesday morning, assembled in great numbers. About half past nine o'clock it was reported that the police were taking the men down the road, and a tremendous rush was made towards them. They were overtaken just opposite the factory where the obnoxious characters above alluded to were employed, and the two prisoners were instantly released. An attack was then made upon the police, who had the men in custody. Those who worked in the mill appeared at the different windows, brandishing bludgeons, shaking their fists, and making other gestures of defiance. This, to an already exasperated crowd, was more than they could bear, and the consequence was, stones and other missiles were hurled at them. An attack was also made upon the house of the 'black sheep', and the latter rushed out of the back of the mill with fire-arms, and shot several times amongst the crowd. When they had discharged their pieces they retreated back into the mill, loaded again, and then returned and fired as before . . . it was blank shot that was fired. At length one of the party, who can be identified by half a dozen persons, advanced, and deliberately levelling his piece towards a party who stood at a distance quietly looking on, fired, and the contents, seemingly slugs, entered the breast of a person names James Bentley. He staggered a little, then fell, shook his head, sobbed and died. The cry was instantly raised 'a man is shot', and he who had done the fatal deed changed colour, turned on his heel, and retired. The work of demolition then commenced in earnest – the windows were all smashed in – the houses of both masters and men were entered – . . . All the time this was going on some of the most intelligent amongst the operatives were endeavouring to get the crowd away from this place, showing them the consequences of such like conduct. They at last succeeded, and the people assembled in a vacant piece of ground behind the Albion Inn. They were addressed by several persons who recommended that Lodge meetings should be forthwith held. . . .

By this time some of the 'guards, garbed in red-blood livery' had arrived, but fortunately there was nothing for them to do! In the course of the evening and next day, about fourteen persons were apprehended on a charge of rioting. [. . .]

A meeting of about 15,000 operatives was held at halfpast five o'clock on Wednesday morning on Oldham Edge, and the following resolutions were adopted.

1st That this Meeting pledges itself to prevent, as far as possible, any disturbances of the public peace.

2nd That the Trades' Unions, always wishing to maintain harmony and social order in society and preserve the public peace, deprecates the conduct of the Oldham Police in breaking into their peaceable meetings and disturbing the proceedings.

3rd That this Meeting also deprecates any conduct that is likely to lead, or has led, to the destruction of property.

4th That this Meeting deems it advisable and expedient not to return to labour until justice be rendered them for the outrages that has [sic] been committed upon their 'order'.

On Thursday morning another meeting was held at the same place, and by half-past six, upwards of 25,000 persons were assembling. They were addressed by some of their own body, and also by some of the friends from Manchester, Mr Doherty, Mr Grant and Mr Rigby. The subjoined resolution was passed with greatest enthusiasm:-

Resolved, That this Meeting, both Individually and collectively, again express their firm determination not to return to their daily avocations until full and perfect justice is done to the working-men of England – those of them who have been dragged from their homes, their families, and their country, *for no crime*, be restored – and those who have committed violence and outrage upon them be punished – and they call upon their brethren, in all parts of the country to follow their example. And they further declare that when *they do return to work*, they will not labour more than eight hours per day.

31) *The Great Meeting at Copenhagen Fields, 1834*
(*The Voice of the West Riding*, 26 April 1834)
THE GREAT MEETING IN COPENHAGEN FIELDS AND
PROCESSION OF THE TRADES' UNIONISTS TO
WHITEHALL
On Monday last the Unionists of London went in procession to
Whitehall with another petition to the King, in favour of the Dor-
chester convicts, the prayer of those they had sent before not having
been complied with. We give from the *True Sun*, the following account
of the procession, and the reception they met with at the Home Office.

Scarcely had day dawned this morning before the metropolis, in all
its principal streets began to present the busy note of preparation for
the impending great meeting in Copenhagen-fields, and the procession thence to Westminster, as an escort to the five deputies
appointed to convey the petition on behalf of the Dorchester
labourers to Lord Melbourne, for his lordship in his official
capacity, to lay before the King. Persons were to be seen with the
appointed distinguishing ribbon of the Union in almost every street
at six o'clock in the morning, hastening to their respective lodges.
[. . .] On reaching the opening to Copenhagen-fields, bodies closely
compacted and walking in strict order, were to be seen crossing the
fields on all points towards the general point of conveyancing,
leading to the Copenhagen-house, namely, the new Caledonian
asylum. These bodies, as they were thus seen advancing had a most
beautiful and orderly appearance. [. . .] A similar large body was to
be seen advancing along the road over the Maiden-lane bridge. At
six o'clock a town cart was sent from the Rotunda, in the
Blackfriars-road, laden with the banners and distinguishing trade
insignia, as agreed upon. These banners were planted in the open
space in front of Copenhagen-house, which had been hired for the
occupiers at considerable spaces apart, so as to admit of the various
bodies as they arrived, each ranging himself under the appropriate
trade banner.

(Copenhagen-field, Nine o'clock)
The whole of the Unions are now on the ground and have been
arranged in most admirable order. The banners inscribed with the
name of the respective trades, have been planted 20 feet apart, on

parallel lines on either side of the road-way [. . .] The appearance, as viewed from the windows is particularly pleasing. Neither police nor soldiers are to be seen in any direction, and every thing at present wears the dress of a gay spring holiday. The men appear to be all sober. None but Unionists are allowed to join the ranks.

Arrival of 3,000 Weavers

Since the above was written, a body of about 3,000 weavers from Spitalfields have arrived, and take their prescribed station. Not a policeman or soldier to be seen in any direction.

(Communication from Lord Melbourne)

Lord Melbourne is said to have written a second letter to the central committee last night, stating that if the procession approached any of the government offices he would not receive the petition. It is said that the final determination of the committee was to adhere to the original arrangement, with the slight exception that the car containing the petition should be deposited by the bearers at the side of the road, or on some convenient place near Whitehall, and the procession pass on, and take their stand by New Bedlam, or, as some say, disperse altogether, and that in about half an hour after the last of the procession had passed Whitehall the deputation should take the petition to Lord Melbourne.

32) *An Odious Document, 1834*
(Deposited in Calderdale branch of West Yorkshire Archives, Halifax)
WE whose Names are hereunto subscribed, do declare, that from and after the twenty-fourth Day of May, 1834, we shall cease to be Members of Trades' Unions, or have before disunited ourselves from the Body, and that so long as we continue in the Employment of Benjamin Mellor [of] Stainland we will not be Members of the Union, or contribute in any way to the Support of that, or any similar Association.

William Lawson	John Lumb
Jos Schofield X his mark	John Iredale
John Brooks	George X Gill
Robt Ashworth	George X Raincliffe

[And more than 100 other names, half of whom signed with an X.]

33) *G.J. Holyoake on Trade Unions, 1841*

(Lecture addressed to the 'Trade Unions of Sheffield', 28 November 1841, quoted in W. Milne Bailey, *Trade Union Documents: Compiled and Edited with an Introduction by W. Milne Bailey* (London, G. Bell & Sons Ltd, 1929), p. 47)

The advantages of Trades' Unions will be seen from the remarks made. Being founded in justice, as we have shown, they must have produced good as no just thing is lost to the world. They have generated a love of freedom, have knit together the victims of capital, when masters have forgotten honour and justice, and the world. They have generated compassion and sympathy. When governments and religion were ranked with the oppressors, Unions were the only barriers between the desolation of capital and machinery, starvation and the poorhouse.

34) *The Potters*

(i) (*The Potters' Examiner and Workman's Advocate*, 13 January 1844)
It is well known that the strike of 1836 was to obtain two things. First an equitable form of agreement between masters and men. . . .

The causes made by the men ... were – first a form of agreement that guarantees to the Potteries at least 16 days work a month, instead of the uncertainty that before existed when agreement only bound the employers to find as much work as he conveniently could which sometimes only meant one day a month. Now if the employer finds himself unable by any cause to find the stipulated amount of work the workers have the power to dissolve the contract by giving one month's notice.

(ii) (*The Potters' Examiner and Workman's Advocate*, 27 April 1844)
Everything we are happy to say connected with the union is going prosperously. Never in the history of the Staffordshire potteries was a better spirit developed among the combined Potters of the neighbourhood than at the present time. Never indeed was such a union as the present known to exist at this time of year before. All our previous unions were, as some of our friends remark, 6 weeks before Martinmass Unions which invariably met with sudden and unfortunate deaths almost 6 weeks after Martinmass. They were merely unions of excite-

ment – bubbles on the surface of Trades agitation, called into existence by the fear of 'missing time', and a little passing declamation. The present is the first systematized union in the Pottery trade.

(iii) *(The Potters' Examiner and Workman's Advocate*, 8 June 1844)
[. . .] Central Committee also to take steps to regulate the approaches so as to stop the growing evil of surplus labour.
It is a matter of regret that no step has yet been taken to avoid the influx of agricultural labourers and children of the same into the pottery business of the Kingdom. The children of those who have worked at the trade have priority of claim to employment in the trade.

(iv) *(The Potters' Examiner and Workman's Advocate*, 6 July 1844, on The United Branches of the Operative Potters)
It will be recollected that the former union of our trade was grounded on the principle of one general fund, subscribed to by every branch of the trade and placed in the hands of a single individual and one General Board of Management in whom were invested the Government of the Society both local and general.
This gave rise to various events, among others . . . dishonesty from the accumulation of large funds in the hands of a few individuals, and the Society not being entrusted under the hands of a few individuals.
The concentration of power in the hands of a few.
The inevitable destruction of the Society in the event of the disturbance of its General Executive.
This is now all altered in the present Union. The Society is now governed on the same principle as the U.S. of America. Each branch is a separate state, and each branch Board a State's Congress. All the funds and executive power of the branch is vested in its Board. A Central Committee, a General Board of Management is established . . . is invested with the general management of the United branches of the Operative Potters. This Committee controls all the branches, with the exception of ½d per member to defray all incidental expenses.

35) *The National Association of United Trades for the Protection of Labour, 1845*

(From the *Northern Star*, 29 March 1845)

Report of the Committee appointed at the Inaugural Conference of the National Association of United Trades for the Protection of Labour to consider plans of activity.

The *immediate* measures which it appears to your committee that conference might usefully take into consideration are the following:-

1. A society to be called the Association of United Trades for the Protection of Industry.

2. A Central committee to carry out the objects of the said Association, and the formation of a fund to defray the necessary expenses.

3. The leading objects of the Association may be divisable into two departments – the first having reference to the influence of the Legislature on the conditions of the industrious classes; the second internal, or the effects made by the Trades to improve their own conditions.

With respect to the first of these divisions, your committee suggests that the Central Committee should be empowered and instructed to take every opportunity, by means of petitions to Parliament, deputations to the Government and members of both houses of the Legislature, cheap publications, public meetings, and to other legal, reasonable and peaceable measures to enforce the adoption of shorter hours of labour wherever practicable. . . .

4. Another measure to which serious consideration should be directed is, the establishment of local Boards of Trade, similar to those which have so long existed in France and Belgium, composed of masters and operatives, to whom all matters affecting the regulation of wages, duration of labour, disputes etc. should be referred, and their decisions have the authority of law. . . .

5. The second division of the Association should be the collection and diffusion of information, as to the means by which the capital skill and labour of the trades can be applied for their own benefit, and especially to enable them to abstract from the labour market and set to profitable employment, the redundant hands, who, if suffered to remain in it, would reduce the wages of the whole trade to which they belong. . . .

6. The Central Committee should be instructed to carefully prepare a constitution for concentrating the energies, legalising the proceedings, and giving practical effect to the growing desire for location in the land, and other measures for the profitable employment of the funds of such Unions as might be desirous of using them.

'NEW MODEL UNIONS' AND CRAFT UNIONISM *c.* 1850–1887

The Webbs coined the phrase the 'New Model Unions' almost a century ago in their pioneering effort to map out the pattern and development of British trade unionism. Ever since that time historians, such as G.D.H. Cole and A.E. Musson, have been at pains to stress that there was nothing particularly new about the 'New Model' of unionism. In addition, it has been pointed out many times that the amalgamated societies were not necessarily pacific in their industrial intent and were prepared to strike, that many of them did not have central funds, which might inhibit their strike activities, but were in fact federal in organization and that a large and increasing number of trade unions were, in the 1850s and 1860s, organizing unskilled and semi-skilled workers. Not all trade unionists were 'Labour aristocrats' in any meaningful sense of the phrase. What is clear is that a more powerful form of trade unionism emerged during the prosperous years between the 1850s and the early 1870s which provided the basis of a meaningful and powerful trade-union movement, despite the ravages imposed upon the movement by the depression and deflation of the 1870s and 1880s.

The distinctive feature of this period is that trade unions began to form as national organizations again, on a more permanent and often more trade-orientated basis than ever before. However, they were by no means guaranteed a favourable response and many unions were quickly involved in industrial conflict after their formation. Engineers throughout the country came together to form the Amalgamated

Society of Engineers (1), and with a commitment to getting rid of 'systematic overtime'. It was soon involved in an unsuccessful fight against the lock-out of its members by the engineering employers in London and Lancashire, after which many of its members were forced to sign an 'Odious Document' by which they withdrew from trade-union membership. The Preston cotton weavers also fought for more than seven months for a restoration of wage reductions which had previously been imposed at some firms (2). The South Yorkshire Miners' Association and the West Yorkshire Miners' Association, both formed in 1858, arose out of strike situations. The formation of the London Trades Council (3) was the response on many unions involved in the London Building dispute of 1859 to 1860; its objective came to be the amalgamation of trade unions in order to reduce the likelihood of strikes. As George Odger wrote: 'It is worthy of remark that Societies if they amalgamated, or otherwise become large, steer clearer of strikes and yet raise and sustain wages much easier and with less expense than small societies have done, or we believe, will do.' The fact is that trade unionism, in this period, was openly militant when the need arose. Any doubts on this score could be dispelled by the events which led to the investigation into the 'Sheffield Outrages' (4) in 1867, when the violent tactics used by the light metal unions were exposed.

Despite the greater confidence that many trade unions developed, their position was still precarious. This was revealed by the Sheffield Outrages, and was further revealed by the Hornby v. Close Case (5) where it became obvious that trade unions could not protect their funds under the Friendly Societies Act. The situation of the Bradford Typographers (6) is also interesting, for this skilled group of well-paid workers were still approaching their employers in a tentative manner in the mid-1860s. And one must always remember that the 1867 Master and Servant Act (7) was a disadvantage to workers If they were dismissed they had to pursue redress in the civil courts whereas if they left work without notice they would be deemed to have broken their contract and would be subject to the criminal law.

The situation of trade unions was therefore considerably improved by the recommendation that workers should be allowed to combine, although it was felt that picketing was an interference with individual rights. The Trade Union Act of 1871 (11), which was nearer the minority report view, established the legal status of trade unions but it was coupled with the Criminal Law Amendment Act which created a number of offences which made it difficult for trade unions to conduct strike and picketing activity. This difficulty was exposed in the case of the London gas stokers in 1872 (13) but partly resolved by the Conspiracy and Protection of Property Act, 1875 (15) which redefined molestation, obstruction and intimidation, and also by the passing of a Master and Servant Act in 1875, which made breach of contract a purely civil offence. There was also the Trade Union Act (1871) and Amendment Act, 1876 which clarified what was meant by trade unionism.

The late 1860s and early 1870s were, indeed, exciting years for the trade unions. The Trades Union Congress (9) was effectively formed, without the immediate support of the main London-based amalgamated societies, in Manchester in 1868. The Amalgamated Society of Engineers struck for the nine-hour day in Sunderland and the North East (10). The first serious attempts were made by Joseph Arch to organize the agricultural labourers into the Agricultural Labourers' Union (12) and the Yorkshire miners became particularly aggressive in their demand for wage increases (14). By the late 1870s and early 1880s Emma Paterson was leading attempts to organize women into trade unions (16).

Between the 1850s and the 1870s the British trade-union movement had risen from an estimated 100,000 or so in the early 1850s to more than one million in 1874. From then onwards, certainly for the next twelve or thirteen years, economic and industrial conditions worsened and the membership of trade unions fell substantially by the mid-1880s, recovering to about 750,000 by 1888. In these difficult years trade unions found themselves fighting protracted strikes against wage reductions and facing dramatic membership losses. Many unions went out of existence. In this situation the TUC complained of over-production (17) due to the use of new machinery and the 'systematic working of overtime'. Tom Mann advocated the introduction of a legal eight-hour day and emigration was advocated by some. Increasingly, a new breed of trade unionists, such as Tom Mann, began to demand that trade unions should become less exclusive and that all workers should be organized if the threat of capitalist exploitation was to be avoided (18, 19). At this point the future became clear – trade unionism was to be for everyone not just for the few.

1) *The Amalgamated Society of Engineers*
(From the Rules of the Amalgamated Society of Engineers, 1850)

Rule XXII

[. . .]

1. A committee of seven members shall be appointed in each locality or district where there is more than one branch of our society, each branch as nearly as practicable, appointing an equal number. . . .

2. A secretary and president shall be appointed by each local committee every quarter. The secretary shall write to the General Secretary on the 1st of every month, stating the business transacted by the committee, the numbers of members in receipt of 15s. per week . . . .

3. Any member being discharged in conformity with this rule shall be entitled to the sum of 15s. per week until he again obtains employment; and if it is proved to the satisfaction . . .

4. No committee shall expand of this fund a greater amount weekly than is contributed by the members they represent, at the rate of 5d. [2p] per month, unless by the consent of the Executive Council.

5. If any circumstance takes place in a locality which jeopardizes the situation of a number of members, the local committee shall refrain from advising them until the Executive Council shall have been consulted and their opinions ascertained. [. . .]

Rule XXIII

[. . .]

1. That in order to secure to our members a good general prospect of employment, we repudiate 'systematic overtime', as being the cause of much evil, through giving to a number the privilege of working more than a legitimate week's time whilst doing so deprives other members of situations . . . and causing a great expenditure of the Society's funds. [Threats to exclude members who continue to work overtime.]

2. That the same steps be taken to abolish piecework, to destroy the practice of working more than one lathe or machine, to prevent a greater number of apprentices or admissions into one trade than are likely to find employment therein – apprentices to be in proportion of one to four journeymen. . . .

2) *The Preston Lock-Out, 24 November 1853 to 24 June, 1854*
(National Association for the Promotion of Social Science, 'Report on Trade Societies' (1860), p. 223)

Preston Lock-Out. – To the British Public. – In consequence of the various misrepresentations which have so unblushingly been put forth by the 'Masters' Association', we, the Weavers' Association, feel it to be a duty to ourselves and the public to publish the following answers:-
[. . .] 2nd – We repeat, that we have been 'locked out', in order to starve us into submission, not because we objected to the advances made upon the price paid in 1852, for the great body of us were perfectly satisfied with the advances given, but because we thought fit to give our own money to support some four mills' hands that had disputes with their employers, the primary cause of our sympathy being, that these workpeople had been denied the opportunity of explaining, or coming to an arrangement with their employers. . . .

3rd – They say, 'We at once admit that, owing to the depressed state of trade in 1847, a general reduction of wages took place'; but with respect to the promise of restoring it when trade revived, they say, 'We deny, however, that any such promise was made by the masters generally, although this might have been done by some individual firms'. We are prepared to admit that every employer in the town did not make that promise . . . but the promise given at firms where the masters allowed some little 'freedom', was justly considered applicable to all, and consequently, to those firms where the hands did not ask, at that time, to be other than degraded slaves. [. . .]

5th – We repeat that the wages paid in Preston are less than what are paid in other districts, and this is the secret cause of the determination of the workpeople to improve their condition.

7th – We beg to say that in this struggle the masters are the aggressors; we were (with the few exceptions referred to) satisfied with the wages given us before the 'Lock-Out'; we understand that we must not resume work unless we submit to a reduction of ten per cent; we have offered to have the question settled upon reasonable terms, but 'no concession' is the terms of our employers; they have forced us to rely for an existence upon aid from other towns, and now tell us, that we can only resume work upon condition that we will degrade ourselves in the eyes of the world, by accepting a reduction in the wages of those who have generously saved our children from starvation. Are these the only terms of honourable men? Will it be the interest of the employers of Preston to see their workpeople both degraded and dishonest? – We think not; but if it be, we tell them that we will suffer much more before we submit to such depravity.

In conclusion we again reiterate, that we are prepared at any time to bring this dispute to an honourable and reasonable arrangement.

By Order of the Power-Loom Weavers' Committee,
JAMES WHALLEY, sec.

COMMITTEE ROOM, PRESTON.
Dec. 28th, 1853.

3) *London Trades Council in the 1860s*
(i)   *Second Annual Report, 1861/2*
       (*Report of the Trades Council of London, Annual Report 1861*)
       Gentlemen,
       I[n] presenting to you the Second Yearly Report of the Council, we would for a moment draw your attention to the circumstances which brought it into existence. Most of you are aware that during the winter of 1859–60 delegate meetings were held weekly for the purpose of aiding the Operative Builders of London in defending what is popularly termed the 'odious document'. That document was a blow aimed at the Trades' Unions of this country, and the trades generally came forward nobly in support of those who were opposing it. The result was a complete triumph. The triumph may be attributed chiefly to the delegate meetings held week after week in Shaftesbury Hall.
       At the termination of the struggle it was felt that something should be done to establish a general trade committee, so as to be able, on emergency, to call the trades together with dispatch, for the purpose of rendering each other advice and assistance, as circumstances required. A Committee was therefore elected to draw up a code of rules, which was done, and after being amended at a delegate meeting was adopted and the Trades Council established.
       The first fruits of the Council was the publication of a Trades' Directory, a work of great value, though not without

mistakes. Previous to this there was no means of extensive communication between the trades, except through a few individuals, who had the good fortune to possess a large number of addresses to all parts of the kingdom. [. . .]

The next subject of importance which came before the Council was the employment of the Sappers at the Chelsea barracks, where a dispute existed between the employer and his workmen. This was a question of great importance, not only to the building operatives but to the whole of the workmen of the country. It was a direct interference on the part of the Government and the Council took immediate steps to effect their removal. And here was shown the great value of the Council. . . .There was no other body likely to take the subject up with the promptitude and probable success as our Council. They therefore called a delegate meeting, at Shaftesbury Hall, on July 30th, 1861, at which meeting 50 societies were represented, sending 70 delegates, and representing a total of 50,000 men. This meeting passed resolutions condemnatory of the government, sent a petition to Parliament, . . . and sent a deputation of fifteen to the Secretary of War, and received in Parliament a promise of their removal. The whole of this was effected in ten days, which show plainly the capabilities of the Council. . . .

The Sheffield outrages was a subject that claimed our early attention. Our Secretary wrote letters in answer to the charges brought against us, which were inserted in the Builder, Daily News, &c. Many delegates thought that a delegate should have been sent down to investigate the affair, but our funds were too low to do so. [. . .]

We cannot close our report without referring to some matters of a political character. The Trades' Council of Glasgow and some other places came forward as the champion of Reform. Your Council was urged to give their support and to take up political questions as a council; but as most of the members of the Council are in favour of Reform, they determined to co-operate with other bodies, not as a Council, but as individuals. Circumstances have arisen which have kept them from doing so, but their sympathies are still for Reform. We hope, however, that the trades will not suppose that the Council will take up politics. They will strictly adhere to their functions of watching over the interests of Trades' Unions, and confine themselves to such measures as affect us all as workmen. [. . .] The number of paying members is at present 11,300, but we find that we should at least have double that number. And what is there to prevent it? The Council is not established for any party purposes; nor is there any undue influence on the part of the trade. One object is the welfare of all, and each trade has the right to be represented on the Council . . . .

THE TRADES COUNCIL OF LONDON
GEO. HOWELL, Secretary
18, Albert Street, Islington, N.

(ii)   *The Third Annual Report, May 1862–May 1863*
[. . .] The first subject which came under our notice was the unfortunate dispute which raged so severely between the Iron Ship Builders and the Shipwrights. The Council, after fully considering the question, thought that arbitration if accepted, would be the best and most effectual mode of bringing the dispute to a satisfactory issue. We therefore offered our services to the contending parties for the purpose of calling together Delegates from the various Societies in London to hear the facts of the case stated, discuss them, and then decide the question by votes of the Delegates. We are sorry to say that our offer was not accepted, therefore the hoped for principle of settling disputes by arbitration is put off to a future time.

GEORGE ODGER
6 Park Lane, Kennington Gore

(iii) *Fourth Annual Report of the London Trades Council, May 1863–April 1864*

To the Metropolitan Trade Societies
GENTLEMEN,

   In placing before you the doings of the Council, we feel much pleasure in stating that the past year has been one of peace in the metropolis, in so far as strikes are concerned when compared with many preceding years. [. . .] It is worthy of remark that Societies if they amalgamate, or otherwise become large, steer clearer of strikes and yet raise and sustain wages much easier and with less expense than small societies have done, or we believe, will do. This may be accounted for through the power, in the shape of money and men, which large societies have at their command, and which never fail to be appreciated by the employers, whenever the contending parties confront each other. We therefore would advise all societies to amalgamate, should circumstances favour them for so doing. [Discussion of industrial actions and success elsewhere in the provinces.]

The Puddlers' and Nailers' Societies, and Iron Ship Builders, have very properly taken advantage of favourable opportunities and secured great advances in wages.

GEORGE ODGER,
Secretary,
2 Park Lane,
Kennington Gore.

4) *The Sheffield Outrages of the 1860s and the Commission of Enquiry, 1867*

(i) *Trades Union Commission: Sheffield Outrages, 1867*
(Report presented to the Trades Union Commissioners by The Examiners appointed to Inquire into Acts of Intimidation, Outrage, or Wrong Alleged to have been promoted, encouraged , or connived at by Trades Unions in the Town of Sheffield, Vol I – Report, 1867)
Evidence of Thomas Fearnehough

10,451 You say that on 8 October you were blown up? – Yes.
10,452 Is that the outrage at Hereford Street? – Yes?
10,453 There has been a reward of £1,100 for it? – Yes.
10,454 To who do you attribute the blowing up? Have you any reason to suspect any person or any body of persons of being the cause of the blowing up? – I have as much right to back my opinion as Broadhead to deny the truth.
10,455 What is your belief? – I believe Broadhead knows all about it, and knows the men that did it, if it is not himself.
10,476 Has Broadhead ever used any threat to you at any time? – Yes. I had one about 11 years ago, and I had one either the second or third day after they blew me up.

10,477 From whom was the threat 11 years ago? – I suspect from Broadhead.

Evidence of William Broadhead

[Second day of evidence when Broadhead declared his involvement in the intimidation.]

12,579 (Chairman) I think it is my duty in the interest of both yourself and of public justice, and in the interest of those whom you might implicate to give you a warning. I dare say you may have a false sense of honour that you will not implicate others; but I have looked over my notes and I find that you have not told us the name of a single person who you have caused to do rattening. You have never disclosed a single fact which has not been proved by two witnesses. You have never admitted anything which could not have been proved without your evidence. Remember, that to obtain a certificate you will have to tell us all that you know. It is not merely telling about those things which you have mentioned, but if it should turn out in the result that there are other things with which you are proved to be associated, and you have not told us about them, unquestionably your certificate will be withheld. [. . .] – Pardon me. Will you permit me to ask you one question?

12,580 Yes. – Can I rely upon it that the same mercy will be extended to those men that will be extended to myself, provided I will own to the truth?

12,581 Undoubtedly? – Then I will give you a true statement. (Mr. Chance) It is your only chance, you must do it.

12,582 (Chairman) Is there any statement which you would like to make before I put questions to you? – Yes; to begin with, the statement which I made to you yesterday relative to the Helliwell affair was untrue; I hired Dennis Clark.

12,583 To blow up Helliwell? – Yes.

12,682 Was not your object in talking to Crooks this morning to decide between yourselves how much you should confess, and how much you should withhold? – Yes.

12,683 What did you agree to withhold? – We agreed to withhold the Hereford Street outrage.

12,687 Who committed it? – Samuel Crooks.

[Examination of the shooting of Elisha Parker and the shooting of Linley and others in 1859.]

12,878 On October the 8th 1866 Thomas Fearnehough's house in Hereford Street was blown up? – Yes.

12,879 Who caused that to be done? – Me.

12,880 Whom did you employ? – Crooks.

12,881 Who did that? – Crooks.

12,882 You said just now that Copley did it? – Copley was with him. He told me so; I do not know that he was, but I have no doubt that it is correct.

12,883 Copley is a member of the Union I believe as well as Crooks? – Yes.

12,884 Have you ever seen Copley on the subject? – No, Copley and I never exchanged a word on the subject at any time.

12,885 How much did you give Crooks for doing that? – I think it was £15.

[Then the witnesses mentioned by Broadhead were allowed to declare their guilt in return for a certificate.]

Evidence of Samuel Crooks (recalled)

13,509 Quite so. If you only tell us what has occurred we shall look over that falsehood in your previous statement. With respect of Linley's case you have already stated that you were the person who shot him? – Yes.

13,510 Now you have stated that you shot him in the shoulder? – No, I shot at his shoulder.

13,540 Do you know Samuel Baxter of Loxley? – Yes.

13,541 Did you blow him up? – Yes.

13,542 By putting a quantity of gunpowder down his chimney? – Yes.

13,543 Who was with you? – Thomas Needham.

13,544 Who employed you to do that? – Broadhead.

13,545 How much did he pay you? – Well, I cannot say. I think it would be £15; that was about the regular sum, I think generally. I might have had less on different occasions, but I think at that time it would be £15, but I cannot positively swear to that.

13,637 Now the next thing which I will ask you is the Hereford Street outrage. Did you blow up Fearnehough? – Yes, I am sorry to say that I did.

13,638 Who employed you to do that? – Broadhead.

13,641 How much did he pay you for that? – Well, I think it was £15.

13,648 Did he tell you why he wanted Fearnehough blown up? – Yes, he was doing us a deal of injury. He did not say particularly; I understand that he was doing wrong in some way according to the rules, you know of the trade. I did not ask him any very great particulars about it I think.

13,649 Did he tell you whether it was a joint business of the saw smiths and the saw handle makers and the saw grinders, or whether it was a private matter? – I could not say, I never asked him that.

13,722 Do you know who did the Acorn Street murder? – No. I had nothing to do with it; I never knew anything about that.

13,723 Are you sure about that? – I am certain; I am innocent of that.

Evidence of William Dronsfield [a printer who was hon. secretary of the Sheffield Trades Defence Committee and also the U.K. Alliance of Organized Trades.]

15,369 This is a respectable thing, 'The question too, of more fully legislating for trades unions so as to give powers for compelling payment in the country courts by defaulting members, is one to which they attach much importance, and would, respectfully recommend the same to your lordships most serious attention. Your lordships will see from the accompanying documents the steps the executive have taken in reference to those most disgraceful and abominable outrages attributed to trades unions, and their utter abhorrence of all such acts of violence, and they beg to assure your lordships that they should be only too glad to co-operate in any movement for their suppression, being fully convinced that such acts are not only a disgrace on those who commit them, but also an injury on the town and trade of Sheffield, in the prosperity of which none are more deeply interested than the working community of this large and populous borough. The fact that their secretary is also honorary secretary to a committee appointed at a public meeting to take steps for the suppression of these outrages, and is now in communication with the mayor thereon, will, it is hoped, convince your lordship of their sincerity on this matter? – Yes, I was the secretary to that committee. We had some correspondence with Mr. Brown, who was then mayor; that was immediately after the Acorn Street outrage.'

(ii)   (*Sheffield Independent*, 30 September 1867)

Isaac Ironside: That this meeting, having considered the acts and charges of the unconstitutional Commission of Enquiry which recently held its sittings in Sheffield, desires to express its firm conviction that the present movement against trades' unions is a conspiracy (hear, hear) of the Governing and employing classes to curb the liberties of the working men and their means of defence (cheers) and to reduce them to a conditions of serfs; – . . . and that the meeting . . . resolves that all trades' outrages, strikes and rattenings, are the inevitable consequence of the one-sided . . . legislation. . . .

(5) *The Hornby v. Close Case*
(*Bradford Observer*, 24 January 1867)
The case of Hornby (appellant) v Close (respondent) heard in the Council of Queen's Bench, on Wednesday, was an appeal from a decision of the magistrates at Bradford dismissing an information under the Friendly Societies Act against the treasurer of a society of working men, on the grounds that the objects of the Society, being partly those of a trade union, were not within the act. The information was for wrongfully withholding the sum of £24 belonging to the Society. The Society was the Leeds Branch of the United Society of Boilermakers and Iron-Shipbuilders of Great Britain and Ireland, instituted in 1834 (as stated on the title page of its rules), for the purpose of mutual relief of its members when out of employment, the relief of their sick and burial of their dead, and other benevolent purposes inserted in their rules. [. . .] Such, however, being the professed, and perhaps the original objects of the society, the rules, which have been revised and remodelled in 1862, contained several which were relied upon as showing that the present objects of the society were, in part, those of a trade society. . . . The Lord Chief Justice at once said 'We cannot hesitate for a moment in saying that we thought the magistrates were right in holding that a society did not come within the operation of the Friendly Societies Act. . . . I am far

from saying that a trade union constituted for such purposes would bring the members within the criminal law, but the rules are certainly such as would operate in restraint of trade, and would therefore, in that sense, be unlawful.

6) *The Bradford Typographers, 1866–1867*
(Bradford Typographical Society records, deposited with the J.B. Priestley Library, University of Bradford)
(i)   *Circular to employers, 17 August 1866*
        SIR,
             You are respectfully informed that a Conference of Employers and Employed in the Printing Profession of Bradford, will be held on MONDAY, August 27th, 1866, at LAYCOCK's (late Goodchild's), TEMPERANCE HOTEL, Old Manor Hall, Kirkgate, at Five o'clock in the Evening, to consider the position of their business.
             The following Employers have signified their intention to be present:-

JOHN DALE & CO	WILLIAM BYLES & SON
HENRY GASKARTH	SQUIRE AUTY
H. O. MAWSON	MARTIN FIELD
MICHAEL NELSON	WILLIAM LOBLEY
CHARLES DENTON	JAMES HANSON
W. COOKE & SONS	GEO. F. SEWELL
GEORGE W. DALE	

(ii)   *Meeting of Employers and Employed*
        Meeting of Employers and Employed at Laycock's Temperance Hotel Old Manor Hall, Kirkgate held August 27th 1866.

Employers present	Employees present
Mr. Wm Byles	Mr. Cudworth
Mr. Henry Gaskarth	Mr. Munro
Mr. Wm Lobley	Mr. Freeman
	Mr. Burrows (acting Sec. for Meeting)
	Mr. Hustler (Secretary to Society)

After a long conversation respecting the hours to be worked, and the wages to be paid, per week, and the amount to be paid for overtime, &c, Mr. Munro put the following question – 'Had the Employers come to any arrangement when Mr. Byles wrote out the following –'

'The Masters after mature consideration think

1st That 57 hours will be a fair arrangement of the hours per week men are expected to work.

2nd That there is no good reason for departing from the customary rate of 24/- per week as the minimum rate of wages.

3rd That 6d per hour for corrections and overtime is a fair and sufficient rate.

4th That they agree to 2d extra after 10 o'clock and 3d after 12 o'clock to 5 a.m.'

It was agreed that a statistical table be prepared by Mr. Burrows of the number of hours worked and the wages paid in the various towns.

(iii) *Circular to Masters, 23 November, 1867*

To Mr. . . . .

Sir,

The Letter Press Printers in your employ respectfully desire to call your attention to a question oft mooted but still unsettled, viz., the Weekly Rate of Wages, and the Hours to be Worked for those Wages. Nothing daunted by the result of the recent Conference, and the negotiations incident thereto, but relying on the justice and reasonableness of their request, they now desire to renew those negotiations, in the sincere hope and expectation that a more satisfactory result may be arrived at.

While it is but proper to state that this movement is being renewed throughout the profession in the town, your employees now seek an adjustment of the points at issue betwist themselves and you, their employer; trusting that, thus personally addressed you may be better disposed to consider the matters referred to on their merits.

Your employees, then, ask that they may in future be paid at the following rate:- Not less than 27s per week for 55 hours' labour; Overtime, 2d per hour extra from Seven to Twelve o'clock, 3d per hour after; Casual Hands, 6d per hour if employed less than a week; English and Long Primer, $5\frac{1}{4}$d per

1,000; Bourgeois, 5½d Brevior and Minion; Nonpareil, 6¼d.

It is not attempted in this circular to enter into arguments in support of this revised and slightly-increased scale of payment, inasmuch as you will doubtless give us an opportunity to do this in person. It is but right to say, however, that while your employees do not wish to press their claims arrogantly, nor do they intend to use anything but moral suasion to attain their object, the time has come when it would be wrong to themselves, and to those dependent on them, not to press those claims to the utmost of their power.

In concluding this necessarily formal statement, your employees earnestly appeal to you to take the matter into your serious consideration; and solicit an interview that they may convince you that while they are morally entitled to all the items named in this circular, they are not indisposed to treat amicably with you with a view to a settlement of this vexed question.

Trusting shortly to meet you,

We respectfully remain,

Your Employees.

P.S. It is respectfully requested that an answer be given not later than the first Saturday in December.

7) *The Master and Servant Act, 1867*
(30 & 31 Vict. *c.* 141)
[Under this Act if a workman broke his contract of service the act was criminal, and punishable by fine or imprisonment If, on the other hand, the employer broke his contract the master was only liable to civil action, giving rise to damages. This meant that a master could give evidence in his defence whilst a workman, charged with a criminal act, could not.]
4. Whenever the Employer or Employed shall neglect or refuse to fulfil any contract of service, or the Employed shall neglect or refuse to enter or commence his service, according to the contract, or shall absent himself from his service . . . the Party feeling aggrieved may lay an Information or Complaint in writing before a justice, magistrate or sheriff, setting forth the Grounds for Complaint, and the amount of Compensation, Damage, or other Remedy claimed for the 'Breach or Non-Performance' of such contract . . . .

9. Upon the Hearing of any Information or Complaint under the Provisions of this Act two Justices, or the Magistrate or Sheriff, after due Examination either shall make an abatement of the whole or part of any Wages then already due to the Employed, or else shall direct the Fulfilment of the Contract of Service [or introduce a variety of other decisions, including fines up to £20]; and if the Order shall direct the Fulfilment of the Contract, and direct the Party complained against to find good and sufficient security as the aforesaid, and the Party complained against neglect or refuse to comply with such order, a Justice, Magistrate, or Sheriff may, if he shall think fit . . . commit such Party to the Common Gaol or House of Correction . . . there to be confined . . . , but nevertheless so that the term of Imprisonment, whether under One or several successive Committals, shall not exceed the whole Period of Three Months; . . .

8) *Royal Commission on Trade Unions, 1867–1869*
(i) (*Eleventh Report of the Royal Commission on Trade Unions (1869)*, p. xix)

RIGHT TO COMBINE

(60) With regard to the general question of the right of workmen to combine together for determining and stipulating with their employer the terms on which only they will consent to work for him, we think that, provided the combination be perfectly voluntary, and that full liberty be left to all other workmen to undertake the work which the parties combining have refused, and that no obstruction be placed in the way of the employer resorting elsewhere in search of a supply of labour, there is no ground of justice or of policy for withholding such a right from workmen. . . .

PICKETING

(70) So far as relates to members of the union promoting the strike, the pickets cannot be necessary if the members are voluntarily concurring therein; so far as relates to workmen who are not members of the union, picketing implies in principle an interference with their right to dispose of their labour as they think fit, and is, therefore, without justification; and so far as relates to the employer, it is a violation of his right of free resort

to the labour market for the supply of such labour as he requires. . . .

(ii)   (As above, p. xxix)

We, the undersigned, Commissioners appointed by Your Majesty, found ourselves reluctantly compelled to dissent from the foregoing Report, in which we were unable to concur for the following reasons:-

It is in our opinion essential to any serious amendment of the law relating to trade unions that the doctrine of Common Law whereby it is presumed that all combinations, whether of workmen or employers, are unlawful, and according to some authorities are punishable as conspiracies . . . . should be broadly and unequivocally rescinded. [. . .]

We are further of opinion that simple registration and protection for property should be equally accorded to all associations alike, whether of workmen or employers, with the sole condition of their proving themselves to be free from criminal design. [. . .]

Signed by Frederic Harrison, Thomas Hughes, and the Earl of Lichfield.

9) *Trades Union Congress*

(i)   *Circular from the Manchester Trades Council inviting delegates to the first Trades Union Congress, 1868*

(The Beehive, 25 April 1868)

TO THE SECRETARY OF THE –

MANCHESTER, April 16th, 1868

SIR, – You are required to lay the following before your society. The vital interests involved, it is conceived, will justify the officials in convening a special meeting for the consideration thereof. The Manchester and Salford Trades Council, having recently taken into consideration the present aspect of Trade Unions, and the profound ignorance which prevails in the public mind with reference to their operation and principles, together with the probability of an attempt being made by the Legislature, during the present session of Parliament, to introduce a measure which might prove detrimental to the interests of such Societies, unless some prompt and decisive action be taken by the working classes themselves, beg most respectfully to intimate that it has been decided to hold in Manchester, as the main centre of industry in the provinces, a Congress of the Representatives of Trades Councils, Federations of Trade, and Trade Societies in General. [. . .]

(ii) *TUC, 1869: Discussion on Conciliation and Arbitration*
(Handwritten Annual Report of the Second Trades Union Congress, TUC, p. 39)

Mr. W. Owen representative of the Potteries Trades Council read a paper on Courts of Arbitration and Conciliation. He said that these courts could at best be palliatives. They could not join those whose selfishness, class laws and an unjust social system had so long sustained – but if rightly used they may smooth away difficulties and be profitable to local parties. At Nottingham, Courts of Arbitration had made a radical change in the operation and spirit of workmen and masters to each other. There were Board of Arbitration at Nottingham, Wolverhampton, the Potteries, Walsall, Coventry, Worcester, Bristol, Leeds, Manchester, Oldham, Huddersfield, Wakefield, Derby, Leicester, Birmingham, and elsewhere and the trades ruled by these boards were hosiery, lace, iron working, glass bottle making, cotton, pottery and some branches of the building trade. From personal observations of the actions of the board of Arbitration in the potteries, he was convinced that these boards, who conducted impartially, were far more likely to result in justice than the arbitrary action of strikes and lock- outs, and they were thus calculated to do away with destruction and irrational perspectives on either side.

Mr. Walton, of Brecon, with a view to giving practical effort to the paper just read, proposed the following resolution: 'That this Congress is of opinion that the establishment of Courts of Arbitration and Conciliation will greatly conduce to the just and peaceable settlement of all disputes between employers and employed, and by means of preventing strikes and lock-outs, as well as being conducive to industrial and commercial enterprise of the nation.' Mr. G. Howell (London), who had intended to submit a proposition similar to that of Mr. Walton, seconded the resolution.

10) *The Nine-Hour Movement, 1870–1*
(Amalgamated Society of Engineers, *Abstract Report of the Council's Proceedings from June 1st, 1870, to December 31st, 1872*, p. 184)
... a report will be found of a meeting of the Newcastle Central District Committee, wherein the nine hours system was mooted, but by a resolution it was not considered the proper time to move in the matter. . . .

This meeting was held in June, 1870, and in the following April the engineering trade in Sunderland, on their own account, struck for the nine hours system. [. . .]

The engineering firms in Sunderland granted the workmen the terms they asked, and therefore the system was inaugurated.

The movement then extended to Newcastle and resulted in one of the most memorable strikes on record. At first our society had difficulties to meet from the fact that upwards of 8,000 men had struck, whereas only 500 belonged to our society, and very few of them to any other. With wonderful celerity the men on strike joined the nine hours league. . . . Mr Cohn was dispatched at the society's expense to the Continent to intercept the foreign workmen that the employers were engaging. . . . The contest went on and the workmen ultimately triumphed. [. . .] The same concessions that were made by the Newcastle employers to their workmen were rapidly granted by others all over England and Ireland.

11) *The Trade Union Act, 1871*
4. Nothing in this Act shall enable any court to entertain any legal proceeding instituted with the object of directly enforcing or recovering damages for the breach of the following agreements, namely,
1.   Any agreement between members of a trade union as such, concerning the condition on which any member for the time being of such trade union shall or shall not sell their goods, transact business, employ, or be employed:
2.   Any agreement for the payment by any person of any subscription or penalty to a trade union:
3.   Any agreement for the application of the funds of a trade union, –
     (a) To provide benefits to members; or
     (b) To furnish contributions to any employer or workman not a member of such employer or workman acting in conformity

with the rules or resolutions of such a trade; or
(c) To discharge any fine imposed upon any person by sentence of a court of justice; or

–

4. Any agreement made between one trade union and another; or,
5. Any bond to secure the performance of any of the above-
mentioned agreements.
But nothing in this section shall be deemed to constitute any of the
above-mentioned agreements unlawful.

12) *Constitution and Rules of the National Agricultural Labourers' Union,
1872*
(Printed in P. Horn, *Joseph Arch* (Kineton, The Roundwood Press,
1971), pp. 222–228).
(i)   *Constitution and Rules*
        Central Office: Balm Cottage, Forfield Place, Leamington.
        To the Members of the National Agricultural Labourers'
        Union.

In submitting to their brethren the Rules of the 'National
Agricultural Labourers' Union,' the Members of the 'National
Executive Committee' have added certain Supplementary Rules
for the use of Districts and Branches, These Rules are not
regarded by the National Executive as exhaustive, but simply
fundamental. It is felt that the Districts should have perfect
liberty to frame such laws for their own guidance as their own
special circumstances may suggest; that liberty is freely
accorded, and the National Executive hope it will be exercised
on the basis of the Rules for Districts and branches, and in
harmony with the General Rule of the National. The National
Executive hope soon to see a Branch Union in every parish, and
a District Union – that is a combination of Branches – in every
county or division, all communicating with a common centre, all
observing the same principles, and all working for the same end.
[. . .] We must have no local jealousies, no self-seeking, no
isolation. Unity of action is, above all things is necessary, and this
can be secured only as all Branches and Districts work through
a common Representative and Executive Committee. We must

have money, and we must have it in one central fund, to which all shall contribute, and from which, in time of need, all shall in turn be aided. The strength of the great trade societies is their central funds. [. . .]

[. . .] Let it be clearly understood, then, that the Branch remits its funds to the District; that the District remit three-fourths of their receipts to the National, and that any Branch or District failing to do this, has no claim whatever on the general resources of the Union. The fourth, allowed to be retained by the Districts, can be disbursed at the discretion of the District Committee in meeting current expenditure and in promoting the general objects of the Union. [. . .] Let us cleave to and work for the Union. Let peace and moderation mark all our meetings. Let courtesy, fairness, and firmness characterize all our demands. Act cautiously and advisedly, that no act may have to be repented or repudiated. Do not strike unless all other means fail you. Try all other means; try them with firmness and patience; try them in the enforcement of only just claims, and if they fail, then strike, and having observed Rule 10, strike with a will. Fraternize, Centralize! [. . .] Nine and a half hours, exclusive of meal-times, as a day's work, and 16s. a week's pay, are not extravagant demands. Society supports you in making them, and they will be met soon. Brothers, be united, and you will be strong; be temperate, and you will be respected; realize a central capital, and you will be able to act with firmness and independence. Many eyes are upon you; many tongues are ready to reproach you; your opponents say that your extra leisure will be passed in the public-house, and your extra pay be spent in beer. Show that their slander is untrue! Be united, be sober, and you will soon be free.

(Signed) JOSEPH ARCH,
Chairman of the National Executive Committee

Rules and Constitution

NAME

1   The National Agricultural Labourers' Union

OBJECT

2 (A) To improve the general condition of Agricultural Labourers in the United Kingdom.

   (B) To encourage the formation of Branch and District Unions.

   (C) To promote co-operation and communication between Unions already in existence.

COUNCIL

3 A Council, consisting of one Delegate from each District Union, shall meet at Leamington, or elsewhere, as may be determined by the preceding Council, on the third Tuesday of May in each year, for the following purposes:-

   (A) To elect an Executive Committee, together with a Treasurer, Secretary, and four Trustees. [. . .]

NATIONAL EXECUTIVE COMMITTEE
– COMPOSITION AND FUNCTIONS

4 The National Executive Committee shall consist of a Chairman, who shall have a second or casting vote, and twelve Agricultural Labourers, seven of whom shall form a quorum. [. . .]

SETTLEMENT OF DISPUTES

10 All cases of dispute between the members of the National Agricultural Union and their Employers, must be laid before the Branch Committee to which such members may belong; and, should the Branch Committee be unable to arrange the question to the mutual satisfaction of the parties interested, in conjunction with the District Committee, recourse shall be had to arbitration. Should the district Committee be unable to arrange for such arbitration, an appeal shall be made to the National Executive Committee for its decision. Any award made by arbitration or by decision of the National Executive, shall be binding upon all Members of the Union; and in no case shall a strike be resorted to, until the above means have been tried and failed. [. . .]

Rule 2
OBJECTS

To improve the conditions of Agricultural and other labourers in the United Kingdom, Members of the Union, by:-

1 Increasing their wages, and lessening their hours of labour.
2 Protecting their trade interests, and securing them legal redress against oppression.
3 Assisting them to migrate from one part of the Kingdom to another, or to emigrate to other Countries.
4 Providing for all those Members who shall pay the Benefit contributions hereinafter mentioned, a weekly allowance during sickness and the payment of a sum of money at death.

(ii)   *Membership of the National Agricultural Labourers' Union*
(From P. Horn, *Joseph Arch* (Kineton, Roundwood Press,1971), p. 222, the information of which is largely drawn from the Returns submitted to the Chief Registrar of Friendly Societies)

Year	Membership	Year	Membership
1873	71,835	1885	10,700
1874	86,214	1886	10,366
1875	40,000	1887	5,300
1876	55,000	1888	4,660
1877	30,000	1889	4,254
1878	24,000	1890	8,500
1879	20,000	1891	15,000
1880	20,000	1892	15,000
1881	15,000	1893	14,746
1882	15,000	1894	1,100
1883	15,000	1895	None given
1884	18,000	1896	Dissolved– October, 1896

13) *London Gas Stokers, 1872*
(*The Illustrated London News,* 14 December 1872)
[. . .] At the Thames Police Court, on Monday, four of the men in the service of the Commercial Gas Company, at Stepney, were summoned

for wilful and malicious breach of contract, and were each sentenced to six week's imprisonment. At Woolwich Police Court, on Tuesday, six men of the Chartered Gas Company were committed for trial.

14) *A Great Mass Meeting of Miners in Barnsley, 1874*
(Barnsley Chronicle, 11 July 1874)
Mr. John Normansell, secretary of the South Yorkshire and North Derbyshire Miners' Association. 'I want you to know then, that in a couple of days hence, 76 branches of the Association will probably be on strike or locked out. Some one has suggested we should change the word. I do not care what you choose to call it, but . . . let me tell you if you are out it will be your own fault. You have nothing to gain by being out on strike or locked out. You have twelve branches which have made a compromise of 10 per cent on the 1871 prices. I know some employers have offered terms, but they will want to get as much as they can get from you. They are like some of our own men, they are wishful to gain something at the expense of some of the other employees. [. . .] I may also tell you that we have three collieries at work at 10 per cent from the gross, and there are something like 1200 men out in the district for a greater reduction of even 12½ per cent. We have had a meeting of the Council to-day and have passed a resolution which some of you may not like. (A voice: What was passed last Monday?) (Another voice: That was not in your favour. Uproar.) The resolution passed this morning was for 10 per cent from the gross wages. [. . .] I will tell you again that the country generally had a reduction three months ago. [. . .] There have been strikes all over the country during the past three months, and not one single district has been able to resist a wage reduction.

15) *Conspiracy, and Protection of Property Act 1875*
3. An agreement or combination by two or more persons to do or procure to be done any act in contemplation or furtherance of a trade dispute . . . shall not be indictable as a conspiracy if such act committed by one person would not be punishable as a crime.

Nothing in this section shall exempt from punishment any persons guilty of a conspiracy for which a punishment is awarded by an Act of Parliament.

Nothing in this section shall affect the law relating to riot, unlawful assembly, breach of the peace, or sedition, or any offence against the State or the Sovereign. [. . .]

5. Where any person wilfully and maliciously breaks a contract of service or of hiring, knowing or having reasonable cause to believe that the probable consequences of his doing, either alone or in combination with others, will be to endanger human life, or cause serious bodily injury, or to expose valuable property whether real or personal to destruction or serious injury, he shall on conviction thereof by a court of summary jurisdiction, or on indictment as herein-after mentioned, be liable either to pay a penalty not exceeding twenty pounds, or to be imprisoned for a term not exceeding three months, with or without hard labour.

7. Every person who, with a view to compel any other person to abstain from doing or to do any act which such other person has a legal right to do or abstain from doing, wrongfully and without legal authority, –

1. Uses violence to or intimidation such other person or his or injures his property; or

2. Persistently follows such other person about from place to place; or,

3. Hides any tools, clothes, or other property owned or used by such other person resides, or works, or carries on business, or happens to be, or the approach to such house or place; or

4. Watches or besets the house or other place where such other person resides, or works, or carries on business, or happens to be, or the approach to such house or place; or

5. Follows such other person with two or more other persons in a disorderly manner in or through any street or road,

shall on conviction thereof by a court of summary jurisdiction, or on indictment as herein-after mentioned, be liable either to pay a penalty not exceeding twenty pounds, or to be imprisoned for a term not exceeding three months, with or without hard labour.

16) *Women's Trade Societies, 1881*
(*The Times*, 5 September 1881)
To the Editor of the Times,
Sir,

Will you kindly grant me space for a few words with reference to the mention made in *The Times* of yesterday of the woman's trade societies represented at the Trades Union Congress? The statement is that 'the women's societies appear to be numerically the weakest, the smallest numbering only 30 members, the largest but 460 members, while the largest workmen's association, represented, the Amalgamated Society of Engineers, return 45,000 members.'

I wish to point out that the women's trade societies are but recently established, the oldest of which I am one of the representatives – having been formed in only 1874, and that they are at present limited to the place in which they started. The Amalgamated Society of Engineers have been in existence 30 years, and its 45,000 members are made up of branches all over the country, some of the branches having, however, but only a small number of members. I may also point out that one of the men's societies represented at the Congress has only 40 members – a fact not mentioned in the passage I quoted – and that many of these societies are much older than the Engineers' Society.

From the progress already made in the women's union movement, with all its special difficulties and drawbacks, there is every reason to hope that in 20 years time the numerical strength of the women's societies will have largely increased.

I am Sir, your obedient servant
EMMA A PATERSON

17) *The TUC and Overproduction*
(i)　　*The TUC and Overproduction, 1885*
(*The Times*, 8 and 10 September 1885 reporting on the 16th Conference of the TUC at Southport)
T.R. Threlfall, Presidential Address.
'What was their duty now in respect to the present universal depression in trade which had lasted fully eight years and the cause of which was ascribed to overproduction? [Actions include the introduction of the eight-hour day, the re-organization of the home market, though not state-aided emigration.]
One of the most active causes of over-production was the invention and use of labour saving machinery, but what had been omitted was a reduction in the ... number of hours of each labourer, and as a consequence the market had been flooded with unemployment. They must be alive to this fact in

future, and the only way in which they will apply the lesson effectively was through Parliament. Thus their individual votes would soon be equal to . . . the millionaires.'

J. Mawdsley

'That this Congress, believing that the present stagnation in trade is largely due to over-production, a remedy for which is not to be found in a curtailment of the earnings of workers, tenders its sympathy and support to the cotton operatives of Oldham in their effort to prevent reductions of wages which is not accompanied by some measure upon the restriction upon the output, having for its relief of the present glutted condition of the cotton trade.'

(ii) *Trades Union Congress, Hull, 1886*
(*The Times*, 11 September 1886)
Mr. Broadhurst

'That in the opinion of the Congress the systematic working of overtime in many of the skilled trades of the country is an evil on the person engaged, and an injustice to the large body of unemployed, and shall therefore be discontinued, wherever the unions have sufficient influence for the purpose.'

(iii) *The TUC on Land and Emigration, 1886*
(*Report of the 19th Annual T.U.C. held at Hull, 17 September 1886*)
Resolution 3 Land Question

That this Congress is of opinion that the Legislation at once take in hand the Reform of the Land Laws of Great Britain, and should open communication with the various Colonial Governments to ascertain the extent of free grants of land available for colonization purposes, so that on the one hand the agricultural population may become more firmly planted on the land, by the acquisition of property rights at home, and on the other hand our unemployed surplus population, who wish to do so, may proceed to British colonies, and become peasant proprietors in other portions of the British Empire, where their location will not interfere with the Colonial Labour Markets.

18) *The Sectional and Exclusive Attitudes of the Amalgamated Association of Cotton Spinners in the 1870s and 1880s.*
(Evidence of James Mawdsley, Secretary of the Cotton Spinners to the *Royal Commission on Labour*, 1892, XXXV [6708-VI] Group C Evidence, 789–801. Mawdsley was being questioned by Tom Mann.)
Every six years a piecer becomes able to do a spinner's work. . . . Then such spinner would train . . . at least three? – Yes, that is so. – And there would be only work for one of these? – That is so. – What becomes of the other two? . . . The employers have had a splendid selection and they select the giants . . . in the working capacity, as spinners to begin with. . . . The others, the next best, plenty of them drift into miscellaneous occupations, some go as labourers at foundries, some go to hawking, others go in for portering, others in the coal trade it is the same as in other occupations. [. . .]

If the piecers wanted to better their position, would your society help them? – That would depend on the circumstances. If they want to better their position at the expense of spinners, we might object, but if they want to better their position at the expense of employers, we are quite willing they should do so.

19) *Tom Mann and the Eight-Hour Day*
[Tom Mann, *What a Compulsory Eight-Hour Day Means to the Workers* (1886). Original copies in a number of libraries, including the British Library of Political and Economic Science and Leeds Reference Library.]
None of the important societies have any policy other than that of endeavouring to keep wages from falling. The true Unionist policy of *aggression* seems entirely lost sight of; in fact the average trade unionist of to-day is a man with a fossilised intellect, either hopelessly apathetic, or supporting a policy that plays directly into the hands of the capitalist employer.

'OLD UNIONISM' AND THE EMERGENCE OF 'NEW UNIONISM' *c.* 1888–1909

The late 1880s and early 1890s saw the widening of the trade-union movement, with existing unions, such as the Amalgamated Society of Engineers (10), altering their rules in order to admit less skilled workers and new unions, often organized on general lines, attempting to organize all those who would wish to join. Trade unionism was becoming much broader and less exclusive. There had always been unions of the unskilled and the semi-skilled but the number and size of them increased in the late 1880s encouraged by key events such as the organization of the gasworkers (1), the great London dock strike of 1889 (2) and the Match Girls' Strike of 1888. The organizing of the unskilled and semi-skilled moved apace between 1888 and 1893 before the renewal of economic depression and the defensive responses of the employers checked the pace of progress. The Liverpool Tailoresses' and Coatmakers' Union fought for the reduction of working hours (6), the Amalgamated Labourers' Union improved working conditions in the ports of Cardiff, Penarth and Barry (7), and the Leeds tailoresses, led by Isabella O. Ford, fought for improved conditions in the Leeds tailoring trade. The developments were so pervasive that the tide of the 'new unionism' could not be turned back. The whole structure of trade unionism began to change, gradually but almost inexorably. Trade unions became increasingly linked with the demand for state intervention, began to associate with the emergent politically-independent political Labour movement, and began to widen their remit – organizing more women into the movement and white-collar workers.

In this new climate, even the state began to consider the need for a closer involvement in the development of the new, more assertive and more pervasive type of trade unionism which was emerging, showing particular interest in recording and measuring the extent of industrial strike activity through the Labour Department of the Board of Trade (3). In addition, the Royal Commission on Labour surveyed the whole trade-union movement between 1891 and, producing 58 volumes of published evidence between 1892 and 1894 (6, 11) which has still barely ever been tapped by trade unionists. The Royal Commission encouraged the development of conciliation procedures on a regional basis, recognizing that many new unions had not yet been able to establish direct formal arbitration and conciliation agreements with their employers, but the government legislation in this direction did not achieve much in the way of improvements in industrial relations.

The new movement was led by a coterie of young trade unionists, many of whom were also active in the socialist movement. Tom Mann, a skilled engineer, and Ben Tillett, the dockers' leader, were amongst these. In their writings on 'new unionism' (4), they argued that it meant open as opposed to closed trade unionism. To them the new unionism looked to the needs of all the working class while the old unionism looked only to trade-union members. New unionism, because of Mann's advocacy of the eight-hour day, was soon associated with that issue: those who opposed state intervention for the eight-hour day were deemed to be 'old' trade unionists whilst those who supported the demand were considered to be 'new' trade unionists.

The turning point in trade unionism for many writers was the London dock strike of 1889 which saw badly organized and relatively unskilled workers defeat the employers and gain improved conditions and wages. But there were many other developments. The miners' leaders, politically associated with the Liberal Party and deemed to be very much 'old' unionists in their attitude, continued to fight for the eight-hour day for their members (5, 15) and they became embroiled in the 1893 miners' lockout (14, 16) which was settled by the intervention of the government. Also, of great importance was the developments of trade unionism amongst white-collar workers, most particularly the clerks who formed the National Clerks' Association in June 1893 (17) whose main concern, in its early years, was to raise wages by reducing the number of women working for low wages in offices.

By the late 1890s most of the established unions had come to accept that a more open attitude to trade-union membership was necessary if employers were to be resisted. The Engineers' lockout of 1897 (18) revealed that even a powerful union, with large funds and a highly-skilled membership, would find it difficult to resist powerful and determined employers – even though it was clearly the case that engineers, and skilled unionists, were able to continue to meet their employers on something approaching equal terms (21).

During this period, especially after 1893 when the Independent Labour Party emerged and the economic conditions worsened, British trade unions began to move towards a closer association with the forces of political independence. The formation of the Labour Representation Committee in 1900, a body which aimed to unite socialists and trade unionists in a viable independent political party for the working class, provided another stimulus for this connection although the prospects for this at first looked bleak. But many trade unions were motivated to join the LRC due to the Taff Vale case of 1900 and 1901 (19), which eventually saw the House of Lords uphold an injunction from the Taff Vale Railway Company permitting it to sue for damages from the Amalgamated Society of Railway Servants due to the strike action of some of its members. Many trade unions recognized the need to protect their interests through the politics of the LRC. However, this link was threatened by the Osborne Judgement of 1909 (22) which robbed the Labour Party of much needed finance by forcing trade-union members to contract into the political levy arrangement rather than to contract out. Despite this limitation the link between the trade unions and the Labour Party remained firm, as it has done ever since.

1) *The Gasworkers Organize in 1889*
(Extract from Will Thorne, *My Life's Battles*, p. 69)
A few of us got together: I gave them my views and we held a meeting.

This was on March 31st, 1889. . . . A resolution was passed in favour of a gasworkers' union being formed, with the eight-hour day as one of its objects. [. . .]

Sunday morning, March 31st, 1889 . . . – was the birthday of the National Union of Gasworkers and General Labourers of Great Britain and Ireland. . . .

After the speeches were over, I called for volunteers to form an organising committee, of which George Angle was appointed the secretary; then we started to take down the names of the men who wanted to join up. Eight hundred joined that morning. The entrance fee was one shilling, and we had to borrow several pails to hold the coppers and other coins that were paid in. . . .

The meeting over, we had to get down to business. Ben Tillett, Byford and myself formed ourselves into a 'provisional committee' to draft a set of rules and to discuss ways and means of getting . . . the workers in the other gasworks around London. Byford was made treasurer. He was a proprietor of a temperance bar at 144 Barking Road. He had a good knowledge of trade union administration because for many years he had been secretary of the Yorkshire Glass Bottle Workers' Association. [. . .] Sunday after Sunday we would start off from 144 Barking Road, our headquarters, to encourage the men at other gas-works. [. . .] The idea caught on; enthusiasm was at a high pitch, and within two weeks we had over 3,000 men in the union.

Never before had men responded like they did. For months London was ablaze. The newspapers throughout the country were giving good reports of our activities. They were curious to know what we wanted and what we were going to do.

I knew what we were going to do. I kept in mind all the time the pledge to the men at the first meeting. To work and fight for the eight-hour day – that was my first objective, soon to be won.

2) *The London Dock Strike of 1889: The Strike Committee's Manifesto, issued in the fourth week of the strike.*
(The History of the TUC 1868–1968: A Pictorial Survey of the Social Revolution Illustrated with Contemporary Prints, Documents and Photographs, p. 42)

SOUTH SIDE
CENTRAL STRIKE COMMITTEE
SAYES COURT, DEPTFORD.
SEPTEMBER 10, 1889

GENERAL MANIFESTO

Owing to the facts that the demands of the Corn Porters, Deal Porters, Granary Men, General Steam Navigation Men, Permanent Men and General Labourers on the South Side have been misrepresented, the above Committee have decided to issue this Manifesto, stating the demands of the various sections now on Strike, and pledge themselves to support each section in obtaining their demands.

DEAL PORTERS of the Surrey Commercial Docks have already placed their demands before the Directors.

LUMPERS (Outside) demand the following Rates, viz: 1. 10d per standard for Deals. 2. 11s per stand for all Goods rating from 2 x 4 to 2½ x 7, or for rough boards. 3. 1s standard for plain boards. Working day from 7 a.m. to 5 p.m., and that no man leave the 'Red Lion' corner before 6.45 a.m. Overtime at the rate of 6d per hour extra from 5 p.m. Including meal times.

STEVEDORES (Inside) demand 8d per hour from 7 a.m. to 5 p.m. 1s per hour overtime. Overtime to commence from 5 p.m. to 7 p.m. Pay to commence from leaving the 'Red Lion' corner. Meal times to be paid for. Holiday & Meal times double pay and that the rules of the United Stevedores Protection League be acceded to in every particular. (Conceded)

OVERSIDE CORN PORTERS (S.C.D.) demand 15s 3d per 100 qrs. for Oat. Heavy labour 17s 4d per 100 qrs. manual, or with the use of Steam 16s 1d. All overtime after 6 p.m. to be paid at the rate of ½d per qr. extra.

QUAY CORN PORTERS (S.C.D.) demand the return of Standard prices previous to March 1889, which had been in operation for 17 years.

TRIMMERS AND GENERAL LABOURERS demand 6d per hour from 7 a.m. to 6 p.m. and 8d per hour Overtime; Meal times as usual; and not to be taken on for less than 4 hours.

WEIGHERS & WAREHOUSEMAN demand to be reinstated in their former positions without distinction.

BERMONDSEY AND ROTHERHITHE WALL CORN PORTERS demand: 1. Permanent Men 30s per week. 2. Casual Men 5s 10d per day and 8d per hour Overtime. Overtime to commence at 6 p.m. Meal times as usual.

GENERAL STEAM NAVIGATION MEN demand: 1. Wharf men, 6d per hour for 6 a.m. to 6 p.m. and 8d per hour Overtime. 2. In the Stream, 7d per hour ordinary time, 9d per hour Overtime. In the dock, 8d per hour ordinary time, 1s per hour Overtime.

MAUDSLEY'S ENGINEER'S MEN. Those receiving 21s per week now demand 24s, and those receiving 24s per week demand 26s.

ASHBY'S LTD, CEMENT WORKS demand 6d per ton landing Coals and chalk. General Labourers 10% rise of wages all round, this making up for a reduction made 3 years ago.

GENERAL LABOURERS, TELEGRAPH CONSTRUCTION demand 4s per day from 6 a.m. to 5 p.m., time and a quarter for first 2 hours Overtime, and if later, time and a half for all Overtime. No work to be done in Meal Hours.

Signed on behalf of the Central Committee, Wade Arms,

BEN TILLETT
JOHN BURNS
TOM MANN,
H.H. CHAMPION,
JAS. TOOMEY.

Signed on behalf of the South side Committee.
JAS SULLIVAN
CHAS H.
HUGH BRO

3) *Strikes and Lockouts*
(Board of Trade, *Strikes and Lockouts Report, 1889*, C 5809, with an introduction by John Burnett, the Labour Correspondent and ex-trade union leader)
Report by the Labour Correspondent of the Board of Trade.
Labour Disputes 1888
It is certain that all such industrial struggles represent the conflict of

employers and workmen upon matters which one or the other consider to be vital to their interests, and while engaged in this, the participants concerned are really in a state of moral if not actual warfare. [. . .]

As a rule, however, even the largest labour fights are little more than a nine days' wonder, and when they terminate nothing much is heard of them. In the case of lesser disputes, where the interest around is comparatively local, they break out, run for a week or month may be, and no one outside the locality is aware that they have taken place. Nor in any case is any general record kept of them for the enlightenment and instruction of those who may come after. Even the contestants themselves are seldom anxious to put their experiences into a statistical form, but, on the contrary, seem anxious to put away out of sight as speedily as possible all memories connected with the ordeal. . . .

The right of labour to do as it pleases with its own has long been recognised. [. . .] Masters are at liberty to form organisations for all kinds of trade purposes, likewise the same privilege is freely accorded to the workmen. [. . .]

4) *Tom Mann and Ben Tillett on 'New Unionism'*
(Tom Mann and Ben Tillett, *The 'New' Trade Unionism* (1890), p. 15)

In conclusion, we repeat that the real difference between the 'new' and the 'old' is that those who belong to the latter and delight in being distinct from the policy endorsed by the 'new', do so because they do not recognise, as we do, that it is the work of the trade unionists to stamp out poverty from the land. They do not contend, as we contend, that existing unions should exert themselves to extend organisations where they as yet do not exist. They know the enormous difficulties under which hundreds of thousands labour, and how difficult it is for them to take the initial steps in genuine trade unionism and how valuable a little 'coaching' would be from those who have experience in such matters; but they have not done what they might to supply this – we shall. A new enthusiasm is required, a fervent zeal that will result in the sending forth of trade union organizers as missionaries through the length and breadth of the country. Clannishness in trade matters must be superseded by a cosmopolitan, brotherhood must not be talked of but practised; and that real grit exists in the 'new' unions is evident, not only from the manner in which they are perfecting their organisations, but also from the substantial way in which they have contributed to the support of others shows that the 'new' unions were much more prompt in rendering monetary aid than the 'old' ones. Nevertheless, what we desire to see is a unification of all, a dropping of the bickerings, and an earnest devotion to duty taking the place of the old indifferences. The cause we have at heart is too sacred to admit of time being spent quarrelling amongst ourselves, and, whilst we make no pretence to the possession of special values are prepared to work unceasingly for the economic emancipation of the workers. Our ideal is a Co-operative Commonwealth.

5) *Benjamin Pickard on the Eight Hours Question and the Miners*
(*Barnsley Chronicle*, 8 November 1890, reporting on a meeting with the Denaby Main miners at Mexbro)
The officials were empowered to go over Yorkshire and were pledged to this position whether they liked it or not – that a question must be put to the candidate on the eight hours question. They must not give the candidate their support if he would not support them – whether Liberal or Tory. There were plenty of men willing to come forward to support such a bill, and in Yorkshire there was no need to fear a splitting up of the Liberal party. They had never said the men were to vote for a Tory, but they were pledged to abstain from voting for a Liberal who would not agree to the matter. They need not be afraid of what the Tories would do for them. He (Mr. Pickard) liked men to be clear and outspoken, and then they knew the exact position. The Tory party, from the commencement, had been hostile to the movement, and after this their pledges were not worth anything. . . . Mr. Gladstone had spoken on the eight-hour question, and it was now under the Liberal banner to-day . . . and he (Mr. Pickard) was glad to be a humble follower of his.

6) *A Women's Union in Liverpool*
(*Royal Commission on Labour*, 1893 (6894–xxiii), p. 70. Also quoted in Eric J. Hobsbawm, *Labour's Turning Point 1880–1900* (second edition. Brighton, Harvester, 1974), p. 90)
The president and secretary of the Liverpool Tailoresses' and Coatmakers' Union gave the following account of its formation and progress. It was formed in the summer of 1890 ; the Jewish tailors had formed a society and gained a reduction in hours. The women

coatmakers thought that 'what a foreigner could do a woman could'. They therefore prepared slips of paper and went round to the workshops and persuaded 260 women coatmakers to sign their names and addresses in favour of a trade union and a reduction in hours. The Trades Council assisted them and they called a meeting at the Oddfellows Hall and formed themselves into a Union and elected a president, a secretary and a committee. They then sent a memorial to the Middleman's Society asking for a two hours' reduction. No notice was taken of their request. They therefore blocked two shops and sent a letter saying that the reduction of hours must be given without any reduction in wages and without adopting the piecework system.

They had so far no funds. . . .The middlemen held a meeting and decided to lock them out, thinking that without funds they would be frightened. The Trades Council had, however, promised them support and the girls kept together and patrolled the streets to show what respectable-looking people they were, as statements to the contrary had been made. . . .

As soon as the reduction of hours had been granted the numbers in the union began to diminish. . . .'The women are kept combined' now by tea-parties and picnics given them in many cases by a few persons interested in the trade union movement.

7) *The Amalgamated Labourers and militant trade union action in Cardiff, 1891.*
(*Rise and progress of the National Amalgamated Labourers' Union of G.B & Ireland*, by T. J. O'Keefe, District Secretary, Cardiff, 1891, extracts pp. 7–16)
And this it was that caused the rise of THE NATIONAL AMALGAMATED LABOURERS' UNION. All honour to man, or men, that were the instigators of its existence. Proud many they will be of the name it became. Proud . . . to know that from the success which it has acclaimed, and in the majority of cases without a single day cessation of labour on behalf of its members, it has already earned itself a name which will be indelibly stamped upon, not only the annals of Trade Unionism, but upon the minds and hearts of those whoever had a connection with it. [. . .] That memorable night in our history will not be forgotten, when the little band of founders met together, full of longing, full of hope, yet mingled with fear, at the Wyndham

Arcade, Cardiff on the 6th of June, 1889, and gave birth to an organization which soon surpassed their most vital expectations [. . .]

. . . Soon, too, the name of the Union became a household word in Newport, Swansea, Chepstow, and many other places. [. . .] Why? Because the object and benefits extended to the worker for the contribution he paid were such as no other organization in the land had guaranteed. [. . .]

In Cardiff, Penarth, Barry . . . and Walnut Tree, decided benefits were gained for the men. Port rules were drawn up between the Master and the Union benefiting the Labourers of the Fitting Shop and Drydock yards. A code of Working Rules was drawn up affecting the Builders' Labourers, and agreed to by the Masters, by which the men were advanced from three farthings to a penny per hour, or an equivalent of 20 per cent. [. . .]

At Newport the Iron ore, the Iron Workers and the Stevedores obtained an increase in their wages of 35 per cent. The Timber Men after a short, but decisive, struggle gained a victory and an increase of 1/6 per day. [. . .]

Out of several minor disputes . . . only one of importance is worth relating. It was the strike of the THARSIS COPPER WORKS at Cardiff, in April 1890. The men were all in the Union, and they desired that their wages should be increased. Their employment was hard and laborious; and the recompense for their labour was totally insufficient to provide for themselves and their families. . . .

The pickets did their duty well and peaceably, and after sixteen weeks of turmoil and anxiety, sixteen weeks of almost starvation, which the men nobly and uncomplainingly endured, the strike was given over, the firm remaining inflexible to the last; and with the help of those skunks of humanity, the blacklegs, they managed to get their works once more ahead. It is worth stating here that the men, seeing no chance of victory, and all of them not being able to find employment elsewhere, applied for re-engagement, and were taken on; and strange to say, were given an advance of 3d per day.

8) *Amalgamated Society of Dyers, 1891*
(*Yorkshire Factory Times*, 21 February 1891)
To the Editor of Factory Times,
Sir, – A correspondent in last week's issue directs your readers

attention to the fossil type of dyers in the Bradford district and seeks an improvement for their present condition. I think it is next to useless to try and convert such men from their evil ways; but constant effort should be made to induce good men to join the union.

I will not exactly say I am in favour of boycotting but I am strongly of the opinion that, like unruly neighbours, fossils should be kept at respectful distances.

A Dyer

9) *Leeds Tailoresses' Union*
(*Yorkshire Factory Times*, 24 June 1892)
Sir, – Can you kindly answer these questions? There are girls working in one of the tailoring shops in town who are engaged at a weekly rate of 10s. If they get through more than is represented by 10s, the master refuses to pay them the extra amount, but when there is not enough work in the shop to bring in 10s they are sent home, and he takes off so much an hour. Is this legal? Can it be successfully disputed by us in a court of law?

There is also another shop where the power is turned off at 12 o'clock on Saturday. Half an hour is allowed for cleaning the machine, and after that the girls wait for their wages, sometimes until half past one or quarter to two. The wages are only made up to 12.30. The half hour till one is deducted off. Is this legal? Of course, in this case the workers are time hands.

The third question is this: One of the members of our union, who is a good worker, can earn £2 a week when left an hour overtime. But only once has she ever been paid as much as 25s working from six till eight. The employer refuses to pay her more than a certain amount, however much she may earn. He says he can afford no more than £1 and never pays her more unless she works overtime. But however much there is to be done, even if it is three pounds work, she has to do it and does it too.

10) *Engineers alter their rules, 1892*
(Recruiting leaflet, *To All Classes of Workmen in the Engineering Industry*)
Having these objects [the unification of workers and financial security] in view, our delegates meeting held in Leeds in June, 1892 ... gave the subject of more perfect organisation their special

consideration and after lengthy and exhaustive discussion, founded on practical experience and knowledge of trade customs, decided to remove all barriers that prevented or retarded the admission into our society of any workman, who in following the engineering trade, can claim to be a skilled artisan. . . .

11) *An Attack upon Sliding Scale Agreements in the Iron and Steel Industry, 1892*
(Evidence of William Snow, General Secretary of the National Association of Blastfurnacemen, *Royal Commission on Labour,* Group A, II, 1892, C6795–1,XXXVI)
Whilst believing in the principle of a sliding scale, I do not exactly believe in the basis upon which they are formed at the present time; I think the way that they are formed at the present time is sometimes the means of the employer, when trade is bad, competing too keenly against one another for orders. If they sell their iron, say 1s per ton less they will get a reduction of wages comparatively with the reduction that they have made with their iron, and if they knew that there was no sliding scale, and that the men were likely to resort to a strike sooner than submit to a reduction, I think it is possible they would not compete so much against one another as they do, and bring down prices as low as they do.

12) *Wiltshire General and Agricultural Labourers*
(Webb Collection, Coll E, B, CV, 10, Wiltshire General and Agricultural Workers' Union, *The Report of the Inaugural Meeting held at Swindon, 12 December 1892; Speeches by Mr. Keir Hardie MP, Mr. J. E. Dorking . . .*)
Meeting held at Swimming Baths, Swindon – December 12th 1892. Chairman [. . .] He knew something of the agricultural labourer – he could almost say he had been one himself . . . , and he concluded there were amongst that class individuals who would be, if their qualities were developed, among our best men. But how, he asked, were men to develop their good qualities on the miserable food on which the agricultural laborer too often had to subsist? (Shame) There had been years ago an attempt by Joseph Arch to start a union in Wiltshire, but the scheme was on too large a scale to succeed. The one in which the present meeting was interested was, however, at their own doors, and

every man who subscribed to it would know how and by whom his money was spent. As a small employer himself, he should be glad to see his own men join the Union.

13) *The Glass Bottle Makers of Yorkshire United Trade Protection Society, 1892–3 and the Glass bottle makers of Scotland*
[The Yorkshire Society was a body of highly-skilled men which attempted to protect its members through apprenticeship rules, high unemployment benefits to dissuade glass bottlemakers from accepting lower wages, and strike action when necessary. In June 1892 there were 3,300 journeyman glass bottle makers in Yorkshire, about half of them working in the Castleford district of Yorkshire. The source is the Glass Bottle Makers, *National Conference Reports, 1893–5, Vol. 1 (First to Twenty-Third Inclusive)*, (1908).]

(i)   *Apprenticeship and wages issue raised at Castleford, 17 Dec. 1892*
       The employers have declared that the wages shall, and must be reduced that the working regulations shall be altered so that they shall *get better profits* which means *indirect and additional reductions* after reducing the standard rates 3/- a week per man – that they shall work their furnaces as many journeys and shifts in a week as they think proper – and shall cram the men and lads into as small compass as they choose – that they shall put up as many lads into trade as they can get and discharge them on becoming 21 years of age unless they will work for apprentice wages after they become men – or discharge men who have wives and families depending upon them in order to make room for other lads who in their turn may be discharged to make room for others, and carry on this system until they have flooded the labour markets with hands and then starve them all into submission to any terms and conditions they think fit to impose upon them, and reduce them to a condition of *absolute white slavery.*

(ii)   *The Glass Bottle Makers' Lock Out, Yorkshire & Dublin, circular from A. Greenwood, Secretary, 3 February 1893*

TO THE TRADE UNIONISTS OF THE UNITED KINGDOM
An appeal for moral and pecuniary support

FELLOW WORKERS,

We now beg to inform you that the Yorkshire Glass Bottle Makers have been locked out five weeks and the Dublin Glass Bottle Hands three weeks, and it has been resolved by the Yorkshire Delegate Meeting and the Council of the International Union of Glassworkers to appeal to the workers throughout the United Kingdom to render them assistance during their present struggle, not only for the protection of fair wages, but also for the maintenance of the principles of trade-unionism.

. . . some 1,500 Bottle Hands in Yorkshire alone are locked out. [. . .] Suffice it so say there is every reason for supposing that the employers have taken advantage of the depressed condition of trade to lock the men out under the impression that they would submit to their terms before being locked out. In this they have been mistaken. [. . .]

[. . .] As soon as the employers sent in their agenda for this year, the workmen resolved to raise the weekly payment of contribution from 2s to 3s a week although a large number of them had not averaged more than £1 a week wages and 30 per cent of them were out of work. . . .The payment to the unemployed during the last 25 years is upwards of £34,000 and the amount paid in connection with trade disputes, lock-outs and strikes is upwards of £21,000. [. . .]

THE DUBLIN GLASS BOTTLE HANDS

It has been resolved to couple the appeal of the Dublin Bottle Hands with the Yorkshire appeal, who all belong to the International Union. The Dublin Glass Bottle Makers are resisting a reduction of 20 per cent. [. . .] They are locked out, 150 of them. It is therefore understood that they shall have a share of the money received.

(iii) *Glass Bottlemakers of Scotland: Lock-out and Strike, 1 July 1893*
To the Trade Unionists of the United Kingdom
AN URGENT APPEAL FOR MORAL AND PECUNIARY ASSISTANCE

FELLOW-WORKERS, – It is with much regret that we make this, our first and urgent appeal to the various Trades of the United Kingdom for their sympathy and support in our present struggle for existence, forced upon us by our employers attempting to crush our Union and reduce our wages. Not satisfied with the men working on an average of about 25 per cent less than Lancashire and Yorkshire Bottlemakers, they also further attempted to further reduce our wages, in some instances about other 12½ per cent.

A number of our employers have already conceded the just and exceedingly reasonable request of the men. Whilst there are others who have not only admitted that our demands are just, but are really less than what is reasonable, and yet they keep their men on strike. For what? Simply to try to break up our combination and drain our funds. This quarrel has been forced upon the workmen by the employers refusing to meet the representatives of the men to consider the question at issue, with a view to a settlement. We, therefore, had no alternative but to fight, or continue in a state worse than slavery.

Fellow-Employers, just to give an instance of what our employers are doing rather than give their men an advance averaging about four-fifths of a halfpenny per hour. They have not only sent moulds to Germany and England, but they are paying the English rates, also the freights to Scotland in addition thereto, and fostering and encouraging foreign competition in a trade already ruined thereby. (Vide employers.)

Fellow-Workmen, in asking for your support and assistance, we beg to state with the exception of a small number in Glasgow, where employers have conceded the advance, and who are not otherwise objected to by the Society, every Bottlemaker in Scotland is out – not a blackleg amongst them. And of the apprentices, there are only a few at Alloa working. There are upwards of 290 men on our pay sheets . . . it takes upwards of £220 per week to clear our expenses, etc. We have been out five weeks. . . .

Fellow-Workmen, we therefore call upon you to render us assistance, and by your help to gain the victory over the unscrupulous employers, and thereby prove to all that are unorganised that there is no power on earth by which the workers can obtain fair wages and reasonable working conditions than by the power of combination and consolidation.

Yours on behalf of the Glassbottlemakers of Scotland,
JOHN LINN, Secretary.
JAMES SHEFFIELD, President.

14) *Benjamin Pickard and Aggressive Trade Unionism, 1893*
(*Barnsley Chronicle*, 8 April 1893. This deals with the attack upon the Miners' Federation of Great Britain by the Miners' National Union and its 'What Trade Unionism should Be' Conference, which had been held in Barnsley that week.)

He had nothing to say whether he was an 'old' or a 'new' unionist. The position he took up was that a union to be anything at all must be aggressive – there could be no conservatism in the strict sense of the word in trade unionism. The good of the largest number must be the aim of and object of trade unionism. To preserve the fossilised idea of conciliation, as understood twenty years ago, arbitration or any other board which meant letting well alone in order that the well 'be-ers' might receive full benefits, whilst the toilers received what the 'well be-ers' dropped from the table was out of the question now. The difference between the National Union and the Miners' Federation of Great Britain might be said to be that the policy of the National Union was to 'let sleeping dogs lie', to let well alone, to allow the owners to prosper and disperse. That was the be-all and end-all of the National Union. The Miners' Federation of Great Britain believed in conciliation which should secure a higher rate of pay to the miners than the public would be otherwise be prepared to give; which should secure for the colliery owner a profitable concern, whether the colliery owners liked to have their concern profitable or not. The Federation believed to-day that conciliation meant no alteration in the present rate of wages. They did not believe in a race for output; the race they believed we are in is for good wages and for profits; selling coal and not giving it away. Mr. Burt held a very responsible position in the present Government . . . (but) Mr. Burt, in his address, treated the eight-hour question in a 'gingerly fashion'. [. . .]

If Mr. Burt was in accord with the decision of the Trades Union Congress, of which he was chairman in 1891, and in accord with the decision of the Miners' Federation executive and the Trades Union Parliamentary Committee, then he (Mr. Pickard) would be in perfect accord with him.

15) *Support for an Eight Hours Bill*
(*Barnsley Chronicle*, 12 August 1893, reporting on a resolution passed at a Barnsley Trades Council demonstration)
Councillor Frith: That this meeting of combined trade unions of Barnsley and district strongly urge upon the Government the necessity of the Miners' Eight Hour Bill being passed into law as speedily as possible, and also a general reduction in the hours of labour in various industries of the country, on the lines laid down by the T.U.C.

16) *National Coal Strike of 1893*
[The dispute began in July 1893 and was settled, after Government pressure on both sides, on 17 November 1893, with the men returning at the old rates of pay until 1 February 1894]

(i)   (*Barnsley Chronicle*, 22 July 1893 and Yorkshire Miners' Association, Minutes (printed), 21 July 1893)
Resolution 'That we do not accept 25 per cent reduction in our wages, or any part thereof. We also reassert that any district not under notice, which has submitted to any reduction of wages during the last two years be requested to ask by notice for such an advance in wages as will bring the wages of such district up to 40 per cent advanced obtained in the Federation districts.

(ii)   (Miners' Federation of Great Britain, Minutes and Correspondence, copies in the Miners' Offices, Barnsley, a letter from Mr. Gladstone, in the Printed Minutes, 15–18 November period.)
Sir, – The attention of Her Majesty's Government has been seriously called to the widespread and disastic effect produced by the long continuance of the unfortunate dispute in the coal trade which has now entered its sixteenth week.

It is clear, from information which has reached the Board of Trade, that much misery and suffering are caused not only to the families of the men directly involved, but also to many thousands of others not engaged in mining, whose employment has been adversely affected by the stoppage. The further prolongation of the dispute cannot fail to aggravate this suffering . . . .

(17) *The Clerks*
(Various items on the Clerks, Webb Collections, Coll. E, B. cviii, British Library of Economic and Political Sciences.)
(i)   *The National Clerks' Association, 1893*
[. . .] On the 2nd June 1893, a few reforming individuals here in Yorkshire launched this Association, having for its object the co-operation, combination, and mutual protection of the vast body of clerical labour in this country, at present so utterly helpless, and so abjectly at the mercy of capital.

This Association has been steadily growing since its initiative, but we have to regret the same apathy and even greater indifference which so characterises the workers in almost all other branches of skilled and unskilled labour, and our membership, consequently, is far from satisfactory. [. . .]

Yours fraternally,
A. E. Allen, President
Jos. Hazelip, Secretary

(ii)   *The Clerk's Charter*
(Walter J. Read [editor of *The Clerk*], The Clerk's Charter, Webb Collection, Coll E, B, cviii, item 3)
1. A *Wage* that will enable them to live as educated citizens;
2. Healthy and comfortable *Offices* wherever they can work and keep sound minds in healthy bodies;
3. *Hours* that will not leave their minds and bodies exhausted at the end of the day but will leave them *Leisure* to develop them further and their individuality. [. . .]

Women's Place is not in the Office
Plenty of employers will agree to that in principle, but women are cheaper, after all 'Business is business' and there is competition to face.

What is just? Many thousands of women did not come into the clerical world for the love of it, but because they must earn their living, and support others dependent upon them. Men have no right to dictate to women how and where they shall earn their living. On the other hand, women should not cut salaries, for their own sake as well as that of the men. Men are willing to meet competition on fair terms, and, if women prove themselves better clerks, to give way; but women should not compete unfairly. They should not make themselves too cheap.

The competition also decreases the chance of young women marrying. Few will marry on a wage that means certain misery, and if young women compete by cheapening themselves more and more of them will be left 'on the shelf'. Many firms forbid marriage to the clerk who has not reached a certain salary, and many clerks are stopped nowadays before they reach it, so that every girl who accepts a low salary is thereby helping to reduce, under existing conditions, the number of male clerks who will attain a position enabling them to marry.

Sound Business to Get a Good Clerk and Keep Him
[. . .] No woman should make herself too cheap. Some can hardly help themselves, but every woman with a comfortable home, who only works as a clerk to get pocket money, can 'play the game'. Her favoured economic position enables her to demand a full salary . . .

Stand Out for Equal Pay for Equal Work
Once she understands that by working at a sweating wage she is lowering the standard of life of clerks who are obliged to work for a living her sense of fair play will compel her to help her fellow-clerks to obtain a living. Women and men have equal rights and equal votes within the Union. Many women held office, and I hope even that one or two women with sufficient income to live on, when they understand the position, will voluntarily devote themselves to organising women clerks in the N.U.C. [. . .]

18) *The Engineers' Lock-out, 1897*
(*The Clarion*, 21 August 1897)
As the trial of strength between the masters and men in the engineering trade seems likely to be longer and sterner than many at first

anticipated, it may be as well to tell the general reader how the struggle arose, why it is being carried on, and what either side hopes or expects to gain by it.

It commenced as a purely London struggle, where the men . . . demanded a reduction of hours from nine to eight per day. . . .The struggle would have ended as a London battle, had not the masters' federation chosen to make a national fight of it. . . . How [was] a local struggle . . . made national, and for what purpose [is] it . . . being waged? The answer is briefly as follows: the masters' federation, professing to fear that the London eight-hour demand might, if successful, lead to an extension of the demand in the provinces, called upon the employers in the engineering trade to lock out 25 per cent of their men all over the country until the London dispute was ended. . . .

The men contend that the provincial lock-out could not be to combat a demand for an eight-hour day . . . and that in reality the desire of the masters' federation is to crush the engineers' union, of the power and stability of which they are jealous. The strike in London is practically over. . . .The men in the provinces are willing to return to work, . . . having no dispute with their own masters, who are thus simply acting as the tools of a federation. . . .

19) *Taff Vale Case, 1900*
(Sir G. Lushington, article in the *National Review*, vol 38, 1901, p. 563, also quoted in E. J. Hobsbawm, *Labour's Turning Point 1880–1900* (Brighton, Harvester Press edition, 1974) p. 161)
In my opinion it is just and salutary law. On principle I know of no reason why Trade Union funds should be exempt from liability, and very strong ones why they should not be exempt. [. . .] The law will be a great protection to the public; perhaps the chief suffered; to the employers it will secure some portion of the redress to which they are entitled . . . even to the Trade Unions themselves it should be a blessing in disguise. [. . .]

For the moment the law laid down by the House of Commons is much resented by Trade Unionists. But it will be useless for them to ask Parliament to abolish it. It is founded on justice and the public good. [. . .] So a Trade Union will be answerable in its funds for any wrongful act done by its officers 'acting within the scope of their employment' whatever their instructions.

20) *Trade Unions and the Labour Representation Committee: The Labour Representation Committee and the parliamentary election, 1900*
(Labour Party Archive)

LABOUR REPRESENTATIONS AND THE ELECTIONS

The Elections which are just over have not been regarded with much satisfaction by Progressive politicians, but the Labour Representation Committee desire to bring before your notice the remarkable success which has met those candidates who have stood in harmony with the resolutions passed by the Conference of Labour Representation called in London last February by the Parliamentary Committee of the Trade Union Congress. Those resolutions declared in favour of uniting the Labour movement politically, not merely as a wing of any one of the existing parties, but as an expression of the necessity which has now arisen for Trade Unionists and others working for the emancipation of Labour, to adopt political efforts in order to assist their other efforts.

Although there have been Labour members returned by various constituencies, and although individual Unions, as, for example, the Miners, have been directly represented in Parliament, there has been no united Labour movement in the country, advocating systematically the political claims and ideals which naturally supplement the economic claims and ideals of the working class and Trade Union organisations. There have been men, but there has been no movement. [. . .]

Issued on behalf of the Committee
J. RAMSAY MACDONALD
Hon. Secretary

21) *Meeting between the Halifax Branch Engineering Employers' Federation and the Amalgamated Society of Engineers (Halifax Branch), 22 June 1906*
(Calderdale branch of the West Yorkshire Archives, TU 1/6)

(Trade unionists) [. . .] Of course, in the first place, we think that the present and prospective state of trade warrants us in asking for an advance, and we would take the opportunity of reminding you that it is a long time since we had any change in this particular direction. It is something like nine years since we had an advance in the rate of wages . . . there have been changes in several directions, and would point out that the cost of living to us has been increased. It is no exaggeration – in fact, a low estimate – to say the rent of cottage houses has gone up six pence [2½p] per week, and in some cases nine pence [3¾ p] per week. Then again, we are in recent times having to pay more for the food that we get, and the clothes we wear, . . . there has been no increase in the wherewithal to meet same. There is one other matter we desire to point out . . . the changes which have taken place in the changed mode of production, that are acknowledged to have effected a revolution, that is, with the introduction of speeds cut steel, and also improved and labour saving machinery, the productivity has been increased to an amazing extent, and up to the present we do not see that we have reaped any advantage from these benefits, and we do think, as workers, we are entitled to a little consideration on that account. [Discussion of the wage levels in other towns.] Halifax figures amongst the lowest paid districts, and we think that accordingly there is room for improvement. [Wages were apparently 38s per week in Sheffield, Rotherham and Portsmouth. Bradford paid 34s, Leeds paid 33s and Manchester 36s. Halifax pay seems to have been 33s per week. Keighley paid 28s to 30s and Wakefield 31s.]

A MASTER [. . .] You must remember in Halifax there is a very large export trade, and not only Halifax but Keighley and one or two other places do very largely an export trade, and others in competition not only with each other, but with other nations. Only quite recently we had considerable competition from Germany. [Some discussion about the good industrial relations in the trade.]

A MASTER [. . .] You refer to the continuation of the cordial feeling existing between the masters and men. This feeling has existed during very trying circumstances. It has really existed on account of the forbearance of the masters. During the past few years three tool firms have gone under. . . .

A MASTER I am afraid you are really out of touch with the general conditions of trading as reductions at our place have recently been necessary, and we have often been busier than now. [. . .]

A MASTER [. . .] There have been now for something like twelve years cordial relations between us, though it is not that we have not always had nothing like friction. [. . .]

22) *The Osborne Judgement, 1909*
(The Osborne Judgement of 1909 made illegal the political levy – the trade union contribution to the Labour Party – and led to a loss of income to the party and a loss of membership)

(i) *Lord MacNaghten, in the Osborne Case, Amalgamated Society of Railway Servants v. Osborne, 1909*

It is broad and general principle that Companies incorporated by Statute for special purposes, and societies, whether incorporated or not, which owe their constitution and their status to an Act of Parliament, having their objects and powers defined thereby, cannot apply funds to any purpose foreign to the purposes for which they were established, or embark on any undertaking in which they were not intended by Parliament to be concerned.... This principle is not confined to Corporations created by special Acts of Parliament. It applies, I think, with equal force in every case where a society or association formed for the purposes recognised and defined by an Act of Parliament places itself under the Act, and by so doing obtains some statutory immunity or privilege.

(ii) *How the Osborne Judgement dooms Trade Unionism*
(Labour Party, *Labour Party Leaflet, no. 49*)

A few Judges have decided that Trade Unions must not defend their members and advance their interests by political means.
Landlords,
Railway Directors, can go to the House of Commons
Brewers,
Rich men generally
But Labour is forbidden by the Judge to adopt the only means by which working men can get there. [. . .]
How can Trade Unions do their work with this power taken from them? Parliament has become the field upon which the great battles between capital and labour are to be fought. By using its political power, Trade Unionism has won the

> *The Workmen's Compensation Act,*
> *Factory and Mining Legislation*
> *Unemployed Workmen's Act,*
> *Fair Wages in Government Contracts*

and similar Working-Class benefits.

They have secured freedom of combination, and they repelled the last attack made upon their liberties by the unjust Taff Vale Decision.

SYNDICALISM, MASS UNIONISM AND THE GREAT WAR, 1910–1918

Industrial conflict began to increase dramatically on the eve of the First World War. There were many reasons for this. In the first instance the improved economic conditions encouraged trade unions to attempt to win back the wage reductions which they had suffered in the previous decade. In addition, trade unions were better organized and many were moving towards amalgamation. It is fair to assume that the rising level of strike activity would have occurred in any case since the improving economic conditions were more propitious for strike action. Nevertheless, and rather misleadingly, this period is identified with the activities of the industrial syndicalists – who aimed to obtain workers' control through the reorganization of the trade-union movement and the organization of a general strike to bring down capitalism. Few industrial disputes were actually organized, or even influenced, by syndicalists but the violent industrial action of the pre-war years is associated with syndicalism just as the continued industrial conflict of the war years is often seen, again misleadingly, as an extension of the shop-stewards' movement on Clydeside and in Sheffield.

Part of the reason for the undue attention given to the industrial syndicalist movement is that it was, temporarily at least, led by Tom Mann, one of the great international figures of socialism and trade unionism. His reports on the violence and conflict against the Cambrian Combine's mines at Tonypandy in South Wales (1), his involvement in the Liverpool dock strike, and his imprisonment for publishing the 'Open Letter to British Soldiers' (2), raised both his profile and the attention paid to the syndicalists. In fact there were few syndicalist activists outside the Liverpool docks, and mining in South Wales and their activities were very largely confused with those normal industrial and amalgamation activities which would have occurred without their presence. *The Miners' Next Step* (3), the one significant document produced by the British syndicalists, did not appear until early 1912 just as Tom Mann began to withdraw from active involvement in the movement and when his supporters began to divide and disperse. Nevertheless, it lays down the programme and tactics which the syndicalists intended to use.

Syndicalism in fact received scant attention from many trade-union and Labour leaders who saw it as less of a danger than did the capitalist press. Their attention was drawn to the far more mundane issues of improving the working conditions and reducing the hours of work of their members. The winning of the eight-hour day was the prime interest of the Amalgamated Society of Railway Servants (5). In Liverpool the Anti-Sweating League was concerned to improve the organization of women in trade unions in order to improve wages and conditions (6). The trade unions were far more interested in securing the connection with the Labour Party, a parliamentary party whose actions syndicalists dismissed as ineffective, than in pursuing industrial conflict for workers' control. The Trade Union Act of 1913 (4) allowed this connection to be re-established through a political levy, subject to a ballot of trade-union members and removed the restrictions which had been imposed by the Osborne Judgement.

The outbreak of the First World War, in 1914, fundamentally strengthened the position of trade unions. There was a shortage of skilled workers, particularly in trades such as engineering where there was a labour shortage. Consequently, trade unions won wage increases, their members were generally wealthier and membership rose from about four million in 1914 to six million in 1918, and eventually to eight million in 1920. The trade-union movement was quickly recognized as part of the apparatus of government, its leader, such as George Barnes the engineer, were drawn into government and they undertook to suspend trade-union rights until the end of the war– in return for a promise that there would be a return to pre-war conditions. The Munitions of War Act of July 1915 (7) also created a structure of delays and interventions by government which would effectively reduce the possibility of strike action. For many trade unionists these arrangements were satisfactory. But in some areas, and particularly amongst the engineers working on munitions in Glasgow and Sheffield, the actions of their union leaders were ignored and regarded as 'treachery to the working class'. Appointing shop stewards as their representatives many engineers, ignoring their union membership, fought on the Clydeside for better wages and some type of workers' control on a shop or plant basis (8). They were led by members of the Clyde Workers' Committee such as David Kirkwood, Willie Gallacher and James Messer.

The array of documents listed here reveals the concern of the authorities to increase output by strengthening the hand of the employers and by introducing dilution – the employment of female labour to replace male engineers and to make good the labour shortage. It is clear, however, that the Clyde Workers' Committee were not prepared to capitulate easily and Lloyd George's attempt to appeal to their patriotism was unsuccessful. In the end, the authorities simply imprisoned some of the chief members of the Clyde Workers' Committee and the resistance to dilution and the employers' demands was soon dismissed. Elsewhere, and particularly in Sheffield, J.T. Murphy and the shop stewards called the engineers out on strike in order to prevent their fellow workmen being conscripted and sent to the Front. In fact this strike won war exemptions for some skilled men, although these were of a temporary nature, and led to the popular catch 'Don't send me in the Army George'. J.T. Murphy, Willie Gallacher, John Paton and many other shopstewards subsequently wrote up their vision of how workers' committees would work and how workshop control would operate to undermine, if not to remove, capitalist control.

Potentially one of the most important developments of the war years was the agreement of three of the major unions – the Miners' Federation of Great Britain, the National Union of Railwaymen, and the Transport Workers' Federation – to form a 'Triple Industrial Alliance'. The idea was that these unions would come to the aid of each other during industrial disputes. For instance, the railwaymen might decide not to remove coal from the pit heads when the miners were on strike. To many contemporaries this had revolutionary overtones: here was the potential for a general strike. In reality as can be seen from the document (9), the constitution was extremely cautious and all three unions were anxious to maintain their autonomy of action. It is thus not surprising that when the Triple Alliance was called to operate for the first time in 1921 it failed to function on 15 April, a day which has since become known as 'Black Friday'.

1) *Symposium on Syndicalism. By Active Workers. Editorial Notes by Tom Mann*
(*The Industrial Syndicalist*, November 1910)

Hurrah! Gallant Little Wales

It so happened that I was due for a meeting in Tonypandy Rhondda Valley, on Sunday 6th inst. Arriving there on the 5th, I learned of the result of the mass meetings held earlier in the day, and of the arrival of police from other districts. I had the advantage of several conferences with the most influential men and was thus able to gauge the situation.

The one thing that stood out more glaringly than all the others combined, was the absence of that thorough solidarity which, working in clockwork fashion, can alone ensure success.

Already the miners – over 11,000 in number – were out, after having given notice in accordance with the conference decision, and the full vote of the members in the South Wales coalfield. This was unanimously acted upon, but here comes

The Damaging Item

The hauling engine men, who haul the coals to the pit shaft, belonged not to the Miners' Federation, but to a separate union, known as the Hauling Engine Men's Stokers' and Craftsmen's Union, and the winding engine men, those who drive the engines that wind the coal up the shafts, lower and raise the men, etc., belong to still another union. Each of these unions having entered into undertakings with the management, prevented them making common cause with the miners.

The miners had ceased work some five days before the Sunday, and during the interval had met the representatives of the two enginemen's unions in order to secure their co-operation, and with whom, by the way, they had long before entered into what was considered a working understanding. But the enginemen stated that they had separate agreements, had not given notice, and could not, therefore, take action by making common cause without incurring legal liabilities.

Anyway, here was the evil: out of a total of 12,000 men, including officials, over 11,000 belonged to and acted loyally as members of the Miners' Federation; but directly and solely because of the isolated action of the two small unions named, complete isolation of the mines was impossible; it, therefore, became necessary that all who worked at the mines under the Cambrian Combine, should know from the miners themselves that their co-operation was desired; therefore picketing became necessary, and in accordance with decision, not less than 8,000 men were on picket on Monday the 7th, at the three groups of mines belonging to the combine.

It had been resolved at public meeting, by solemn vote, that on the men's side everything should should be perfectly peaceable. I put the matter to the vote on the Sunday night in the Tonypandy Town Hall, and it was unanimously agreed to.

With the Pickets

I was with the pickets early next morning, and can vouch that they behaved in accordance with the vote. I witnessed the only departure therefore near the Cambrian Mines, at 6.30 am; this was when two enginemen were slinking past some houses in High Street, near to where the men were processioning, and some of the miners' wives standing at their doors, called out to these men who were making towards the pit. The pickets, who were near by, commenced to speak to the men in a perfectly peaceful fashion, simply saying they 'hoped they would not start work but that they would join the general body'; a number by this time had gathered round, perhaps 60 to 70 persons, when two mounted police, near to whom I had been for some time, swerved towards the bunch of people and knocked down two of the women. There was not the slightest necessity for this, and naturally it was resented by the men who saw it, and they shouted at the police to clear out, and booed a little; a stone was thrown that hit no one, and a little empty milk-tin hit a foot constable; but instantly several of us exerted our influence and, in spite of the provocation, all was quiet in a few minutes, and the men marched along singing choruses.

On the Tuesday, the police successfully became the aggressors, often enough, and vicious enough, to cause a considerable retaliation on the men's side, who foolishly played into the hands of the reactionaries by demanding more police and military.

I am writing this on Tuesday, the 15th inst., at the time a

Conference of delegates is being held from all the disaffected collieries in South Wales at Pontypridd.

We heartily congratulate our Welsh comrades on this step, and upon their pluck and solidarity in this struggle.

We admire and congratulate CHARLES STANTON for his determined stand in the Aberdere district; and we rejoice to know that there is a strong movement already shaping, with Pontypridd as the centre, for pushing ahead at once with Syndicalist principles throughout the Welsh coalfield.

The workers are not entirely void of genuine fighting grit, and, with a little more experience, we shall avoid the unnecessary, and centre on the capitalists' citadel.

Working-Class Socialism
By E. J. B. ALLEN

Industrial Unionism is working-class Socialism; it is the only logical form of working-class organisation able to cope with the conditions that have been inaugurated by the great development of machinery, and the minute sub-division and simplification of the industry attendant thereto. The Industrial Unionist seeks to unite all the workers of an industry into one union, and so establish a complete co-operation of all the industrial organisations, with the object of not only obtaining the best results in the daily wage-wars, but also to effect their emancipation from the system of wage slavery.

The union movement is the only one capable of uniting the workers as a class on grounds of their economic interests. The real interests of the workers are the full proceeds of their labour, their productive energy; and this necessarily means the taking into possession of the mines, railways, factories, and mills by those who operate them.

We have seen that Labour legislation is of little use without an adequate organisation to see that the reform regulations are properly enforced. We have seen, further, that an adequate organisation can enforce reforms, whether on the Statute Book or not.

Many working-class representatives have been elected to public bodies, and after some time have passed 'to the other side of the barricade'; the industrial union is the only safeguard against wholesale treachery that the workers can have. It is the bulwark alike against a State bureaucracy or a military despotism.

A State within a State

The industrial union organisation when completed will be the embryo of a working-class republic. Our national unions, local unions, and other bodies will be the administrative machinery of an Industrial Commonwealth. We claim that no 670 men, elected to Parliament from various geographical areas, can possibly have the requisite technical knowledge to properly direct the productive and distinctive capacities of the nation. The men and women who actually work in the various industries should be persons best capable of organising them. [. . .]

2) *Open Letter to British Soldiers, 1911*
(*Tom Mann's Memoirs* (1923), pp. 237–8)
Men! Comrades! Brothers!
You are in the army.
So are we. You are in the army of Destruction. We, in the Industrial, or army of Construction.
We work at mine, forge, factory, or dock, etc., producing and transporting all the goods, clothing, stuffs, etc. which makes it possible for people to live. You are Workingmen's Sons.
When We go on Strike to better Our lot, which is the lot also of Your Fathers, Mothers, Brothers, and Sisters, YOU are called upon by your Officers to MURDER US
Don't do it.
You know what happens. Always has happened.
We stand out as long as we can. Then one of our (and your) irresponsible Brothers, goaded by the sight and thought of his and his loved ones' misery and hunger, commits a crime of property. Immediately you are ordered to murder Us, as you did at Mitchelstown, at Featherstone, at Belfast.
Don't You know, that when you are out of the colours, and become a 'Civvy' again, that You, like Us, may be on strike, and YOU, like Us, be liable to be Murdered by other soldiers.
Boys, Don't Do it.
'Thou shalt not kill' says the Book.
Don't forget that!
It does not say, 'unless you have a uniform on'.
No! MURDER IS MURDER, whether committed in the heat of

anger on one who has wronged a loved one, or by the clay-piped Tommies with a rifle.

Boys, Don't do it.

Act the Man! Act the Brother! Act the Human Being.

Property can be replaced! Human life, Never!

The Idle Rich Class, who own and order you about, own and order us about also. They and their friends own the land and means of life in Britain.

You Don't! We Don't!

When We kick they order You to murder Us.

When You kick, You get court-martialled and cells.

Your fight is Our fight. Instead of fighting Against each other, We should be fighting With each other.

Out of Our loins, Our lives, Our homes, You came.

Don't disgrace Your parents, Your Class, by being willing tools any longer of the Master Class.

You, like Us, are the Slave Class. When We rise, You rise; When We fall, even by your bullets, Ye fall also.

England with its fertile valleys and dells, its admired resources, its sea harvests, is the heritage of ages to us.

You no doubt joined the army out of poverty.

We work long hours for small wages at hand work, because of our poverty. And both your poverty and Ours arises from the fact that, Britain with its resources, belongs to only a few people. These few, owing Britain, own Our jobs. Owning Our jobs they own Our very lives. Comrades, have We called in vain? Think things out and refuse any longer to Murder Your Kindred. Help Us to win back Britain for the British, and the World for the Workers.

3) *The Miners' Next Step*
(Reform Committee of the South Wales Miners, *The Miners' Next Step* 1912)

PROGRAMME

Ultimate Objective

One organization to cover the whole of the Coal, ore, Slate, Stone, Clay, Salt, mining or quarrying industry of Great Britain, with one Central Executive.

That as a step to the attainment of that ideal, strenuous efforts be made to weld all National, County, or District Federations, at present comprising the Miners' Federation of Great Britain, into one compact organization with one Central Executive, whose province it shall be to negotiate agreements and other matters requiring common action. That a cardinal principle of that organization to be: that every man working in or about the mine, no matter what his craft or occupation – provisions having been made for representation on the Executive – be required to both join and observe its decisions.

IMMEDIATE STEPS – INDUSTRIAL

1. That a minimum wage of 8s per day, for all workmen employed in or about the mines, constitute a demand to be striven for nationally at once.
2. That subject to the foregoing having been obtained, we demand and use our power to obtain a seven-hour day.

PROGRAMME – POLITICAL

That the organization shall engage in political action, both local and national, on the basis of complete independence of, and hostility to all capitalist parties, with an avowed policy of wrestling whatever advantage it can for the working class.

In the event of any representative of the organization losing his seat, he shall be entitled to, and receive, the full protection of the organization against victimisation.

GENERAL

Alliances to be formed, and trades organizations fostered, with a view to steps being taken, to amalgamate all workers into one National and International union, to work for the taking over of all industries, by the workmen themselves.

The Programme is very comprehensive, because it deals with immediate objectives as well as ultimate aims. [. . .] The main principles are as follows:

Decentralization for negotiating

The Lodges, it will be seen, take all effective control of affairs, as long as there is any utility in local negotiations. With such a policy, Lodges become responsible and self-reliant units, with every stimulus to work out their own local salvation in their own way.

Centralizing for fighting

It will be noticed that all questions are ensured a rapid settlement. So soon as the Lodge finds itself at the end of its resources, the whole fighting strength of the organization is turned on. We thus reverse the present order of things, where in the main, we centralize our negotiations and sectionalize our fighting.

The use of the Irritation Strike

[. . .] The Irritation Strike depends for its successful adoption, on the men holding clearly the point of view, that their interests and the employers are necessarily hostile. Further that the employer is vulnerable only in one place, his profits! Therefore if the men wish to bring effective pressure to bear, they must use methods which tend to reduce profits. One way of doing this is to decrease production, while continuing to work. Quite a number of instances where this method has been successfully adopted in South Wales could be adduced. [. . .]

Industrial Democracy the objective

[. . .]

Our objective begins to take shape before your eyes. Every industry thoroughly organised, in the first place, to fight, to gain control of, and then administer, that industry. The co-ordination of all industries on a Central Production Board, who, with a statistical department to ascertain the needs of the people, will issue its demands on the different departments of industry, leaving the men themselves to determine under what conditions and how, the work should be done. This would mean real democracy in real life, making for real manhood and womanhood. Any other form of democracy is a delusion and a snare.

Every fight for, and victory won by the men, will inevitably assist them in arriving at a clearer conception of the responsibilities and duties before them. It will assist them to see, that so long as shareholders are permitted to continue their ownership, or the State administers on behalf of the shareholders, slavery and oppression are bound to be the rule in industry. And with this realization, the age-long oppression of labour will draw to its end. The weary sigh of the over-driven slave, pitilessly exploited and regarded as an animated tool or beast of burden; the medieval serf fast bound to the soil, and life-long prisoner on his lord's domain, subject to all the caprices of his lord's lust or anger: the modern wage-slave, with nothing but his labour to sell selling that, with his manhood as a wrapper, in the world's market-place for a mess of pottage: these are the three phases of slavery, each in their turn inevitable and unavoidable, will have enhanced the possibilities of slavery, and mankind shall at last have leisure and inclination to really live as men, and not as beasts which perish.

4) *The Trade Union Act 1913 (2 & 3 Geo. V)*

3 (1)   The funds of a trade union shall not be applied, either directly or in conjunction with any other trade union, association, or body, or otherwise indirectly, in the furtherance of the political objects to which this section applies (without prejudice to the furtherance of any other political objects), unless the furtherance of those objects has been approved as an object of the union by a resolution for the time being in force passed on a ballot of the members of the union taken in accordance with this Act for the purpose by a majority of the members voting; and where such a resolution is in force, unless rules, to be approved, whether the union is registered or not, by the Registrar of Friendly Societies, are in force providing –

(a)   That any payments in furtherance of these objects are to be made out of a separate fund (in this Act referred to as the political fund of the union) . . . ; and

(b)   That a member who is exempt from the obligation to contribute to the political fund of the union shall not be excluded from any benefit of the union . . . .

(3)   The political objects to which this section applies are the expenditure of money –

(a)   on the payment of any expenses incurred either directly or indirectly by a candidate or prospective candidate for election to Parliament or to any public office, before, during, or after the election in connexion with his candidature or election; or

(b)   on the holding of any meeting or the distribution of any literature or documents in support of any such candidate or prospective candidate; or

(c)   on the maintenance of any person who is a member of Parliament or who holds a public office; or

(d)   in connection with the registration of electors or the

selection of a candidate for Parliament or any public office; or
(e)   on the holding of political meetings of any kind, or on the
distribution of political literature or political documents of any
kind, unless the main purpose of the meetings or of the
distribution of the literature or documents is the furtherance of
statutory objects within the meaning of this Act.

5) *The Railwaymen's Eight-Hour Bill, 1913*
(Amalgamated Society of Railway Servants, Misc. Coll. 487, British
Library of Political and Economic Science)

> Amalgamated Society of Railway Servants
> Walsall Branch
> 158 Wednesbury Road,
> Walsall.
> 1. 5. 1913

R. A. Cooper Esquire MP
Dear Sir,
> Meeting Sunday May 11th.

   Yours of the 18th ulto was duly placed before the Committee who
have this matter in hand, and in reply I desire to say the chief matter
for decision will be the 8 hour Bill, the Minimum Wage question will
no doubt be touched, as also will the Railways No 2 Bill, though I
cannot see that much good can be done now the latter is passed, the
only thing is are the Government going to bring in another Bill to
Safeguard the Men Connected with the Trade Union Movement, a
general discussion on the lines I have mentioned will be the Order of
the day, . . .

> Yours faithfully,
> H. Hucker

6) *Women's Trade Unionism, Liverpool, 1914*
(Webb Collection, Coll. E, section A, xlvii, 13)
> Liverpool Anti-Sweating League

> 10/1/1914

Dear Madam [Beatrice Webb],
1. The numbers [of women in trade unions] vary greatly from
practically every woman in the trade, as the Upholsters Union to about
10% on the Cafe Workers.

2.   In some Trades like the Tailors the women have a great distrust of the men (for the most part) and will not go into their organisations, most of the skilled workers prefer to be quite separate. Postal employees, Clerks, Shop Assistants exceptions. I think perhaps the presence of men gives a greater feeling of strength to the Unions.

3.   I will answer this in respect to *Women's* Organization only. The Upholsterers' Union has been in existence for nearly twenty years. When we started work in L'pool in 1909 there were no other purely women's unions, there had been one or two but they had flickered out. We started a dress makers' union which is still flourishing . . . though only about 5 per cent of the dressmakers in the town are in it & Cafe Workers' Union which has dwindled to very small proportions, but some of the original members are enthusiastic about it.

4.   The Upholsterers' Union being strong has secured a working week of 48 hours & a minimum wage of 15/-. The others have in many cases improved the condition of their work.

5.   The Clerks' Union the women who are greatly in the minority are on the Executive as well as the men. The idea is to have equal numbers of the sexes but as the men so greatly outnumber the women this would not be fair at the present.

6.   Some are quite indifferent but others are very keen to manage their own affairs entirely. It is here that the benefit of women alone appears as they are then obliged to come forward & are not over powered by the . . . method of the men.

I will now amplify one or two of my answers. Besides these unions I have mentioned there have been others in the last five years, which started hundreds strong & have lapsed for several causes. Two very strong Unions who started, one among the rubber workers, one the Automatic Wire Workers. In one of them the women urged by the men came out on strike, had no funds, got dispersed & the Union fell to pieces. In the other there was a strong feeling against the Union expressed at the works, one or two of the girls were victimised.

This is one of the great difficulties of Women's Unions, the fear of victimization. With unskilled labour the women's place is easily filled that her work is very precarious. If the foreman or forewoman sets his or her face against a Union it is therefore no wonder that the woman worker is too much alarmed at losing her place to insist on being a member. In my answer to No 2 I said the Tailoresses distrusted the men, numbers of women do. The men for a long time did not trouble to look after the Woman worker & now in some trades are trying to organise her with a view to forcing her out of the trade altogether (not the Tailors alone). Fear of strikes is another reason for preserving their independence.

Some who join the Union expect everything to be improved at once, & if not fall out again or perhaps they obtain some benefits & think everything is coming – it is not worth while remaining in. This was the case with the Cafe Workers who started with a strong Union. They get a remission of fines through the Union in the first year.

The Insurance Act has had a bad effect on the Unions, the very poorly paid women find they cannot keep up with both payments. In many instances too, they had looked at the Union very much in the light of a sick benefit club & for them there is not the necessity. There is a great deal of bullying in the workshops encouraged by the foremen & forewomen. I touched upon the point earlier. This has been shown very strongly lately. [. . .] It is fear that is the root cause of lack of organisation. [. . .]

A. Billinge

7) *Munitions of War Act July 1915*
PART I

1. (1) If any difference exists or is apprehended between any employer and persons employed, or between any two or more classes of persons employed, and the difference is one to which this Part of this Act applies, that difference, if not determined by the parties directly concerned or their representatives or under existing agreements, may be reported to the Board of Trade, by or on behalf of either party to the difference. . . .

   (2) The Board of Trade shall consider any difference so reported and take any steps which seem to them expedient to promote a settlement of the difference [and recommend a settlement under the various parts of the act].

   (4) The award of any such settlement shall be binding both on employers and employed and may be retrospective; and if any employer, or person employed, thereafter acts in contravention of, or fails to comply with, the award, he shall be guilty of an offence under this Act.

2. (1) An employer shall not declare, cause, or take part in a lock-out, and a person employed shall not take part in a strike, in connection with any difference to which this Part of this Act applies, unless the difference has been reported to the Board of Trade, and twenty-one days have elapsed since the date of the report, and the difference has not been during that time referred by the Board of Trade for settlement in accordance with this Act.

PART IV

3. No person employed shall insist or attempt to insist on the observance either by himself or by any other person employed of any rule, practice, or custom tending to restrict the rate of production on any class of work, or to limit the employment of any class of person, or otherwise tending to restrict production or employment.

PART VII

'A person shall not give employment to a workman who has within the last previous six weeks . . . been employed on or in connection with munitions work . . . unless he holds a certificate from the employer by whom he was last so employed that he left work with the consent of his employer. . . .

8) *The Shop Stewards' Movement and Workers' Control during the First World War*

(i)   *Sir Hubert Llewelyn Smith, Memorandum of Labour for Armaments, 9 June 1915*

(Copy in engineering records, Calderdale Archives, West Yorkshire.)

The shortage of labour directly delays production. It is, however, at the present time having direct effects perhaps even more serious. Practically any workman of any pretensions to skill at all in the engineering and shipbuilding trades has so little difficulty in finding work the moment he wants it that he has little economic motive left for remaining with his employer, if he is in any way dissatisfied, whether with good reason or without.

On the other hand, the employers, constantly urged by the Government to increase their output, do not feel themselves really in a position to bargain with the men, and have, indeed, in many cases owing to the terms of their contracts, little incentive to do so.

The ordinary economic control of the individual workman has practically broken down. The result is that to a very considerable extent men are out of the control of both employers and of their own leaders. The question is whether some exceptional form of control or motive not of a purely economic character can be effectively substituted.

(ii) *Letter from William Weir, employer, to Christopher Addison, 8 October 1915 regarding his dislike of the fact that he was opposed to the Lloyd George and the government negotiation with the trade unions.*
(Records of the Ministry of Munitions in the Public Record Office, Mun. 2)

[Weir quotes Lloyd George, August 1915] 'I think if it (the dilution of labour) is fought out in one good case in each district then the Trade Unions will give in to the rest, but if there is real trouble, you (the employers) must call the Ministry in, and we must make it a national issue. If the trade unions resent it, if they carry it to the extent of threatening to strike, then we shall have to be called in, and the whole influence of the Government must be brought to bear upon it.'

[Weir attacks the Ministry for a want of sincerity.] Every delayed decision of the nature I give shows to the working man that the State – or rather the leaders and advisers – are not in earnest. [. . .] Every additional example of vacillation increases the gravity of the inevitable re-adjustment. Efficiency cannot exist apart from discipline, and discipline is non-existent in our shops now. [Weir attacks the Government for having chosen to negotiate with the Unions.] The fallacy was the belief that bargaining was necessary . . . the bargaining spirit became rife. The actual position was that the men would have loyally done whatever the country required of them, if the position had been clearly put to them, as they have done as soldiers.

(iii) *J.W. Muir's Statement to Lloyd George on Friday, 24 December 1915*
(*The Worker*, 15 January 1916)

Now we have sufficient intelligence not to need any lecturing on the question of the urgency of supplies for military and domestic purposes, and, what is more, we have very strong views on how they can best be obtained. But I will come to that later. There is no need either to take up any time explaining to us the principle of dilution of labour. We are thoroughly conversant with it as are also goodly number of our men throughout the district.

It is not original at this time; it is not the product of any one man's, or any particular group of men's, brains, nor can it be fixed within the limits of any very recent period. It has been going on practically since the Industrial Revolution. (Mr. Lloyd George: Yes with every introduction of new machinery.) Not only so. Every new subdivision of labour and every new adoption of standard parts has made for its extension.

The present demand for widespread employment of unskilled men and women is, therefore, merely an effort to accelerate the extension of an already firmly established custom.

We have no objection to that provided its application conforms to certain clearly defined conditions which I shall specify later. We regard it as progressive from the point of view that it simplifies the labour process, makes Labour mobile, and tends to increase output. In short it is a step in the direct line of industrial evolution. But – and this is where the present difficulty arises – its progressive character is lost to the community unless it is accompanied by a corresponding step in social evolution.

What is the situation just now?

The dilution of labour has been proceeding somewhat tardily, for war purposes, for some months back – not with the good-will and co-operation of the skilled men, but against their sullen and barely concealed opposition. The scheme has been imposed on them without their voice having being heard in the matter, and without provision having been made for them having control over it.

What we (the Clyde Workers' Committee) are fully conscious of, the mass of the workers only feel instinctively. . . .

The employers have long wished for an opportunity to try just such an experiment on a large scale, and the war has given them that opportunity practically free of risk, and on a scale far beyond their dreams. They are taking full advantage of it and they will never go back on it. . . . No – there will be no return to pre-war conditions, and in all circumstances the workers are justified in their resentment at the proposal to impose this dilution scheme on them without real safeguards. You have to remember that for some years past there has been considerable nibbling at the individuality of the worker.

During all his working hours he is merely a cipher – known by a check number.

At the Labour Exchange he had a number, and when he is ill, under State Insurance, he is also known as a number. The Munitions Act and the Defence of the Realm Act have divested him of the last shreds of individuality, and it begins to look as if they were gone permanently. . . .

Trouble can be averted by making the [dilution] scheme conform NOW to certain conditions at which I have already hinted. These are:

That benefits shall not accrue to one class in the community.

That organised labour must have a share in controlling it.

These conditions can only be fulfilled by the Government compliance with the demand of the Clyde Workers' Committee that all industries and national resources must be taken over by the Government – not merely 'controlled', but taken over completely – and that organised labour should be vested with the right to take part directly and administration in every department of industry. I have used the word 'demand' advisedly, as this is no propagandist statement. It is our fixed determination to force the matter to an issue.

(iv)   *Clyde Workers' Committee*
(Leaflet to be found in several collections, including Calderdale Archives and the PRO)

TO ALL CLYDE WORKERS

Fellow-Workers,

Since the outbreak of the European War, many changes have been brought about of vital interest to the workers. Foremost amongst these have been the scrapping of Trade Union Rules, and the consequent undermining of the whole Trade Union

Movement. To the intelligent worker it has been increasingly clear that the officials have failed to grasp the significance of these changes, and as a result, have been unable to formulate a policy that would adequately protect the interests of those workers whom they are supposed to represent.

The support given to the Munitions Act by the Official was an act of Treachery to the Working Class. Those of us who refused to be **Sold** have organized the above Committee, representative of **All Trades** in the Clyde area, determined to retain what liberties we have, and to take the first opportunity of forcing the repeal of all the pernicious legislation that has recently been imposed upon us. In the word of a Manifesto issued by the Trade Union Rights Committee, recently formed in London:-

'Let us preserve what rights still remain and refuse stead-fastly to surrender another inch to our allied foes – the capitalists and politicians. The liberty and freedom of the organized worker is one thing; our fight is the fight that matters, and now is the time to act.'

WHAT THE COMMITTEE IS AND ITS PURPOSE

It is composed of Delegates or Shop Stewards from all Trades in the Glasgow area, and is open to all such *bona fide* workers. The progresses in all Trades are invited to attend. Its origin goes back to the last big strike of February, 1915, when action was taken to force the demand put forward for an increase of 2d per hour in the Engineering industry. At the time a Committee known as the Labour With-holding Committee was set up, representative of the different Trades in the industry, to organise the strikes, and notwithstanding the fierce opposition from public opinion, employers, Government, and our own officials alike, that Committee managed and carried through probably the best organised strike in the annals of Clyde history, and brought about closer working class unity amongst the rank and file of the different Trades than years of official effort. It became obvious then that such a Committee permanently established would be valuable workers, and with that purpose in **view** the Committee was kept in being after the termination of the **strike**.

Recently, when the three Govan shipwrights were locked up under the Munitions Act, many appeals were sent to the Committee to again take action. In answer to those appeals the Committee called its forces together and discussed certain lines of action and, despite all reports to the contrary, it was through 'the powers that be' getting to know that the Committee was again at work, that ultimately forced the release of the three shipwrights.

At this juncture it was considered advisable to change the name of this body, and from now on it will be known as the **Clyde Workers' Committee (C.W.C)**.

Our purpose must not be misconstrued, we are not for unity and closer organisation of all trades in the industry, one Union being the ultimate aim. We will support the officials just so long as they rightly represent the workers, but we will act independently immediately they misrepresent them. Being composed of Delegates from every shop, and untramelled by obsolete rule or law, we claim to represent the true feeling of the workers. We can act immediately according to the merits of the case and the desire of the rank and file.

The following Trades are at present represented on the Committee. All other Trades are kindly invited to become attached. All Shop Stewards welcome: – A.S.E, Toolmakers, Boilermakers, Blacksmiths, Shipwrights, Coopersmiths, Brassfinishers, Patternmakers, Miners, Tinsmiths, Sheet-iron Workers, Electrical Trades, Joiners, Gas and General Workers, School Teachers, Coopers.

For further information see your Shop Steward. Speakers will be sent on request to Work Gates, Districts and generally be at the convenience of the workers.

Signed on behalf of the Committee.
W. M. GALLACHER, President
J. M. MESSER, Secretary.
408 Allison Street

(v) *Letter from Paterson (Glasgow area munitions official) to Ministry of Munitions in London, dated 17 January 1916)*

(The Beveridge Collection on Munitions, iii, p. 111 British Library of Economic and Political Science)

Below I give the names of the gentlemen whose removal from the Clyde district for an indefinite period would go a long way towards helping production, viz: (Kirkwood, Gallacher, Messer, Muir, McManus, Clark, McLean, Petroff).

I am afraid that the removal of almost any one of these men (with the possible exception of McLean and Petroff, who are not working men or officials of societies here) would at once cause a big strike.

When a strike takes place, it is desirable that the Government should have the best case possible to present to the public. Ultimately it will be forced to give some reasons for the removal of these men, and it would then have to be disclosed that action had been taken on general statements, unsupported by real evidence of a convincing nature.

A very much cleaner issue would be a strike against the enforcement of the dilution of labour, as the Government there would be in a position of asking the skilled men of the country to allow their skill to be used to the best advantage, and the public opinion would be overwhelmingly against the men.

If, therefore, definite orders for the dilution of labour are to be given, I think it would be better to delay consideration of the question of removing any men out of the district.

(vi) *Summary of Dilution Programme as based (with modification) on Mr Weir's Memorandum, presented to Lloyd George on 18 January 1916*

(Beveridge Collection on Munitions, British Library of Economic and Political Science, title as above, 22 January 1916)

(1)   An announcement to be made by the Prime Minister . . . that the Government propose now to take steps to bring about dilution of labour wherever possible, in accordance with the necessities of the situation and on the conditions laid down by the Munitions of War and Amending Bill, without permitting further delay on any ground whatever; they are issuing a general

instruction to employers accordingly; and that they are sending a special Commissioner or Commissioners to the most important districts to give effect to this policy.

(2) Commissioners to be sent to the Clyde (& Perhaps the Tyne) to act as follows –

a. They will require selected establishments forthwith to submit their definite dilution proposals, etc.

b. Having done this they will arrange for a meeting representative of the men at the works (the shop stewards) to be called with the employer present. The local trade union officials concerned will also be invited to attend. The Commissioners will then state that a scheme of dilution has been prepared, under the instruction of the Minister, to be put into force on a named date (not more than three days hence). . . .

(3) In the event of a strike taking place or being imminent, the policy will be –

a. To guarantee adequate police and military protection to all who are willing to work;

b. To secure (by an injunction if necessary) that trade unions funds are not used to support the strikers;

c. To take measures under the Defence of the Realm Act against those who incite to strike.

(4) Prosecution of Strikers under the Defence of the Realm Act against those who incite to strike.

(5) . . . no bargaining with the men whilst on strike.

[. . .]

Ministry of Munitions, 6, Whitehall Gdns. 22 January 1916.

(vii) *Report of Macassey (Commissioner) to Ministry of Munitions*
(Ministry of Munitions, Public Record Office, 5, memorandum on the Industrial situation in the Clyde, 5 February 1916)
When we started we found the men rigidly opposed to dilution in any shape or form. [To force through dilution as envisaged in the scheme] would have meant a more or less general strike in the Clyde against the principles of dilution. . . . I have no hesitation in saying that course would have wrecked dilution on the Clyde. . . . We have decided that our right procedure was to convert and persuade men in say half a dozen of the principal

establishments to the principle of dilution, then arrange a scheme for each establishment. [. . .]

That course has avoided numerous strikes. On the mere suggestion of a strike I am down on the spot, at all hours of the day or night. . . . As a result the principle of dilution is now accepted in Langs, Weirs, Beardmores (Parkhead and Dalmuir), Yarrows.

(viii) *Industrial Situation on the Clyde, February 1916*
(Ministry of Munitions, PRO, 5.73, memorandum on the Industrial Situation on the Clyde, 9 February 1916)
[The success of the Commissioners has spurred the Clyde Workers' Committee into fresh activity.] Its tentacles are now fairly widespread and are growing. However, the Committee has not effective control over the workers in more than five or six shops.

The outstanding feature of the position is that the Official Trade Unions in the District are in many works now wholly unable to speak for their members. Agreements arrived at between the Commissioners and the local Trade Union officials or even the shop stewards in the works are promptly repudiated by the instigation of the emissaries of the Clyde Workers' Committee. The authority of the official Trade Unions in the Clyde District is being steadily undermined and will be inevitably ruined unless the Unions quickly rise to an intelligent appreciation of their position, and exert themselves to recover their waning control over their members.

(ix) *Statement issued by W. Gallacher and J. W. Muir*
(*Glasgow Herald*, 30 March 1916)
[Outline of the dispute as seen from the Clyde Workers' Committee]
(1) It has long been the custom of Parkhead Forge, where the trouble first arose, that the convenor of shop stewards has the right to go into any shop in which a dispute is in progress. In accordance with this custom Mr. David Kirkwood, the convenor, went into one of the new departments in which women were at work under the dilution scheme. This was reported to the management, which thereupon refused Mr. Kirkwood permission to enter the department without the sanction of the

management. Mr. Kirkwood resigned his position as convenor. The remainder of the shop stewards then held a meeting, and after a failure to get satisfaction from the management a departmental meeting of the men decided to stop work. [. . .]

(2)   There was no elaborate plot to stop work on a type of gun vitally needed for the Army.

(3)   The Clyde Workers' Committee has not, in fact, embarked on any definite 'policy to hold up the production of the most important munitions of war'.

(4)   It has been said that the C.W.C. is responsible for a deliberate policy of calling men out on strike. In none of the above cases were the men called out by the C.W.C.

(x)   *Don't send me in the Army George*
(Popular catch song sung in Sheffield by unskilled engineers during the May 1917 strike of skilled engineers led by the shop stewards)

> Don't send me in the Army George,
> I'm in the A.S.E.
> Take all the bloody labourers,
> But for God's sake don't take me.
> You want me for a soldier?
> Well, that can never be . . .
> A man of my ability,
> And in the A.S.E.

(xi)   *The Workers' Committee*
(J.T. Murphy, *The Workers' Committee*, published by the Sheffield Workers' Committee, 1918)

The procedure to adopt is to form in every workshop a Workshop Committee, composed of shop-stewards, elected by the workers in workshops. Skilled, semi-skilled, and unskilled workers should all have their shop-stewards, and due regard be given also to the particular union to which each worker belongs.

For example: suppose a workshop is composed of members of the General Labourers' Union, Workers' Union, A.S.E., Steam Engine Makers, Women Workers, etc. each of these unions should have their shop-stewards, and the whole co-operate together, and form a Workshop Committee.

Immediately this will stimulate the campaign for the elimination of the non-unionists. We know of one shop where, as soon as the Workshop Committee was formed, every union benefited in membership, and one society enrolled sixty members.

Where possible, it is advisable for shop-stewards to be officially recognized, and to be supplied with rules which lend support and encourage the close co-operation which a Workshop Committee requires. [. . .]

Local Industrial Committees should be formed in each district. It will be readily perceived that no one firm will be completely organised before the workers in other firms begin to move in the same direction. Therefore in the early stages of development, full shop-stewards' meetings should be held in every district, and an Industrial Administrative Committee to be formed from these meetings.

Works or Plant Committee

The next step is to intensify the development of the workshop committees by the formation in every plant of a Plant Committee. To achieve this all the shop stewards of each firm, from every department of that firm, should meet and elect a committee from amongst them to centralize the efforts or link up the shop committee in the firm.

(xii) *Willie Gallacher and J. Paton on the Collective Contract*
(W. Gallacher and J. Paton, *The Collective Contract: Towards Industrial Democracy: A Memorandum on Workers' Control*, Paisley Trades Council, 1917)

Now the movement for the overthrow of capitalism by an abolition of the wages system must begin, not at Westminster, not in the trade union executive, nor in the trade union branches, but in the workshops. And it should take the form of the assumption by the workers of an ever-increasing share in control.

Not Peace but a Sword. A share in control does not imply that the workers should enter into partnership or any sort of alliance with the employer, or incur joint responsibility with him, or be identified with him in any way. All forms of co-partnership –

collective or individual – are based on the theory that the interests of the employer and exploited are identical, whereas they are, in fact, mutually antagonistic and irreconcilable. All such schemes are cunningly designed by a plausible appeal to individual cupidity to corrupt the worker and seduce him from collective action with his fellows. Co-partnership multiplies profiteers and nourished capitalism. Are we not out to destroy capitalism?

There must be no alliance or compromise with the employer. We shall be obliged, indeed, to negotiate with him through the representatives in the daily routine of the workshop, but not to espouse his interests, or to advance them in any way when it lies in our power to do otherwise. Our policy is that of invaders of our native province of industry, now in the hands of an arrogant and tyrannical usurper, and what we win in our advance we control *exclusively* and *independently*.

The First Step. The first step should be to establish in every industrial area, and for each industry, a system of Workshop Committees. . . .

The Next Step. After all, committees are but machinery and solidarity, a preliminary of action. Let us see, then, what further policy the committee will be.

Only the apathy or disloyalty of the workers themselves can prevent the works committees having in a very short time the experience and the authority to enable them to undertake in one large contract, or in two or three contracts at most, the entire business and production throughout the establishment. Granted an alliance with the organised office-workers – a development which is assured so soon as the Shop Committees are worthy of confidence and influential enough to give adequate protection – these contracts might include the work of design and the purchase of raw material, as well as the operation of manufacture and construction. But to begin with the undertaking will cover only the manual operations. The contract price, or wages – for it is still wages – will be remitted by the firm to the Works Committee in a lump sum, and distributed to the workers by their own representatives or their officials, and by whatever system or scale of remuneration they may choose to adopt. If, as is likely, a great industrial union has by this time taken the place of the sectional unions, these financial intromissions may be carried out by its District Executive (which would succeed the Allied Trades Committee) instead of by the Works Committee. A specially enlightened union of this sort would no doubt elect to pool the earnings of its members and pay each a regular salary monthly, or quarterly, exacting, of course from the recipient a fixed minimum record of work for the period. [. . .]

Knock-out Blow. Now it is true that even when we have got so far we shall not yet have destroyed the wage system. But we shall have undermined it. Capitalism will still flourish, but for the first time in its sordid history it will be in real jeopardy. With such a grip on the industrial machine as we have postulated, and backed by the resources of a great industrial union, or it might even be a federation of Industrial Unions, the committees should soon force up contract prices to a point that would be approximate to the full exchange value of the product, and put the profiteer out of business. In short, we shall have taken to our hands a powerful economic lever which, intelligently and resolutely applied, is easily capable of overthrowing the entire structure of capitalism, and substituting for it a real Industrial Democracy.

9) *The Triple Industrial Alliance 1915–1921: 1915 Constitution*
(Comprising the Miners' Federation of Great Britain, the National Union of Railwaymen, and the Transport Workers' Federation. Quoted from W. Milne-Bailey, *Trade Union Documents* (London, G. Bell & Son, 1929), pp. 148–9)
The Constitution of the Alliance.

1.   That matters submitted to this joint body, and upon which action may be taken, should be those of a national character or vitally affecting a principle which in the opinion of the Executive making the request necessitates combined action.

2.   The co-operation of the joint organisation shall not be called upon nor expected unless and until the matter in dispute has been considered by and received the endorsement of the National Executive of the organisation primarily concerned, and each organisation insti-

tuting a movement which is likely to involve the other affiliated organisations shall, before any definite steps are taken, submit the whole matter to the joint body for consideration.

3.   For the purposes of increasing the efficiency of the movement for combined action, periodical meetings of the three full Executives shall be held half-yearly.

4.   There shall be appointed a Consultative Committee of six, composed of two members chosen from the Executive Committee of each of the three bodies, whose duty it shall be to meet from time to time, and who shall be empowered to call at any time a special conference of the Executives of the three bodies if in their opinion such conference be necessary.

That a meeting be called on application made by one of the three bodies.

5.   With a view to meeting all management expenses incurred each affiliated body shall contribute a sum of 10s. per 1000 members per annum, or such sum as may be decided upon from time to time.

6.   Simultaneously with these arrangements for united action between the three organisations in question every effort shall proceed among the three sections to create effective and complete control of their respective bodies.

7.   Complete autonomy shall be reserved to any one of the three bodies affiliated to take action on their behalf.

8.   That joint action can only be taken when the question at issue has been before the members of the three organisations and decided by such methods as the constitution of each organisation provides, and a conference shall then be called without delay to consider and decide the question of taking action.

9.   No obligation shall devolve upon any other of the three bodies to take joint action unless the foregoing conditions have been complied with.

TRADE UNIONISM DURING THE INTER-WAR YEARS: THE GENERAL STRIKE OF 1926 AND ITS IMPACT

The dominating event of the inter-war years was the 1926 General Strike when, for nine days, the British trade-union movement struck in support of the miners in their attempt to avoid wage reductions and the move from national to local wage agreements (6, 7, 8, 9). But from the start the General Strike meant different things to different people. To the right wing, it was evidence of the revolutionary intent of the workers. For a time, this was a view held by the Communist Party which made great efforts to organize the workers throughout the country during the strike and many of whose members were arrested for their activities. To the TUC and the wider trade-union movement it was merely a national strike in support of the miners, whose wages were about to be unjustly reduced. Indeed, to many trade unionists it was an opportunity to check the reductions of wages which had been imposed on workers since the early 1920s. The defeat of the General Strike was also interpreted in many different ways. According to the Communist Party the miners had been betrayed by the leaders of the TUC. To many historians it represented a defeat for trade unionism which left trade unions at the mercy of the employers. However, this is a view which has been challenged by Professor H. A. Clegg who has noted that in the wake of the General Strike the reductions in wages were less marked than they had been before 1926. In other words, the General Strike was a cautionary tale for both sides in industry and stemmed the haemorrhage of wages.

There are a large number of documents on the General Strike in this section. They deal with the attitude of the Communist Party before, during and after the dispute. They also deal with the organization of the strike in Liverpool and south Lancashire, the position and advice of the TUC and the Samuel Memorandum which was accepted by the TUC as the basis for a settlement to the dispute, though ignored by the Baldwin Government. Extracts from newspapers, such as *The British Worker*, and the records of local trade unions are also included.

Yet one must not focus upon the General Strike alone for it was part of a wider re-adjustment that was occurring in British society, industry and industrial relations throughout the war. The consequence of economic depression and change in Britain between the wars was that governments, particularly Conservative ones, believed that wages had to be reduced and trade-union power reduced if the rationalization and change that was necessary was to occur. In this scenario there was no place for a repeal of the Police strikes of 1919, and the government moved to cut the police off from the wider trade-union movement in 1919 (1). It also passed the Emergency Powers Act of 1920 in anticipation of a major conflict with the unions (2). There were, perhaps, good reasons for this. In 1921 the miners went out on strike on the return of the coal mines to the coal owners; the mines had been taken over by the state during the First World War. Although the Triple Alliance failed to materialize in April 1921, and the miners were forced back to work, the TUC had decided to form the General Council in 1921, in order to facilitate its desire to co-ordinate the industrial muscle of the movement and to prevent a repeat of the debacle of 1921; or as one historian has suggested 'to expiate the guilt of 1921'. Certainly the TUC aimed to create a new industrial alliance to prevent any one group of workers being mercilessly dealt with by employers in the future. The alliance was not fully forged before the 1926 General Strike, largely owing to the reluctance of the miners, but the success of the woollen and worsted textile workers, one of the worst organized groups of workers, created false hopes that the tide had changed in favour of the trade unions (4). This hope was further encouraged by the fact that at more or less the same time the miners, with the support of the TUC, had forced the government to intervene with a subsidy and a royal commission to avert a miners' strike. Friday, 31 July 1925 became known as 'Red Friday' (5) and was seen as a revenge for 'Black Friday', 15 April 1921. But this was only a skirmish and the main battle was enjoined nine months later in May 1926, when the government subsidy ran out, when the Samuel Commission failed to offer acceptable solutions to the problems of overproduction in the coal industry, and when the employers renewed their demands for wage reductions. Although the General Strike lasted for only nine days the coal miners were out for about six months, before they began to drift back in November 1926 (9).

In the wake of the General Strike the government introduced the 1927 Trades Dispute and Trade Union Act (10) which, among its many provisions made secondary strike action illegal and made it more difficult for the trade unions to contribute political funds to the Labour Party. However, it does not appear to have interfered significantly with the conduct of industrial relations and shortly afterwards the TUC and the employers attempted to work together to deal with economic problems through the short-lived 'Mond-Turner' (11) talks.

Throughout the 1930s the trade unions looked towards the new expanding industries, such as the car industry, to increase their membership but even in traditional industries there were, by the late 1930s, some significant recovery in membership figures. Trade-union attention also turned towards the threat of European fascism and the Spanish Civil War (12, 13). Indeed, it was Ernest Bevin and the TUC which encouraged the Labour Party to take a more war-like attitude to the rising fascist threat in Europe.

In the late 1930s the TUC also made one of its most momentous decisions – to accept the principles of what became known as the 'Bridlington Agreement' of 1939 (14). The purpose of the four main principles was to stop wrangles between unions over members and to allow the TUC to intervene to settle inter-union disputes. The Bridlington Agreement has, ever since, been seen as one of the major symbols of authority of the TUC and has been used to expel offending unions from Congress – as will be noted in the final chapter.

1) *Police Act, 1919*
(9 & 10 Geo. V., ch. 46)
1 – (2) The Police Federation and every branch thereof shall be entirely independent of and unassociated with any body or person outside the police service.

2) *Emergency Powers Act, 1920*
(10 & 11 Geo. V., ch. 55)
1. (1) If at any time it appears to His Majesty that [there have occurred, or are about to occur, events of such a nature] as to be calculated by interfering with the supply and distribution of food, water, fuel, or light, or with the means of locomotion, to deprive the community, or any substantial portion of the community, of the essentials of life, His Majesty may, by proclamation (hereinafter referred to as a proclamation of emergency), declare that a state of emergency exists.

3) *The Formation of the General Council of the TUC, 1921*
(*The General Council of the Trades Union Congress; its Powers, Functions, and Work*, London, TUC, 1925)
[. . .]
Centralised Organisation
  The powers, functions, and work of the General Council are, of course, far wider in their range than those of the old Parliamentary Committee which it has superseded. The steps by which the Parliamentary Committee developed its authority until the time came for the General Council to inherit that authority and to carry it still further, brought the Congress to a realisation of the fact that they were no longer members of a voluntary association merely, but units of a closely knit and strongly centralised organisation. Congress has itself assumed a more permanent form, in the sense that it continues to function from day to day through the General Council, which has ceased to be merely an administrative body carrying out the general policy framed by Congress; the General Council is now an actively functioning organ dealing systematically with the problems of Trade Unionism as they arise, and taking action upon its own initiative in regard to a wide range of questions with which Congress may not have been previously concerned, or in relation to which Congress has only laid down guiding principles to the General Council to observe.

[. . .] The advent of the General Council marks a very great stride forward in the direction of a Labour General Staff. That idea has not yet been realised. In the view of many trade unionists, it will not be achieved until Trade Unions assent to the creation of a controlling body sitting in continuous session and devoting its whole time to the tasks of organisation, the co-ordination of effort, and the planning of industrial action on scientific lines.

[. . .] The rise of the Labour Party necessitated the handing over to the political organisation many of the functions and duties which the Congress formerly required the old Parliamentary Committee to discharge; but this has not meant that the General Council has been shorn of powers and responsibilities. On the contrary, it has been acquiring larger powers and accepting far more onerous responsibilities within its proper sphere.

4) *The Wool Textile Dispute of 1925*

[This was the largest lockout and strike that ever occurred in the woollen and worsted textile industry. It was supported by about 150,000 workers, from many unions, who refused to accept wage reductions – although not all of them were involved in industrial action since many employers did not attempt to impose the reductions. A Court of Investigation settled the dispute and decided not to change the wage rates.]

(i)   *Huddersfield Examiner*, 25 July 1925

We deeply regret the action taken by the employers' federation. They may win this fight. They may succeed in imposing their demands on the operatives. If, however, they do so, we venture to find their triumph will be a Pyrrhic victory [one costing more than the gains], and that, setting loss against gain, they will have cause to regret the step which they have taken.

(ii) *The Manifesto*

(Amalgamated Union of Dyers' Collections at Bradford and Huddersfield branches of the West Yorkshire Archives Service) The wages paid to the textile operatives covering all processes to produce one yard of cloth is no more than ¼ of the total cost of the cloth. The proposed reduction in wages will affect the price of a yard of cloth at 8/4 per yard by less than a penny, so we are to have poverty for one penny per yard.

(iii)   Comment in the *Yorkshire Factory Times*, 27 August 1925
         ... General Council's action in support of the miners and wool
         textile workers signalised a turn in the tide, the beginning of a
         definite stand against the policy of wage reductions which
         economic conditions have enabled the employers to impose in
         the last four and a half years.

5) *Red Friday, 31 July 1926*
(*Labour Magazine*, August 1925, copy in the Textile workers records,
Kirklees Archives and Lord Citrine, *Men and Work* (1964), p. 174)
In my opinion it would be mistaken to overrate the apparent success
which attended the General Council's efforts in support of the miners,
and later the textile workers, in their struggle to maintain essential
Trade Union principles. [. . .] I am convinced that in limiting the scope
of the action which it was proposed to take in the mining dispute and in
basing our strategy upon the transport and railway unions – which
incidentally cannot always be expected to act as the storm troops of the
movement – the General Council acted wisely. Had it been necessary to
call a general stoppage we should have realized where our weakness lay.

   Responsibility for calling a strike and for organizing the necessary
financial and other measures is not concentrated in the General
Council to such an extent that many – perhaps the majority – even of
trade union executives could not constitutionally act without the
sanction of a ballot vote of their members.

6) *The Communist Party and the General Strike, 1926*
[The Communist Party of Great Britain initially supported the efforts
of the TUC in the General Strike, with its motto of 'All Power to the
General Council', but after the strike was called off it resolutely
attacked the General Council of the TUC for its betrayal of the
workers]
(i)   *Statement of the Executive Committee of the CPGB, 10 January
       1926*
       (*Workers' Weekly, 15 January 1926*)
       The present industrial situation and the crisis looming ahead
       fully justifies the Communist Party's warning to the workers
       that the Capitalist class is determined to return to the offensive,
       on an even more gigantic scale than last July.

The miners, after breathing space brought for the owners by the means of subsidy, and the sham impartiality of the Coal Commission, are now threatened with an open attack on the seven-hour day, on the Miners' Federation and on wages.

The attack upon the miners is the most violent and unashamed; but workers in most of the industries are faced with similar attacks.

The railwaymen are threatened with wage cuts; the engineers with longer hours; the builders with abolition of craft control won by years of sacrifice. [. . .]

These facts, taken together with the steady, if unobtrusive organisation of the OMS [Organisation for the Maintenance of Supplies], point to a definite determination on the part of British capitalists to, prevent a repetition of Red Friday, to challenge the organised Labour movement and smash it, and to drive the workers down to coolie conditions. [. . .]

The struggle now opening is of a magnitude hitherto unknown. But this enlarged meeting of the Central Committee of the Communist Party believes that the workers can meet the capitalist attack and smash it, as on Red Friday.

(ii)   *Stand by the Miners! An Appeal by the Communist Party of Great Britain*
(Workers's Bulletin, 13 May 1926)
The General Council's decision to call off the General Strike is the greatest crime that has ever been permitted, not only against the miners, but against the working class of Great Britain and the whole world. The British workers had aroused the astonishment and admiration of the world by the enthusiasm with which they had entered upon the fight for the miners' standard of living. But, instead of responding to this magnificent lead by a call to every section of organised labour to join the fight against the capitalists, the General Council has miserably thrown itself and the miners on the tender mercies of the workers' worst enemies – the Tory Government. [. . .]

The Right Wing in the General Council bears direct responsibility for throwing away the workers' weapons and leaving them almost defenceless against the capitalists. Throughout the General Strike they deliberately avoided any pledge to fight against wage reductions. They gave prominence to appeals by Archbishops and County Councils to call off the General Strike without guarantee as to living standards. They suppressed the news that scores, sometimes hundreds, of workers were being arrested or batoned for exercising their right of picketing and propaganda. And most of the so-called Left Wing have been no better than the Right. By a policy of timid silence, by using the false pretext of loyalty to colleagues to cover up breaches of loyalty to workers, they have left a free hand to the Right Wing and thus helped to play the employers' game. Even now they have not the courage to come out openly as a minority in the General Council and join forces with the real majority – the workers – against the united front of Baldwin-Samuel-Thomas.

(iii) *Why the Strike Failed*
(Workers' Weekly, 4 June 1926)

WEAK LEADERSHIP

The response of the workers was beyond all praise. The leadership was beneath contempt.

Once called, the strike should have been readily extended. The General Council hesitated, groping for an excuse to end the strike. The Government, noting the hesitation, were all out to win.

The acceptance of the Samuel Memorandum involving wage reductions followed, and the strike was called off, and the miners were left in the lurch. The Communist Party declares that while it is important to investigate the means by which certain members of the General Council were induced to believe that the Samuel Memorandum had Government backing, that this at best was a side issue. The betrayal of the General Council consists in its acceptance of the Samuel Memorandum at all. This acceptance was not forced upon the General Council by the force of circumstances, it was the logical culmination of its whole policy.

The Communist Party, therefore, declares that the fundamental failure of the General Strike was a failure of leadership. It asks the working class to repudiate with scorn the suggestion that the strike was weakening, and that it should be called off in order to prevent collapse.

7) *The famous circular by the Ministry of Health, 5 May 1926*

Circular 703

MINISTRY OF HEALTH,

Whitehall, S.W. I

5th May, 1926

Board of Guardians

(England and Wales)

Sir,

I am directed by the Ministry of Health to transmit for the consideration of the Guardians the following notes and suggestions with reference to the action to be taken in view of the general stoppage of industry.

The position of the Guardians now becomes one of great responsibility and importance.

It is to be anticipated that there may be large numbers of applications for relief arising directly or indirectly out of the stoppage, and it will be necessary on the one hand for the Guardians to make adequate arrangements for carrying out their statutory duty of relieving destitution and on the other to take all possible steps to conserve their financial resources in face of the demands that may be made upon them, and the possibly prolonged duration of the stoppage. An emergency like the present makes it the plain duty of every Board to keep this second consideration always before them in deciding what they can properly do.

With regard to the limits within which relief may be given to persons who are destitute in consequence of a trade dispute, the Minister desires to draw attention to the declaration of the law contained in the judgement of the Court of Appeal in Attorney-General versus Merthyr Tydfil Guardians (1900).

The function of the Guardians is the relief of destitution within the limits prescribed by law and they are in no way concerned in the merits of an industrial dispute, even though it results in applications for relief. They cannot, therefore, properly give any weight to their views of such merits in dealing with the applications made to them.

The question for consideration of the Guardians on any application for relief made by the person who is destitute in consequence of a trade dispute are questions of fact, namely, whether the applicant for relief is or is not a person who is able-bodied and physically capable of work; whether work is or is not available for him and if such work is not available for him, whether it is or is not so unavailable through his own act or consent.

Where the applicant for relief is able-bodied and physically capable of work the grant of relief to him is unlawful if work is available for him or he is thrown on the Guardians through his own act or consent and penalties are provided by the law in case of failure to support dependents. . . .

[. . .] There is no legal authority for any bulk payment to another agency by the Guardians for the establishment of communal feeding centres, but it is open to them to pay for meals supplied to individual children or adults on the order of a relieving officer or of the Guardians, and the Minister hopes that, wherever this is found practicable, the Guardians will avail themselves of any facilities that may be provided in their Union. He has no doubt that individual Guardians will be prominent in the organisation of arrangements of this kind and that there will be every facility for co-operation between the Guardians and the organisations.

The value of any meals so received, and of any other means of subsistence available to the applicant for relief, should, of course, be strictly taken into account in applying any scale of relief which is adopted.

The Minister would add that he attaches particular importance to close co-ordination and exchange of information between the Guardians and the Local Education Authority as regards the provision of meals by that Authority.

It will be realised of course that the powers conferred upon Local Education Authorities by the Education Act, 1921, in regard to the provision of meals are not intended to be so used as to throw the burden of relief of destitution upon the Education rate.

I am, Sir,
Your obedient Servant,
(signed) W. A. ROBINSON

8) *The TUC, the conducting of the General Strike and the Samuel Memorandum*

(i)   *The Telegram circulated throughout the country to Local Transport Committees informing them that no other body had the right to issue permits allowing the movement of vital supplies of goods, 7 May 1926.*

(Liverpool Council of Action Collection, copies in James Graham College Library, Leeds and Liverpool Library)

Post Office Telegraphs

7.15 PM LONDON C T O
EDWARDS ENGINEERS HALL MOUNT PLEASANT LV WE INSTRUCT ALL LOCAL TRANSPORT COMMITTEES REVIEW ALL PERMITS WHICH HAVE BEEN ISSUED NO TRADES COUNCIL LABOUR PARTY COUNCIL OF ACTION STRIKE COMMITTEE OR TRADE UNION BRANCH HAS AUTHORITY TO DEAL WITH PERMITS PLEASE CONVEY TO ALL CONCERNED + NATIONAL TRANSPORT COMMITTEE UNITY HOUSE LONDON

(ii)   *Extracts from the British Worker. The Official Strike News Bulletin*
(*The British Worker*, Monday 10 May 1926, Manchester edition)

WHERE WE STAND

It is being persistently stated that Mr Ramsay MacDonald. Mr. Herbert Samuel, Mr. Arthur Cook, and other Trade Union leaders have been engaged in an attempt to re-open negotiations with a view to ending the General Stoppage.

The General Council wish it to be clearly understood that there is no truth in this assertion.

No official or unofficial overtures have been made to the Government by any individual or group of individuals, either with or without the sanction of the General Council. Complete control of all negotiations is vested in the General Council, who have had no direct or indirect communication with the Government since they sent their emphatic letter of protest against the Cabinet's wanton action in wrecking the peace discussions that were proceeding.

The position of the General Council may be stated in simple and unequivocal terms. They are ready at a moment to enter into preliminary discussions regarding the withdrawal of the lock-out notices and the ending of the General Stoppages and the resumption of negotiations for an honourable settlement of the Mining Dispute. These preliminary discussions must be free from any condition.

The Government must remember, and the public are asked to remember, that the General Stoppage took place as a result of the action of the Cabinet in breaking off peace discussions and issuing their ultimatum, using as their excuse the unauthorised action of the printing staff of a London newspaper. The responsibility of the present grave situation rests entirely upon the Cabinet. Even the newspapers concerned admits it to be true 'that when the negotiations broke down the trade union representatives knew nothing of the stopping of *The Daily Mail*.'

It is therefore merely fantastic for the Prime Minister to pretend that the Trade Unions are engaged in an attack upon the Constitution of the Country. Every instruction issued by the General Council is evidence of their determination to maintain the struggle strictly on the basis of an industrial dispute. They have ordered every member taking part to be exemplary in his conduct and not to give any cause for police interference.

The General Council struggled hard for peace. They are anxious that an honourable peace shall be secured as soon as possible.

They are not attacking the Constitution. They are fighting the community. They are defending the mine workers against the mine owners.

WHAT THE MINERS EARN
THE LIES ABOUT BIG WAGES

THE real issue in the struggle is Wages – miners' wages. It is important, therefore, to make everyone understand what those wages are and what the proposed reductions mean. [. . .]

We will take South Wales as an example.

The average wage for the whole of this coalfield in the month of February was 10s 6.41d a day. That covers all grades below the under-managers. Based on a 5½-day week, it means an average of 58s a week.

Cut of 16s 11d a Week

The daily average under the owners' proposals would be 7s 5.72d, or for a 5½-day week 41s 1d, a *reduction* of 16s 11d *a week*.

But let us take the various grades of labour separately. We often hear tales of the huge money made by the coal hewers. It is difficult to get an average figure for hewers who are on piece rates.

What they earn depends on the nature of the coal and the supply of trams. And a man in 'a good place' may suddenly find himself up against a 'fault' – a cleavage in the strata – and may have to work many days boring through the disturbed strata for the continuation of the coal seam.

The only definite figure is that whereas he received 62.41 per cent added to the basic rates set out in the colliery price list, the owners propose that the addition should be 10.16 per cent, *which is 32 per cent reduction of the present earnings.*

A guide to the colliers' wages is, however, provided by the rate fixed for those who are on a wage of so much a day.

The rate is 9s 9¼d a day. Assuming that the man worked full time that means £2 13s 9d a week. The owners proposed to reduce this to 7s 2½d a day, equal to £1 19s 8d a week, *a cut of* 14s 1d.

Less than £2 for a full week's work at a hard and dangerous job!

There are deductions for explosives, tools, &c, which make a hole even in that low figure.

And remember, the miners are often idle through circumstances over which they have no control, so that the average over a year will be far less than £2 a week.

Less Than £1 [sic] a Week

Take three other classes – labourers, shacklers (handling the trams at the pit bottom), and the assistant timber-men. The rate for these men was 8s 8¾d a day, equal for a full week's work to 44s 3d. The mineowners want to reduce them to 6s 8d for married men and 5s 9d for single men, equally to 36s 8d a week for married men, and 31s 7½d for single men.

When comfortable opponents of the miners talk about big wages they are either misinformed or lying.

Quote these authentic figures against them, and remember that they are from the district in which the opponents pretend that fortunes are being made by the men.

(iii) *TUC Reply to Mr. Baldwin*
(*The British Worker*, 11 May 1926)
Our Reply to Mr. Baldwin's Broadcast

The workers must not be misled by Mr. Baldwin's renewed attempt last night to represent the present strike as a political issue. The trade unions are fighting for one thing, and one thing only to protect the miners' standard of life.

The General Council never broke off negotiations. This was done by the Cabinet upon an isolated and unauthorised incident at a most promising stage of discussion.

The General Council is prepared at any moment to resume those negotiations where they had left off. It has been urged to do so by the united churches of the country, led by the Archbishop of Canterbury. But his appeal was withheld from the nation by the Broadcasting Company. Why?

The Prime Minister pleads for justice. He can get justice by going back to the Friday before the mineworkers' lock-out notices took effect and recreating the atmosphere of hope which prevailed. [. . .]

The General Council has never closed any door that might be kept open for negotiation. It has done nothing to imperil the food supplies; on the contrary, its members were instructed to co-operate with the Government in maintaining them. No notice has been taken of this offer.

The Prime Minister pleads for peace, but insists that the General Council is challenging the Constitution. This is untrue.

The General Council does not challenge one rule, law or custom of the Constitution; it asks only that the miners be safeguarded. [. . .]

The General Council does NOT challenge the Constitution. It is not seeking to substitute unconstitutional government.
Nor is it desirous of undermining our Parliamentary Institutions.
The sole aim of the Council is to secure for the Miners a decent standard of life.

The Council is engaged in an Industrial dispute.

In any settlement, the only issue to be decided will be an industrial issue, not political, not constitutional.

There is no Constitutional Crisis.

(iv) *Correspondence relating to, and including, the Samuel Memorandum* (TUC Archives and some local collections)

a.   May 12th, 1926

Dear Mr. Pugh,

As the outcome of the conversations which I have had with your Committee, I attach a memorandum embodying the conclusions that have been reached.

I have made it clear to your Committee from the outset that I have been acting entirely on my own initiative, have received no authority from the Government, and can give no assurances on their behalf.

I am of opinion that the proposals embodied in the Memorandum are suitable for adoption and are likely to promote a settlement of the differences in the Coal Industry.

I shall strongly recommend their acceptance by the Government when the negotiations are renewed.

Yours sincerely,

(Signed) HERBERT SAMUEL

A. Pugh, Esq.,

President, General Council,

Trades Union Congress.

b. Sir Herbert Samuel,

London.   12 May. 1926

Dear Sir,

The General Council having carefully considered your letter of to-day and the memorandum attached to it, concurred in your opinion that it offers a basis on which the negotiations upon the conditions in the Coal Industry can be renewed.

They are taking the necessary measures to terminate the General Strike, relying upon the public assurances of the Prime Minister as to the steps that would follow. They assume that during the resumed negotiations the subsidy will be renewed and that the lockout notices to the Miners will be immediately withdrawn.

Yours faithfully.

(Signed) ARTHUR PUGH, Chairman.

WALTER CITRINE, Acting Secretary.

c. Memorandum

1. The negotiations upon the conditions of the coal industry should be resumed, the subsidy being renewed for such reasonable period as may be required for that purpose.

2. Any negotiations are unlikely to be successful unless they provide for means of settling disputes in the industry other than conferences between the mine-owners and the miners alone. A National Wages board, should therefore, be established which would include representatives of those two parties with a neutral element and an independent Chairman. The proposals in this direction tentatively made in the Report of the Royal Commission should be pressed and the powers of the proposed Board enlarged.

3. The parties to the Board should be entitled to raise before it any points they consider relevant to the issues under discussion.

4. There should be no revision of the previous wage rates unless there are sufficient assurances that the measures of reorganisation proposed by the Commission will be effectively adopted. A Committee should be established as proposed by the Prime Minister on which representatives of the men should be included, whose duty it should be to co-operate with the Government in the preparation of the legislative and administrative measures that are required. The same Committee, or alternatively, the National Wages Board, should assure itself that the necessary steps, so far as they relate to matters within the industry, are not being neglected or unduly postponed.

5. After these points have been agreed and the Mines National Wages Board has considered every practicable means of meeting such immediate financial difficulties as exist, it may, if that course is found to be absolutely necessary, proceed to the preparation of a wage agreement.

6. Any such agreement should

(i) if practicable, be on simpler lines than those hitherto followed.

(ii) not adversely affect in any way the wages of the lowest paid men.

(iii) fix reasonable figures below which the wage of no class of labour, for a normal customary week's work, should be reduced in any circumstance.

(iv) in the event of any new adjustments being made, should provide for the revision of such adjustments by the Wages Board from time to time if the facts warrant that course.

7. Measures should be adopted to prevent the recruitment of new workers, over the age of 18 years, into the industry if unemployed miners are available.

8. Workers who are displaced as a consequence of the closing of uneconomic collieries should be provided for by

(a) The transfer of such men as may be mobile, with the Government assistance that may be required, as recommended in the Report of the Royal Commission.

(b) The maintenance, for such period as may be fixed, of those who cannot be so transferred, and for whom alternative employment cannot be found, this maintenance to comprise an addition to the existing rate of unemployment paid under the Unemployment Insurance Act, of such amount as may be agreed. A contribution should be made by treasury to cover the additional sums so disbursed.

(c) The rapid construction of new houses to accommodate transferred workers. The Trades Union Congress will facilitate this by consultation and co-operation with all those who are concerned.

(v)   *The TUC Calls off the General Strike*
(TUC Archives and some local collections contain the following
circular issued on 12 May 1926)
TO THE SECRETARIES OF AFFILIATED TRADE
UNIONS AND FOR THE INFORMATION OF TRADES
COUNCILS AND STRIKE COMMITTEES.
Dear Sir or Madam

The General Council, through the magnificent support
and solidarity of the Trade Union Movement has obtained
assurances that a settlement of the Mining problem can be
secured which justifies them in bringing the general stoppage to
an end.

Conversations have been proceeding between the General
Council representatives and Sir Herbert Samuel, Chairman of
the Coal Commission, who returned from Italy for the express
purpose of offering his services to try to effect a settlement of
the differences in the Coal Mining Industry.

The Government has declared that under no circumstances
could negotiations take place until the General Strike had been
terminated, but the General Council feel as a result of the
conversations with Sir Herbert Samuel and the proposals which
are embodied in the correspondence and documents which are
enclosed that sufficient assurances had been obtained as to the
lines upon which a settlement could be reached to justify them
in terminating the General Strike.

The General Council accordingly decided at their meeting
to-day to terminate the general stoppage, in order that negotiations could be resumed to secure a settlement in the coal
mining industry, free and unfettered from either strike or
lock-out.

The General Council considered the practicability of securing a resumption of work by the members in dispute at
a uniform time and date, but it was felt, having regard to
the varied circumstances and practices in each industry,
that it would be better for each Executive Council itself
to make arrangements for the resumption of work of its
own members. The following telegram was dispatched to you
to-day –

General Council TUC have today declared General Strike terminated. Please instruct your members as to resuming work as soon as arrangements can be made. Letter follows.
Pugh. Citrine.

Throughout the negotiations and during the whole of the stoppage, the General Council have declared that they have been fighting to protect the Miners against an intolerable degradation of their standard of life and working conditions. It was with this object, and with this object alone, that the General Council assumed the grave responsibility of calling upon its affiliated organisations to unite in strike action to inforce the cancellation of the lock-out notices and the withdrawal of the new wages scale posted in the mining districts. No attack was at any time contemplated upon the established political institutions of the country, and it is a testimony to the loyalty and discipline of the Movement that disorders have been practically unknown.

The Unions that have maintained so resolutely and unitedly their generous and ungrudging support of the Miners can be satisfied that an honourable understanding has been reached.

The General Council accept the consequences of their decision with a full sense of their responsibility not only to their own membership but to the Nation at large. They have endeavoured throughout the crisis to conduct their case as industrial disputes have always been conducted by British Trades Unions, without violence or aggression. The General Council feel in taking the last steps to bring the crisis to an end that the Trade Union Movement has given a demonstration to the World of discipline, unity and loyalty without parallel in the history of industrial disputes.

Yours fraternally,
ARTHUR PUGH, Chairman
WALTER M. CITRINE, Acting Secretary

(vi)   *Local Reactions to the General Strike*
    (a) Request for permit to the Liverpool Council of Action
        (Photocopy in the hands of Dr K. Laybourn)

Nottingham Buildings
19, Brunswick Street,
Liverpool,
6th May 1926

W. STONELEY & CO
Corn Merchants
Court of Action,
Clifton House,
Islington,
LIVERPOOL.

Dear Sirs,
   We are anxious to get Maize Meal and Ground Oats carted out to Preston, and our carter will only be too pleased to get the same out provided you give us the permit. Would you kindly do the needful, and oblige.

Yours truly,
(Signed) W. Stoneley Co.

(b) Report of Liverpool Council of Action after the end of the General Strike
[Copy in hands of Dr K. Laybourn]
In submitting this report from the Liverpool Trades Council and Labour Party we realised some 12 months ago that trouble lay ahead in connection with the Mining Industry, and therefore we decided to take what, in our opinion, seemed to be necessary steps for bringing about co-ordination and unification amongst the Trade Union Organisations within the Merseyside areas, and therefore we brought into being the 'Provisional Council of Action'.
   Invitations were therefore extended to Trade Union Organisations and Federations in August last, and the first meeting of the 'Provisional Council' was held on Wednesday evening March 24th 1926. At that meeting representatives were present from all the Trade Union Federations within the Merseyside area. At that meeting a provisional Chairman and Secretary were elected, and the meeting

dispersed with an instruction that the Chairman and the Secretary should convene the next meeting as soon as information and instructions were received from the T.U.C.

In view of the developments that took place, the members of the 'Provisional Council of Action' were called together for Sunday 2nd May 1926, and at that meeting it was decided that the 'Provisional Committee' should become the 'Council of Action' for the area comprising Liverpool, Bootle, Birkenhead and Wallasay.

The Organisations represented upon the Council were as follows: Transport & General Workers' Union, Carters' Union and Motormens' Union, Enginemen and Shipbuilding Federation, Building Trades Federation, N.U.R., A.S.L.E.F., R.C.A., National Union of Distributive and Allied Workers, National Union of General and Municipal Workers, Shipwrights, Boilermakers, Liverpool Trades Council, Birkenhead Trades Council, Bootle Trades Council and Wallasay Trades Council. The three Merseyside Members of Parliament, Messrs Hayes, Gibbins and Secton, were later co-opted members of the 'Council of Action'.

The Council of Action were in continual session from the beginning of the General Strike until its termination, and grouped round them were the respective Strike Committees connected with the following Industries: Transport Trades, Building Trades, Distributive Trades etc., who maintained contact with the 'Council of Action' by the appointment of liaison officers.

A Publicity Committee was set up consisting of 5 representatives and during the period of the strike 500,000 bulletins were issued and circulated throughout the whole of the Merseyside area. This was only possible by mobilising from the respective Trade Union officers, duplicating machines, of which 14 were placed at our disposal.

Arrangements were also made for the holding of meetings etc. and during the period of stoppage 72 meetings were held in the Merseyside area which were attended by thousands of people. In many cases where halls were booked, huge overflow meetings had to be held in the open spaces in the vicinity.

Viewing the position from the Merseyside point of view the response made by the workers to the General Council's appeal was magnificent. The greatest difficulty we had to face during the Strike, was a lack of definite instructions and contact with the Trades Union Congress General Council. Any information and instructions we received were indirect, i.e. from the Trades Union Organisations attached to the Council of Action. This in my opinion was a weakness, all instructions should have been sent from the T.U.C. to the 'Local Council of Action' and the responsibility for carrying out the same should have been theirs.

(Signed) W. H. BARTON

(c) *Special Bulletin issued by the Merseyside Council of Action*

The Council of Action has been in constant session considering the situation arising out of the General Strike order being cancelled. The Council has now ascertained that a large number of employers and Employers' Federations (including the Dock Board, Shipowners, and the Liverpool Cotton Association) have agreed to carry out the resumption of work policy on the old agreements and no victimisation on either side. The Dock Board and Shipowners have already discharged volunteer labour.

The Council of Action feel that this is a practical expression of the Prime Minister's statement that 'neither malice or vindictiveness should be exhibited' and it is hoped that this will be regarded as an example to be followed by all employers on the Merseyside and elsewhere.

The various Unions have therefore decided as follows:-
(1) That those unions who have *National* Agreements are now meeting the Employers' Federation concerned, and the members are to act as per instructions received from their respective National Executives. Work to be resumed as and when ordered by the Executives concerned.
(2) Those unions who have *Local* Agreements with Employers' Federation are now busily in negotiation with the

employers and members will return to work when definite instructions are given by their local officials.

The Council of Action will continue to function until such times as the unions concerned report that they have made satisfactory arrangements as to return of their members to work.

      (Signed) W. H. BOSTON (Chairman)

              W. H. BARTON (Secretary)

May 13th, 1926

PLEASE PASS THIS ON TO ANOTHER MEMBER

(d) Extract from the *St Helens Labour News*, No. 1

Editorial

We regret that the first appearance of the *St. Helens Labour News* has been made under rather adverse circumstances, but for its appearance we make no apology. Indeed, a leaflet of this type is absolutely necessary at the present time, if the workers locally are to know the truth. The Government has issued a daily bulletin, several capitalist papers have appeared in a greatly modified form, and the Wireless is in the hands of the Government. No Labour leader has been permitted to broadcast his views of the present position, and the public are not being given the whole of the facts of the crisis. The *Daily Herald* warned us to beware of wireless messages, and we desire to repeat the warning. As an illustration of the sort of thing we refer to we need only state that though there are eight stations between St. Helens and Liverpool, nobody can reasonably be expected to believe that eight trains run on one journey between these two towns.

Mr. Sexton states that London is at a standstill, and that Liverpool is practically the same. The General Council of the TUC are delighted with the magnificent response of the workers all over the country. Locally, the response has far exceeded the expectations of the Industrial Committee. Our organisation is directed not against the State, as was suggested by the Premier, BUT AGAINST THE POSITIVE ATTEMPTS BY INDUSTRIAL MAGNATES OF THIS COUNTRY TO REDUCE THE WAGES OF MINERS.

(e) *Extract from the Workers' Chronicle* issued by G.H. Laraman for Newcastle Trades Council of Action, No. 5, 8 May, ld

IS TOFFEE FOOD?

Comrades & fellow workers,

The question of the moment is who can handle the food supplies, it is the most important question of today. Will the machinery break down (ask Sir Kingsley Wood). He asks the Workers to handle it, and next month claims all is O.K.

Why? He has to kid his Governmental Bosses that he is doing his job, but we, knowing the position, know he has failed.

It's all very well from a publicity point of view to see all vehicles marked food supplies, but in all my experience as Organiser in one of the main Food Trades I never knew Dainty Toffees, Ice Cream etc could be called food, unless there was a surplus of labels to use up.

Matt Pringle
Bakers' Union.

(f) *Extracts from the National Union off Railwaymen's Strike Committee Minute Book, Birmingham 1926* (Webb Collection, British Library of Political and Economic Science) Minutes (no date given but appear to be 4th or 5th May 1926)

Letter received from Bo. 5 [branch] re position, stating trains arriving into New Street 3.5 returning at 4.20 manned by Station master from Dudley. Three signalmen in at troop(?) house. Assistant Station Master working No.2 New Street.

Letter received from Dudley Branch, Crown Hotel, W'hampton stating all are solid at Dudley. We sent back congratulations from the office.

9) *The Last Flickers of Communist Protest at the end of the Coal Lock-out, 1926*

Circular from Communist Party

NO COMPROMISE   FIGHT LIKE HELL AND WIN

Nov. 10th 1926

STAND FAST

Issued by the Communist Groups in West Yorkshire Pits

These are critical times for the Miners and the whole of the workers after 28 weeks of heroism and wonderful solidarity on the part of the Miners, their wives and children, the Miners stand solid against the attack of the Owners Government, the Boss Press and the whole of the Capitalist State. No stick is too big for the Government to use in attempting to drive the Miners back to work on conditions which will ensure dividends, profits and royalties for the owners and poverty, misery and legislation for the Miners. Imprisonment, ridicule, lies, intimidation, starvation, in fact any weapon is good enough to gain the owners end. The latest move is the conviction of Locked Out Miners for failing to maintain their wives and children.

All these have been to no avail so the old and subtle method of bringing in the so-called leaders of the workers to negotiate a settlement by surrender is being attempted.

THE COMMUNITY PARTY CALLS UPON THE WHOLE OF THE WORKERS TO OPPOSE WITH THEIR MIGHT ANY NEGOTIATIONS THAT CAN ONLY END IN LOWER WAGES, LONGER HOURS AND DISTRICT SETTLEMENT.

The Mine Owners are adamant, they can rely on their Government to see them through, but the whole of industry is calling for a settlement. THE MINERS CAN AND MUST WIN.

SOUTH WALES AGAIN LEADS THE WAY, WE MUST FOLLOW.

The Mardy Lodge of the South Wales Miners has passed a resolution against any negotiations for District Settlements, which can only mean longer hours and lower wages.

Realising the importance of this *The Sunday Worker*, we are informed, has circulated a copy of the resolution to all branches of the MFGB.

FELLOW MINERS SUPPORT AT ONCE THE 'MARDY' RESOLUTION AND SEE THAT THE M.F.G.B IS IMMEDIATELY INFORMED OF THE FACT BY TELEGRAM.

10) *Trade Disputes and Trade Union Act, 1927*

1. (1) It is hereby declared –
     (a) that any strike is illegal if it –
          (i) has any object other than or in addition to the furtherance of a trade dispute or industry in which the strikers are engaged; and
          (ii) is a strike designed to coerce the Government either directly or by inflicting hardship upon the community. . . . and it is further declared that it is illegal to commence, or continue, or to apply any sums in furtherance or support of, any such illegal strike. . . .
          For the purpose of the foregoing provisions –
     (a) a trade dispute shall not be deemed to be within a trade or industry unless it is a dispute between employers and workmen, or between workmen and workmen, in that trade or industry, which is connected with the employment or non-employment or the terms of employment, or with the conditions of labour, of persons in that trade or industry;

7. Without prejudice to the right of any person having a sufficient interest in the relief sought to sue or apply for an injunction to restrain any application of the funds of a trade union in contravention of the provisions of this Act, an injunction restraining any application of the funds of a trade union in contravention of the provisions of section one of this Act may be granted at the suit or upon the application of the Attorney-General.

4. (1) It shall not be lawful to require any member of a trade union to make any contribution to the political fund of a trade union unless he has at some time after the commencement of this Act and before he is first after the thirty-first day of December, nineteen hundred and twenty-seven, required to make such a contribution delivered at the head office or some branch office of the trade union, notice in writing in the form set out in the First Schedule to this Act of his willingness to contribute to that fund and has not withdrawn the notice in manner hereinafter provided; and every member of a trade union who has delivered such a notice as aforesaid, or who, having delivered such a notice, has withdrawn it in manner hereinafter provided, shall be deemed for the purposes of the Trade Union Act, 1913, to

be a member who is exempt from the obligation to contribute to the political fund of the union, and reference in that Act to a member who is so exempt shall be construed accordingly: [. . .]

(2) All contributions to the political fund of a trade union from members of the trade union who are liable to contribute to that fund shall be levied and made separately from any contributions to the other funds of the trade union and no assets of the trade union, other than the amount raised by such a separate levy as aforesaid, shall be carried to the fund. . . .

5. (1) Amongst the regulations as to the conditions of service in His Majesty's civil establishments there shall be included regulations prohibiting established civil servants from being members, delegates, or representatives of any organisation of which the primary object is to influence or affect remuneration and conditions of employment of its members, unless the organisation is an organisation of which membership is confined to persons employed by or under the Crown. . . .

11) *Mond-Turner Talks, 1927–1933*
(Invitation addressed to the General Council of the TUC by Sir A. Mond's Group of Representative Employers, 23 November 1928, quoted in W. Milne-Bailey, *Trade Union Documents* (London, G. Bell & Son, 1929), pp. 253–4)

Dear Sir, – As there appears to us, after investigation, to be no single existing organisation of employers which can take the initiative of inviting discussions to cover the entire field of industrial reorganisation and industrial relations, we desire, as a representative group of employers, to extend to the General Council of the Trades Union Congress an invitation to meet us to consider questions relating to these matters.

The movement towards industrial co-operation has recently received a great accession of strength and there seems to be general agreement that a useful purpose would be served by a consideration of certain fundamental factors in industrial reorganisation and industrial relations with a view to the formulation of definite and concrete proposals applicable to and to be determined in detail by the various industries concerned.

We realise that industrial reconstruction can be undertaken only in conjunction with and with the co-operation of those entitled and empowered to speak for organised Labour. The necessity of every action being taken to achieve the fullest and speediest measures of industrial reconstruction, therefore impels us to seek the immediate co-operation of those who are vitally interested in the subject as ourselves. We believe that the common interests which bind us are more powerful than the apparently divergent interests which seem to separate.

The prosperity of industry can in our view be fully attained only by full and frank recognition of facts as they exist and an equally full and frank determination to increase the competitive power of British industries in the world's markets, coupled with free discussion of the essentials upon which that can be based. That can be achieved most usefully by direct negotiation with the twin objects of restoration of industrial prosperity and the corresponding improvement in the standard of living of the population.

If this is agreed, we would proceed to enumerate the topics which might serve as a basis for our discussion. We hope that you will agree that a useful purpose could be served by representatives of your Council entering discussion with this object in view.

Yours faithfully.

[The letter was signed by Sir Alfred Mond and 20 other employers]

12) *Bradford Trades Council's reflection on some of the events of the 1930s* (Bradford Trades and Labour Council Minutes Books, deposited in the Bradford branch of the West Yorkshire Archives)

(i)   *National Situation*

(Minutes, 17 September 1931)

This Council expresses its distrust and strongest opposition to the present Government and congratulates the National Labour Party on its decision to form itself into the official opposition in Parliament.

Further, it fully endorses the action of the T.U.C. General Council on its attitude to the new coalition government, believing that the proposals to reduce unemployment benefits is only part of the general policy for a further depression in wages. Therefore, we pledge ourselves, on behalf of the Trade Unionists of the City, to resist to the best of our ability this new manifestation of capitalistic dictation.

(ii)   *United Front*
(Minutes, 4 May 1933)
Submitted letter from the Communist Party and the I.L.P. Bradford urging a united front, and stating that a deputation would wait on the Committee. It was agreed to receive the deputation and Mr. M. Ferguson and Mr. E. Wilson attended and stated their case for a United Front against Fascism, War, the Russian Embargo, etc. After consideration it was agreed to recommend the Council accede to the request of the Communist Party and the I.L.P.

(iii) *Proscribed Organisations*
(Minutes, 18 April and 17 October 1935)
This Trades Council, having considered the communication of the General Council of the Trades Union Congress, hereby re-affirms its decision not to interfere with the rights of Trade Union branches to appoint their own representatives to the Trades Council, or to abrogate the right of the rank and file to elect their own representatives.

We hereby declare that this Council is a non-political body, and that during the whole of its existence it has not questioned the political opinions of delegates. [. . .]

That this Council fall into line with the T.U.C. policy as outlined in Circular 16, that affiliated societies be informed accordingly; and that societies which persist in sending delegates connected with proscribed organisations be reported to the General Council of the T.U.C. for them to take the matter up with the National Executive Committee of the Unions concerned.

(iv)   *Fascism*
(Minutes, 15 October 1936)
[The suspension of Standing Orders] was agreed to in order to discuss the question of holding a counter demonstration to Mosley's meeting on the 25 October. It was resolved that the matter be referred to the Joint E.C.s of the Council, Labour Party, and Co-op. Party, with the request that an 'All-in' demonstration be held.

13) *Ernest Bevin, Walter Citrine, The TUC and the Spanish Civil War, 1937*
(Report of the 1937 TUC, pp. 260–7)
[Bevin] With respect to the conflict in Spain we followed last year *with reluctance* the lead of Premier Blum. It certainly appears that his policy gave an opportunity to consolidate the democratic forces in France, held Fascism in check in that country, and has now enabled them to take a stronger line. It probably averted a world war at that time. But it is now recognised that non-intervention has *become* a complete farce. The whole question is now going back to the League. What will become of it?
[Citrine moving the composite resolution]
This Congress expresses its deep abhorrence of the murderous attacks on the defenceless men, women and children in Spain by Franco's Fascists, aided by German, Italian and Moorish forces. It further deplores the fact that the British government and other Governments continue to deny the legal Government of Spain right under international law to purchase necessary arms and equipment, thus affording support to the Fascist rebels.

14) *Bridlington Agreement, 1939*
(Report of the Proceedings at the 71st Annual Trades Union Congress, held at Bridlington, 4 & 5 September 1939 (TUC London, 1939), pp. 105–8)
Main Principle No. 1
The application for membership form of the Union should contain an inquiry to be answered by the candidate as to whether he is or has been a member of any other Union, and, if so, what his financial relationship to the Union is. [. . .]
Main Principle No. 2
As a general principle, no member of any Trade Union should be accepted into membership in another without inquiry from the union concerned. [. . .]
Main Principle No. 3
No member should be allowed to escape his financial obligations by leaving one Union while in arrears and by joining another. [. . .]
Main Principle No. 4
Under no circumstances should a Union accept members from any other Union which is engaged in a trade dispute. It should be a general

understanding that both national and local officials of Trade Unions should refrain from speaking or acting adversely to the interests of any other Union during any period in which the members of the latter Union are participating in a trade dispute. Much trouble could be avoided if Unions about to participate in a trade dispute would take care to inform other unions whose members would be likely to be affected thereby. [. . .]

(21) Proposals

(25) The General Council recommend to Congress that all Unions shall –
- (i) Consider the possibility of joint working agreements with unions with whom they are in frequent contact. Such agreements where possible to deal with –
    - (a) Spheres of influence;
    - (b) Recognition of cards;
    - (c) Machinery in composing difficulties;
    - (d) Conditions of transfer of members. [. . .]

THE TRIUMPH OF BRITISH TRADE UNIONISM c. 1940–1969

The Second World War saw the powerful re-emergence of the trade unions; their memberships increased and their wages and working conditions generally improved. Furthermore, despite some contrary views, the creation of consensus between employers, the state and unions which emerged during the war years appears to have survived until at least the late 1960s. In this situation trade unions became increasingly conscious of their power and authority – seeking involvement in the economic decisions of government, agreeing to wage freezes for the good of the economy and even contemplating the need for new productivity arrangements to ensure the continued health of British industry – whether privately-owned or nationalized (13, 14). They also made a conscious stand for the nationalization of whole industry, 'the socialisation of production' as it was known, much to the annoyance of a Labour Party leadership which was, by the late 1950s, becoming increasingly hesitant of the relevance of that demand (5, 6).

During the war, strike activity was suspended and the trade unions generally obliged in this matter as their attentions were focused upon other issues – most particularly the terms and nature of the post-war reconstruction. The General Council strongly advocated the public ownership of vital industries (1), but the miners missed the opportunity of playing a direct role in running the nationalized coal industry (2) from 1946. In the immediate post-war years the return of a Labour government clearly eased their minds although the government did ask the unions to cooperate in the control of wages. By the late 1940s this understanding was breaking down and the Attlee government became concerned that the industrial unrest which was developing was being stirred up by Communist agitators (3). Nevertheless, the industrial relations of the late 1940s and early 1950s were relatively calm. The only real dangers, as Attlee's Labour government had perceived, was the danger that the rank and file workers would feel increasingly that their interests were not being best represented by their own officials. This concern certainly led to the famous Hull dockers strike of August 1954. Union officials do not appear to have been conscious of their members' fears that the work process and workplace arrangements were causing concern amongst their members.

The return of Harold Wilson's Labour government, in 1964, issued a new period in trade-union relations. The government intended to make British industry more competitive and intended to implement its plan through the National Economic Development Council, where government, employers and trade unionists would meet (7). The government intended to establish a 'Prices and Incomes' policy, which the 1965 TUC conference suggested it would be interested in developing (8). The TUC also became involved in attempts to improve the structure of trade unions through the promotion of amalgamations (9), which would also strengthen its control over its constituent unions.

Unfortunately, Harold Wilson's programme of using 'White Hot technology' to solve Britain's economic problems failed, the pound was devalued and the prices and incomes policy fell into disarray. The high incidence of strikes was considered to be one of the causes of the 'British disease', the failure of industry to compete effectively with other countries, and, as a result the Donovan Commission, the Royal Commission on Trade Unions and Employers' Associations, sat between 1965 and 1968 to investigate British industrial relations (10). It suggested that there were two systems of industrial relations – the formal and the informal. It was argued that the informal system, which operated at the factory level, was undermining the formal arrangements between national unions and employers. In order to rectify this situation it was suggested that employers and trade unions should develop a more comprehensive and authoritative bargaining machinery. These recommendations were generally accepted by most trade-union leaders. However relations between the government and the trade unions worsened with the prices and incomes standstill (11) which was introduced in 1966. Relations soured even further when it appeared that the Labour government might impose controls to restrict the level of unofficial strike activity, although its plans were moderate when compared with the Conservative suggestions for making unofficial strikes illegal and introducing legally-binding contractual arrangements between employers and management (12). Whatever situation was going to develop, it is clear that the trade unions were going to be forced to accept more responsibility for the actions of their members.

1) *General Council of the Trades Union Congress, Interim Report on Post-War Reconstruction, 1944*
Public Ownership
5. Certain industries are of such vital importance to the life and well-being of the community that their immediate transfer to public ownership is essential. They are notably the transport, fuel and power, and the iron and steel industries.
7. The form of organisation for all publicly owned industries should be that of a public corporation, established by Act of Parliament to take over all the undertakings in the industry. Responsibility to the public should be maintained by the appointment of the Governing Boards by a minister responsible for the industry to Parliament. [. . .]
Trade Union Participation
18. The extension of public control must mean an increasing democratisation of economic life. It will be essential for the Trade Union Movement to participate in the determination of all questions affecting the conduct of an industry and the well-being of its workpeople, as well as in the operation of all economic controls.
20. In publicly owned industries the right of the organisation of workpeople to be represented on the governing body should be recognised by statute. [. . .]

2) *Coal Industry Nationalisation Act 1946*
46. (1)It shall be the duty of the [National Coal] Board to enter into consultation with organisations appearing to them to represent substantial proportions of the persons in the employment of the Board, or of any class of persons, as to the Boards's concluding

with those organisations agreements providing for the establishment and maintenance of joint machinery for –

(a) the settlement by negotiation of terms and conditions of
employment with provision for reference to arbitration in
default of such settlement . . . ; and

(b) consultation on –

(i) questions relating to the safety, health or welfare of
such persons;

(ii) the organisation and conduct of the operation in
which such persons are employed and other matters of
mutual interest to the Board and such persons arising out
of the exercise and performance by the Board and their
functions.

3) *Attlee's Labour Government and the Industrial Unrest of 1950*
[Attlee's Labour governments owed some of their success to the
voluntary wages control which they established with the Trades Union
Congress. By the late 1940s, however, that policy was beginning to
break down and there was much consternation that industrial unrest
was being caused by Communist agitators.]

(i) *Letter from Sir Frank Soskice, Solicitor General 1945–1951 and
later Attorney General from April 1951, to Herbert Morrison, Lord
President of the Council, 15 September 1950*
(Cab 124, 1196)

I am writing this letter to you because I have just seen from the
minutes of Thursday's Cabinet that you are presiding over a
Committee which is considering action to counter Communist
manoeuvres directed at causing industrial unrest. I was not
invited to the Cabinet and had not known that the Minister of
Labour was to make a statement in regard to the industrial
troubles but having read the statement before I saw the Cabinet
minister, in the *Evening Standard*, under the headline 'Plot
against the Nation' etc, I asked the Director of Public Prosecution and Thompson of the Special Branch to come to see me
in order to ascertain what, if any, action the Law office were to
take. I now appreciate from the Cabinet minutes, that the
statement was made in furtherance of the Government's determination to counter by strong measures the present Communist

activities, a policy with which, of course, I entirely agree. [There was then discussion of the problem that there was no evidence of the Communist breaking the law, the problems which the Transport and General Workers had faced in keeping industrial order for the last four years, and reference made to the unofficial dock and Smithfield strikes. He went on to argue that Special Branch surveillance of Unofficial Strike leaders was in need of revision.]

At present, as you know, they do not find themselves at liberty to get their agents inside such meetings or, for instance, by disguising themselves or issuing false Union cards, and the result is that it is hardly ever possible to obtain legal evidence of the incitement or illegal action which no doubt occurs when such meetings take place.

(ii) *Prime Minister, Personal Minute, 19 October 1950*
(Cab 124, 1196)
At their morning Cabinet meeting – Cabinet agreed that a Committee of Ministers should further preside for (i) countering Communist endeavours to promote industrial unrest, politically by means of unofficial strikes; and (ii) adapting to the current needs the everyday machinery for the negotiation of wage settlements in industry. [. . .]

(iii) *Letter to Prime Minister from P. Jordan, 6 October 1950*
(Cab 124, 1194)
[Jordan stressed the problem of unrest was not just to do with the Communist Party agitation but the difficulties and frustrations of trade unionists who expect more of a Socialist government]
It is argued that, under a Socialist Government, the power of the Trade Unions to hold the loyalty of their members must inevitably whither, because the Unions are so completely connected with the government that they must attempt the impossible task of running with the hare and hunting with the hounds. The argument concludes that so long as wage restraint is necessary unofficial strikes will become more numerous because men and women who are mainly preoccupied with their immediate living conditions will lose faith in a leadership that must now take account of interests far wider than those they were elected to serve.

4) *The Hull Dockers' Strike, August 1954*
(*The Times*, 18 and 21 August 1954)
[Industrial relations were relatively good during the early 1950s but by the mid 1950s frustrations began to develop amongst rank and file members which led them to question the extent to which their officials represented their interests. In this unofficial strike the men became frustrated with the Transport and General Workers and many were recruited into the Amalgamated Stevedores and Dockers' Union, thus infringing the Bridlington Agreement.]

(i)　Shipping was brought to a standstill at Hull to-day by a dispute which started amongst the dockers on the Seaboard Enterprise, a grain ship berthed in the King George Dock. Four thousand dockers stopped work, and 60 ships were affected ...

Recently 63 dock workers from Cardiff and Swansea were drafted into Hull by the National Dock Labour Board to relieve the labour shortage at a period of peak trade. Twelve Cardiff dockers took exception to the method of filling grain bags followed at Hull, and refused to work on board the Seaboard Enterprise. Their places were taken by local dockers, but after a time these men came into line with the Cardiff men and stopped work. Officials of the Transport and General Workers' Union advised them to continue to work pending negotiations with the port employers, but the men ignored their advice. [...]

The men's solution of the dispute is that the Seaboard Enterprise should be 'boxed up' and sent to a silo berth, to await its turn to unload there.

In Hull it has been the custom to discharge bulk grain cargoes into lighters by manual labour when no silo birth is available to take the grain direct into storage. The dockers have criticized the system, but in the port their objections have been met by granting extra men in the gangs. The system involved filling bags by manual labour in the ship's hold and tipping them into lighters alongside. The men say that this practice is particularly objectionable because of the dust and they are now pressing for the abolition of what they consider to be an obsolete system of dealing with such cargoes.

(ii)　No progress has been made towards ending the unofficial strike that is keeping 4,000 dockers idle in the port of Hull. ...

[Then the strike meetings are described] The unofficial strike leader . . . climbed down from the rostrum to spontaneous cheering. Mr. Arthur Bird, the national docks group secretary of the Transport and General Workers' Union, fresh from a triumph of arbitration in the Southampton dispute, this morning met with different fortunes. The men watched him go to the pulpit for a second or a third time to make an impassioned appeal, a mixture of emotion and reason for work to be resumed on the employers' terms, which happen to be understandably the terms prescribed by the agreement ruling both employers and union.

WALKED OUT

As he spoke the men, without any heart-cry or even murmer, rose listlessly from their seats where they had been glowering for two hours and walked out, with a shrug, into the rain that has been drenching them ever since the strike began.

5) *A Message from Hugh Gaitskell to trade unionists, 1959*
[Extracts from a speech to delegates at the Trades Union Congress, 10 September 1959, about four weeks before the 1959 General Election, produced as a pamphlet under the above title by the TUC, 1959. Although this speech was a rallying speech outlining Labour's commitment to getting a multilateral agreement to end nuclear testing and other election issues, Gaitskell did, briefly, discuss the need for the continued relationship between the Labour Party and the trade unions on pages 6–7.]
Unions and Party

I read a certain amount in the newspapers about the trade unions and the Labour Party. This attempt at giving advice, you know, is an old game. They tell you 'Wouldn't it really be rather better if you kept out of politics altogether? Wouldn't it be rather better if you had no contact with the Labour Party?' They say, 'After all, you have to work with any government.' Of course you do. You always have and you will. But they tell us at the same time that it is really a great handicap to the Labour Party to have anything to do with the trade unions. Don't let us be taken in by this sort of thing.

Let me state very plainly what, as I see it, the true relationship is between the trade unions and the Labour Party. It is quite simple. We are part of the same great Labour Movement in Britain. We are comrades together, but we have different jobs to do. You have your industrial job and we have our political job. We do not dictate to one another. I should get the brush off pretty quickly if I started trying to dictate to Bob Willis. And believe me, any leader of the Labour Party would not be worth his salt if he allowed himself to be dictated to by the trade unions.

I have been leader of the Party for nearly four years now, and I have been in the Labour Party for some time fairly prominently. I have never known an occasion when any trade union leader or any collective body of trade unionists ever attempted to dictate to the Labour Party at all. Let us put that on the record. What we do get and what we shall have is two bodies working together, and we shall get that for the simple reason, as you said, Mr. President, we happen to have common aims and because it is in our interest to work with you and in your interest to work with us.

6) *The Trades Union Congress position on nuclear weapons and national-isation, 1959 and 1960*

(i)   (*Report of Proceedings at the 91st Annual Trades Union Congress, 1959*, pp. 398, motion 35 carried)

This Congress declares its abhorrence at the possibility of the use of nuclear weapons, despite the pollution of the atmosphere by tests and [noting the joint policy statement of the TUC General Council and the Labour Part National Executive Committee] urges that all possible steps be taken to secure its implementation as a step towards not only nuclear but general disarmament.

(ii)   (*Report of Proceedings at the 91st Annual Trades Union Congress, 1959*, p. 415, motion 43, carried)

Congress protests against the desire of the British Government to permit sites in these islands for the launching of the United States ballistic missiles. The White Paper published in February 1958, Cmd 366, entitled *Supply and Ballistic Missiles in the United Kingdom* makes it clear that all nuclear war heads used at these sites will remain in full United States ownership, custody and control.

Congress believes that their policy endangers Britain and that what is needed is not the extension of nuclear bases in Europe but summit negotiations for military and nuclear disengagement.

(iii) *(Report of Proceedings at the 92nd Annual Trades Union Congress, 1960, p. 442)*

Mr. W. E. Peddy, M.P. (Union of Shop, Distributive and Allied Workers) moved the following composite motion [passed with no opposition].

That Congress reaffirms its belief in the principle of common ownership and democratic control of those sections of industry which are vital to the well-being of the country and, recognising the vital contribution that public ownership has to make to the solution of the problem facing the nation, calls for the extension of the principle on a selective and progressive basis. It therefore calls upon the General Council to prepare a comprehensive report on the subject having regard to the general aims and objectives of Congress, the recommendations contained in the Interim Report on Public Ownership adopted at the 1953 Congress, the consultations on certain industries held by the General Council with the unions, and the need to improve the functioning and accountability and public control of nationalised industries. Congress also calls upon the General Council to conduct a vigorous campaign to explain the moral and material benefits that would accrue to all sections of the community as a result of the application of the socialistic principle of control of the means of production, distribution and exchange in the national interest.

7) *Joint Statement of Intent on Productivity, Prices and Incomes 1964* (House of Commons, *Debates*. Fifth Series Vol. 704 Cols 385–8)

THE OBJECTIVES

The Government's economic objective is to achieve and maintain a rapid increase in output and real incomes combined with full employment. [. . .]

THE GOVERNMENT

6. The Government will prepare and implement a general plan for economic development in consultation with both sides of industry through the National Economic Development Council. This will

provide for higher investment; for improving our industrial skills; for modernisation of industry; for balanced regional development . . .

8. The Government will set up machinery to keep a continuous watch on the general movement of prices and of money incomes of all kinds and to carry out . . . other functions. . . .They will also use their fiscal powers or other appropriate means to correct any excessive growth in aggregate profits as compared with the growth of total wages and salaries, after allowing for short-time fluctuations.

[Agreed by representative of the TUC, the Federation of British Industries, the British Employers' Confederation, the National Association of British Manufacturers and the Association of British Chambers of Commerce.]

8) *Prices and Incomes Policy: An 'Early Warning System'*
(Cmnd 2808, 1965)

INTRODUCTION

The Government announced on 2nd September 1965 their intention to seek statutory power to introduce a compulsory 'early warning' system for prices and incomes, i.e. to take power to require advance notification to the Government of an intended increase in prices or charges, of claims relating to pay, hours or other major improvements; and of prospective terms of settlement in such cases. . . .

PURPOSE OF ADVANCE NOTIFICATION

2. The purpose of an 'early warning' system for price increases and for increases in pay, reductions in hours or other major improvements is to give the Government an adequate opportunity to consider decisions concerning prices and pay before they are put into effect. . . .

ACTION BY THE TRADES UNION CONGRESS

16. In accordance with the decision taken at the recent Congress [1965], the Trades Unions Congress has introduced arrangements whereby the General Council is informed by affiliated unions of all impending claims. These claims are examined by a special committee established for this purpose, consisting of one General Council member for each of the 19 Trade Groups of Congress.

17. Where the General Council does not wish to make any comment

on the claim, the union will be informed within about a month of receipt of the claim by the Trades Union Congress. In some cases the General Council may wish to make written observations on the claim or to invite representatives of the unions or unions concerned to meet them to discuss it. In the latter event, the meeting will be arranged as quickly as possible after the committee has considered the claim. In the great majority of cases, not more than five weeks or so at the most should elapse between the receipt of the notification and completion of the procedure. Until then unions will be expected to refrain from proceeding with the claim but thereafter they will be free to proceed, taking account of such considerations as the General Council may draw to their attention.

18. The Trades Union Congress will keep the Government informed of developments, with the object of meeting the Government's 'early warning' requirements in respect of affiliated unions.

[. . .]

PRINCIPLES OF THE WHITE PAPER ON PRICES AND INCOMES POLICY (CMND 2639)

26. It must be emphasised that the new arrangements described above is no way to relieve those concerned with determining prices and incomes of the obligation to act in accordance with the principles set out in Cmnd. 2639. To keep the general level of prices stable, it is vital that price increases should be avoided where possible and that prices should be reduced wherever circumstances permit; and that the overall increase in wages, salaries and other forms of incomes should be kept in line with the growth of real national output. The Government are free to refer appropriate cases to the National Board for Prices and Incomes whether or not they are subject to the 'early warning' system.

9) *The General Council of the TUC and Amalgamations*
(General Council of the TUC, *Report to Congress: Trade Union Structure*, presented to the 1965 TUC Congress)

TRADE UNION STRUCTURE

. . .The General Council believe that the case for amalgamation between certain unions is strong.

(a) Larger unions with greater resources are more able to provide services (research; legal; education) and to develop new services.

(b) Larger unions catering for groups of occupations nationally are in a better position to formulate comprehensive policies and to give effect to them.

(c) Although small unions can make a substantial impact at workshop level they are less effective at industrial and national levels (e.g. in the work of the Economic Development Committees and Industrial Training Boards).

(d) Some unions which in the past catered for separate trades now cater competitively for workpeople whose trade indentities are changing or have been submerged: this leads to duplication of officials each engaged on the same duties for small groups of members in the same establishment.

(e) Competition between unions has not led to higher membership but is one of the reasons why, in some occupations, the level of membership is low. [. . .]

The arguments against amalgamation were partly based on fears of loss of autonomy and of trade identity. Other doubts were financial: it was said, for instance, that marked differences in scales of contributions and benefits make mergers difficult.

10) *The Two Systems of Industrial Relations*
(Royal Commission on Trade Unions and Employers' Associations 1965–1968, *Report* (Cmnd 3623) 1968)

THE TWO SYSTEMS

143. We can now compare the two systems of industrial relations. The formal system assumed industry-wide organisations capable of imposing their decisions on their members. The informal system rests on the wide autonomy of managers in individual companies and factories, and the power of industrial groups.

144. The formal system assumes that most if not all matters appropriate to collective bargaining can be covered in industry-wide agreements. In the informal system bargaining in the factory is of equal or greater importance.

145. The formal system restricts collective bargaining to a narrow range of issues. The range in the informal system is far wider, including discipline, recruitment, redundancy and work practices.

146. The formal system assumed that collective bargaining is a matter of reaching written agreements. The informal system consists largely

in tacit arrangements. In the informal system many important decisions about pay are taken in the factory.

THE REFORM OF COLLECTIVE BARGAINING

182. In order to promote orderly and effective regulation of industrial relations within companies and factories we recommend that the boards of companies review industrial relations within their undertakings. In doing so, they should have the following objectives in mind:

(1) to develop, together with trade union representative of their employees, comprehensive and authoritative collective bargaining machinery to deal at company and/ or factory level with the terms and conditions of employment which are settled at these levels.

[. . .]

191. [. . .] a statute, which might be called the Industrial Relations Act, should lay an obligation on companies of a certain size to register collective agreements with the Department of Employment and Productivity. Initially the limit should be set high, say 5,000 employees, in order to keep the administrative burden within bounds. [. . .]

196. If a company does not recognise trade unions, it will have no agreements to register, and this will have to be reported to the Department of Employment and Productivity with reasons. In this event the company will be failing in its public duty unless it can show that its employees are unwilling to join trade unions and to be represented by them.

201. [. . .] The Industrial Relations Commission should be the body to carry out inquiries into the general state of industrial relations in a factory or an industry. . . . But if it was required to arbitrate on particular disputes about terms and conditions of employment its attention would be diverted from the proper functioning of the machinery, and from long-term objectives to short-term compromises.

203. [. . .] It would be wrong to attempt to lay down a detailed set of rules to which the [Industrial Relations] Commission will be expected to work. [. . .] Equally, however, it will be important that the principles which guide the Commission's work should be known and understood. We suggest that they might be these:

(1) that collective bargaining is the best method of conducting industrial relations. There is therefore wide scope in Britain for

extending both the subject matter of collective bargaining and the number of workers covered by collective agreements;

(2) that, since collective bargaining depends upon the existence, strength and recognition of trade unions, the test in dealing with any dispute over recognition – other than a dispute between unions over recognition – should be whether the union or unions in question can reasonably be expected to develop and sustain adequate representation for the purpose of collective bargaining among workers in the company or factory concerned, or a distinct section of those workers. A ballot may be useful in applying the test, but could rarely determine the issue by itself;

(3) that a system of industrial relations must be judged principally by its effects in the company, the factory, the workshop. Industry-wide procedures and agreements should be confined to those issues which they can effectively regulate;

(4) that wherever possible, collective agreements should be written and precise;

(5) that pay agreements should provide intelligible and coherent pay structures;

204. Failure on the part of a company to register its agreements or to report that it has no agreements and why, will render it liable to a monetary penalty. . . .

11) *Prices and Incomes Standstill (Cmnd 3073) 1966*

1. INTRODUCTION

2. The country needs a breathing space of twelve months in which productivity can catch up with the excessive increases in incomes which have been taking place. The broad intention is to secure in the first six months (which can be regarded, for convenience, as a period to the end of December 1966) a standstill in which increases in prices or in incomes will so far as possible be avoided altogether. The first half of 1967 will be regarded as a period of severe restraint in which some increases may be justified where there are particularly compelling reasons for them, but exceptional restraint will be needed by all who are concerned with determining prices and incomes. [. . .]

PART I
THE NATIONAL BOARD FOR PRICES AND INCOMES

1. (1) There shall be established a body, to be called the National Board for Prices and Incomes (in this Act referred to as 'the Board').

2. (1) The Secretary of State, or the Secretary of State and any other Minister acting jointly, may refer to the Board any question relating to wages, salaries or other forms of incomes, or to prices, charges or other sums payable under transactions of any description relating to any form of property or rights. . . .

PART II
NOTICES AND STANDSTILLS

6. (1) Her Majesty may by Order in Council of which a draft has been laid before and approved by a resolution of each House of Parliament –

   (a) bring the provisions of this Part of this Act into force for a period of twelve months beginning with the date specified in the Order,

   (b) from time to time extend or further extend that period by a further period of twelve months, [. . .]

12) *The Conservative Party and the Trade Unions*

(i) (Stephen Abbott, *Industrial Relations: Conservative Policy*, Conservative Political centre, 32 Smith Square, London, 1966, pp. 3, 17)

At the centre of their [Conservative] proposals is the enforceability of agreed dispute procedures. So many strikes occur because the agreed method of settling an underlying grievance is not used. So often the threat of a strike prevents management from improving efficiency. [. . .] Perhaps Britain's greatest task is to sweep away barriers to greater productivity and industrial efficiency. Our future living standards are dependent on success in this field. And it can only be achieved through the sustained, co-operative effort of management, trade unions and workpeople. [. . .]

Our system of industrial relations is crying out for reform. The Conservative proposals are part of a strategy for the enrichment of the lives of the whole community. In essence, they provide a fair deal for the individual, for unions and employers. . . .

(ii)   (*Industrial Advance: A Report from the Conservative Trade Union-ists' National Advisory Committee together with evidence to the Royal Commission on Trade Unions and Employers' Associations*, Conservative Political Centre, on behalf of the Conservative Industrial Department, 32 Smith Square, London SWI., Summary of Conclusions)

Main Points

(1) Expand membership of Trade Unions but reject compulsion.

(3) Reform of the payment of political levy is long overdue.

(4) Legislation to curb unofficial strikes would merely bring the law into contempt. The union and the TUC should be encouraged to adopt wider powers of control.

(5) Agreements between union and employer should be on a contractual basis enforceable at law.

(6) It may be desirable for a ballot to be taken prior to strike action. . . .

(7) Far too many unions exist in some industries and the TUC should be encouraged to accelerate amalgamations and [examine] the future of the industry in which they work.

(10) Imposing an incomes policy is not in the national interest. Economic taxation is inflationary and exhortation useless. The answer lies with the individual who must be trained, encouraged and given suitable incentive.

13) *Productivity, Prices and Incomes Policy After 1969 (Cmnd 4237) 1969*
D. FRAMEWORK OF THE POLICY
CONTINUATION IN FORCE OF PART II OF THE PRICES
AND INCOMES ACT 1966

28. The Government has always recognised that the full range of powers available under the 1967 and 1968 Prices and Incomes Acts to delay the implementation of pay and price increases was called for only in exceptional circumstances and as a short term measure. The delaying powers under the 1967 and 1968 Acts expire at the end of 1969 and they will not be renewed. The Government has however laid bare before Parliament a draft of the necessary Order in Council

continuing Part II of the 1966 Act in force for a year beginning on 1 January 1970.

E. GUIDANCE FOR PAY NEGOTIATIONS
GENERAL CHARACTER OF PAY SETTLEMENTS

35. In the next few years output per worker is likely to go up by about 3% a year. Therefore if we are to avoid a steep increase in the cost of living money incomes should only rise at about this rate. This was the basis of the 'norm' of 3–3½% for pay increases which formed the starting point of the policy in 1965. If productivity rises faster than expected then so can incomes. The principle was accepted in 1965. It is still true today.

36. This means that most wages and salary settlements need to fall in the range of 2½–4½% increase in a year if this aim of greater price stability is to be achieved. A range within which most settlements need to fall has been given because no single figure can be appropriate to the circumstances of all negotiations. Nor indeed will the average figure be the same from one year to the next. The appropriate level for a particular settlement within this range will depend on a variety of factors. . . .

40. The factors . . . are –
Productivity and Efficiency Agreements
Reorganisation of Pay Structures
Low Paid Workers
Equal Pay for Women
Labour Market Requirements
Pay and Public Services.

14) *The National Board for Prices and Incomes, Report No. 123: Productivity Agreements (Cmnd 4136) 1969*

REVISED AGREEMENTS FOR EMPLOYERS
AND TRADE UNIONS

131. Productivity agreements which specify changes in working practice to be introduced continue to provide an appropriate and effective means of raising productivity and efficiency, especially of manual workers, over much of the economy. But since there are many workers who can contribute to increased efficiency without signing productivity agreements in this narrow sense, a new term may be desirable which

would include productivity agreements in the generally accepted sense within its scope. We think the term 'efficiency agreements' appropriate for agreements in the wider sense. The word 'efficiency' in particular seems to us in many ways more suitable in this context, since there are many workers who are not engaged in production and for whom the concept of efficiency has a much more immediate significance.

THE CHALLENGE TO TRADE UNIONISM AND ITS DECLINE IN THE 'THATCHER YEARS', *c.* 1969–1990

The last twenty-one years have seen the trade-union movement come under increasing attack from both friend and foe alike. The fundamental problem is that both Labour and Conservative governments have realised that industrial disputes are highly damaging in a world where the British economy was, and still is, highly vulnerable to foreign competition. Yet the strategy of various governments has varied widely. On the whole, Labour governments have attempted to work with the trade unions in a consensual voluntary system forming the basis of an incomes policy. This approach has never lasted long and has usually created intense strain within the wider Labour movement. Conservative governments, on the other hand, have on the whole sought to impose legally-binding agreements on trade unions, to weaken them, to strengthen the individual's rights within unions, and to make unions financially responsible for their actions – operating within a voluntary framework of industrial relations. Since the 1980s, this latter policy has imposed severe legal and financial constraints on trade unions and has been effective in reducing trade-union membership and producing some spectacular industrial conflicts. On the whole, trade unions have not fully adjusted to the changing pattern of industrial relations which, with the Labour Party's move away from domination by the trade unions, has been compounded by their falling political importance – although by the 1990 TUC they had come to recognize to operate within the new legal framework.

It was Harold Wilson's Labour government which, in 1969, first threatened to change the pattern of industrial relations with its White Paper, in furtherance of the findings of the Donovan Commission, *In Place of Strife* (1). This advocated the improvement of industrial relations through the increased recognition of trade unions and by the creation of a better and more effective system of conciliation. Although the unions rejected the strategy, the introduction of an Equal Pay Act (2) for men and women, was welcomed. However, the Labour government was replaced by Edward Heath's Conservative government in 1970 and this was committed to reforming the pattern of industrial relations through the Industrial Relations Act of 1971 (3). This Act created an Industrial Relations Court to regulate industrial relations and to impose compensation against unions involved in unfair industrial practice. However, it failed to carry much weight within trade-union circles and was effectively scuppered by the case of the Pentonville dockers (4) who were released from prison for picketing despite the restrictions imposed by the 1971 Act. Also, the 1971 Act did not prevent the miners from effectively defying the government and using 'flying pickets' to close a coal depot during the 1972 miners' strike (5).

The poor industrial relations of Heath's Conservative government forced the Labour Party to think about the need for a voluntary arrangement between trade unions and any future Labour government. As a result the 'Social Contract' was born, based upon a voluntary code of conduct whereby wage increases were held low, on a voluntary basis, in an attempt to curb inflation (6). In order to show good faith, the new Wilson Labour government of 1974 introduced the 1974 Trade Union Act (7), which repealed the 1971 Industrial Relations Act and relaxed the law on peaceful picketing. The 'Social Contract' was accepted at the 1975 TUC conference and subsequently the General Council accepted the government's £6 guidelines for twelve months. Subsequently it agreed to a 5 per cent maximum increase, with a lower limit of £2.50 and an upper limit of £4 for the period 1 August 1976 to 31 July 1977. But many unions were unhappy with the arrangements and the 1976 TUC conference, despite the General Council's attempt to play down its significance, passed a resolution (composite 7) suggesting the need to return to free collective bargaining in 1977. Relations between the government and the trade unions gradually soured as the government attempted to turn a move towards a statutory incomes policy. It was out of the pent-up emotions of trade unionists, who feared what a statutory incomes policy might do, that the 'Winter of Discontent' occurred in 1978–9 (10). Faced with the revolt of its major unions, and rising wage demands, the TUC General Council had no option but to abandon its previous vetting of wage claims (11). There was also some frustration over the failure of the law to ensure that workers could organize into unions if they wished, a situation which became obvious in the Grunwick dispute of 1976–7 (9).

Grunwick was a mail order film-processing laboratory in Willesden, which did not have the benefit of new equipment. In order to compete, it employed a predominantly black and female labour force on a casual labour. The pay was low, the workforce was compelled to work overtime and the employers denied any right to unionization. On 20 August 1976 they walked out after the management refused to accept unionization. On 2 September the management locked out 137 of the work force. The picket was mainly conducted by Asian women, although for four days the Post Office workers refused to handle the Grunwick mail, until there was a threat of a High Court injunction. The management, unsuccessfully, attempted to gain a High Court injunction to stop the strikers picketing retail outlets, such as chemist shops, but Jayaben Desai (one of the strike leaders) was arrested in an exchange with George Ward, the managing director, who took out a private summons for assault. However, the quashing of summonses against six strikers and the award of £3,500 against the police for wrongful arrest raised morale amongst the strikers. But a Court of Inquiry, chaired by Lord Scarman, which recommended the re-instatement of the strikers was ignored by the management and a conciliation report recommending union recognitions was declared null and void by the House of Lords. Even under a Labour government it appeared that trade unions would find the law fighting against their interests.

The Callaghan Labour government lost power in 1979 due largely to its inability to work with the trade unions. With the failure of the 'Social Contract' the Ford workers submitted a claim for £20 per week increase on a 35-hour week, a 25 per cent overall claim on 24 August 1978. They were offered a 5 per cent increase and on 22 September they struck and, four days later, the AUEW made the strike official, followed by the TGWU on 5 October. After a nine-week strike the Ford workers accepted 16.5 per cent. Other unions followed suit. In January (1–14) 1979 20,000 railwaymen held four one-day strikes. There were strikes by haulage drivers and petrol tanker drivers. The former settled for 15 to 20 per cent and the latter for 15 per cent. Secondary pickets at the docks were accused of attempting to starve the country. On 22 January 1979 1,250,000 local authority workers organized a one-day national strike. The most notorious incident which the press picked up on was the grave diggers' strike on Merseyside. A casual remark by a councillor hit the headlines as 'Burial at Sea'. The strike action by poorly paid, essential workers such as the grave diggers, school caretakers, and the refuse collectors, was widely supported. As the crisis deepened, however, and with a hostile media projecting a scenario of death and illness, public opinion was against the strikers. Despite the fact that none of the disasters occurred, the strikers had been identified and pilloried as the new folk devils. The Labour government looked no more capable of dealing with the unions than the Conservative government had been.

With their defeat in the 1974 General Election, many Conservatives began to feel that they could not operate an economic policy without the consent of the trade unions. However, this was not a policy endorsed by some members of the Bow Group who advocated a far more positive attitude towards trade unionism based upon outlawing the closed shop, making postal ballots mandatory for union officials and forcing trade unions to face up to the economic consequences of their action (8). In a general sence this policy has formed the basis of the attack upon trade unions which has been a central tenet of the Thatcher years, from 1979 to 1990 – demanding that trade unions should seek approval for strike action through secret ballots, making secondary strike action, by those not directly involved in the dispute, illegal and introducing the possibility of the fining of unions and the sequestration of their funds for ignoring the courts. The Employment Acts of 1980, 1982 and 1988, plus the Trade Union Act of 1984 (12, 13, 16, 18) have introduced these Conservative policies. The 1980 Act allowed the Secretary of State to permit independent unions to recoup certain forms of expenditure entailed in secret ballots, allowed people to become members of unions and not to be unreasonably expelled from them and made secondary action, by those not directly involved in the dispute, liable to legal action. The 1982 Act dealt with the law of unfair dismissal as affected by closed shops and gave increased compensation for cases of dismissal in a closed shop employment. The 1984 Trade Union Act imposed upon trade unions the responsibility of holding secret ballots before industrial action could be called and periodical ballots on the payment of political funds to any political party. The 'Beloff' amendment in the House of Lords emphasized the need for postal ballots as the normal and primary way of conducting elections, with workplace ballots as a second possible method but subject to strict safeguards. Legal immunities were offered to unions as long as they held a secret ballot not more than four weeks before industrial action. The 1988 Act tightened up on postal ballots for the election of union representatives, for the decision to provide political funds and also allowed union members to ignore majority decisions voted upon without fear of union discipline. The whole package did much to undermine the effectiveness of trade unions and their ability to strike against employers at will.

This package of legislation has successfully limited the operation and the effectiveness of the trade union movement, to a point where its membership and financial health have deteriorated rapidly (19). At all points, however, that legislation has been put to the test by trade unions. This was evident in the National Graphical Association's conflict with Eddie Shah and the enforcement of the Warrington premises of the *Stockport Messenger*. The NGA attempted to enforce a closed shop at Shah's printing works but Shah stood firm, obtained an injunction and, subsequently, a £50,000 fine for contempt. Later the court imposed another £100,000 fine and the union assets were sequested. The union ignored these actions, continued with violent picketing and was further fined £150,000 and £375,000. It called for a national newspaper strike on 24 December, which was at first supported by the TUC's Employment Committee. However, when this action was declared unlawful in the High Court, Len Murray, the TUC's general secretary, had the General Council repudiate the action. In January 1984 the NGA accepted defeat and purged its contempt of court to unfreeze its assets.

In the wake of this the miners' strike, which lasted from March 1984 to March 1985 (15), proved an even bigger conflict and a serious challenge to the Conservative government's trade-union legislation. It began with the closure of Cortonwood colliery but was also fought against a wage offer of 5.2 per cent, which the miners' leaders rejected. Ian MacGregor, the new head of the National Coal Board, announced a programme of pit closures. The strike began on 9 March 1984 at the pits in Scotland and Yorkshire where notification of closures had been made. However, there was to be no national ballot. Instead the NUM sent flying pickets from Yorkshire, Scotland and Kent to persuade the working miners, particularly in Nottinghamshire and the Midlands, to join the dispute. This led to mass picketing and violence, notably at Ollerton in Nottinghamshire and later at Orgeave coke plant. There were many twists and turns in the developments. On 14 March 1984 the High Court gave the National Coal Board an injunction against flying pickets, though the NCB chose not to use it. The government also ensured a police presence to stop the movement of flying pickets. Trade-union support for the miners was mixed although Scargill drew immense personal support at the 1984 TUC conference.

Yet as the strike ground on, court action began to take effect. The South Wales Mineworkers were fined £50,000 for contempt over picketing and when it was not paid the sequestrators seized their funds of £707,000. The national union was fined £200,000 on 10 October, and when the union failed to pay, its assets were seized. There was much violence, many incidents of high emotions but eventually the strike came to an end, in a ragged fashion and without any settlement, when a special delegate meeting of mineworkers decided to return to work without any agreement on 3 March 1985.

The other major dispute which dominated the 1980s was the conflict between Murdoch's News International Group and the Print Unions over the enforcement of new working arrangements and no-strike agreements (17). In effect the print unions were attempting to restrict the use of the new technology and the movement of the newspaper industry from Fleet Street out to Wapping in the East End of London and to Murdoch's other works. The ability of the unions to prevent this was severely hampered by the fact that the Electrical, Electronic Telecommunication and Plumbing Union had made arrangements to operate Murdoch's Wapping plant in the event of a dispute between Murdoch and the print unions. The strike, and the violence associated with it, lasted from January 1986 until February 1987 when, faced with the prospect of sequestration of their assets, SOGAT and the other print unions decided to call off the action. Throughout this period the TUC had been relatively ineffective in resolving the differences between the EETPU and the print unions, despite much negotiation and censure. In the end, for the EETPU's unwillingness to accept the outcome of two inter-union disputes awarded by the TUC under the Bridlington Agreement, it was expelled from the TUC at its 1987 conference.

Since this dispute ended trade unions have proceeded with more caution, especially as their memberships have declined and their finances have dwindled (19). The 1990 TUC conference adopted a policy of accepting and working, in their favour, the employment legislation of the 1980s, expecting no large-scale revocation of the legislation by a future Labour government, and appear to be committed to legal action to press on the Conservative government the European social charter of workers' rights, despite Thatcher's strong opposition to this charter.

1) *In Place of Strife, 1969*
(*In Place of Strife: A Policy for Industrial Relations*, January 1969, Cmnd 3888)
55. The Industrial Relations Bill will lay down the principle that no employer has the right to prevent or obstruct an employee from belonging to a trade union. This principle will become part of the contract of employment . . . .
62. A new Industrial Board will be responsible for dealing with cases under the provisions in paragraph 60 as well as with those referred to in paragraphs 93–98 (conciliation pause and ballots), 109 (registration) and 115–116 (complaints against trade unions by individuals) below. [. . .] The Board will have the power to impose financial penalties on an employer, union or individual striker as it found appropriate. [. . .]

79. Strikes are inevitable in a system of free collective bargaining. But many strikes in contemporary Britain are avoidable. No Government concerned with the economic advancement and prosperity of the country can afford to neglect any reasonable and practical proposal for reducing their incidence and effect.

80. The fundamental solution lies in the re-structuring of our present system of collective bargaining when it is disordered or defective. Many strikes would not take place if there were quick and effective methods of resolving the matter in dispute. Some existing dispute procedures, such as that in engineering, are outdated and no longer provide an adequate means of resolving many of the disputes to which they should apply. Some employers are too ready to take unilateral action on matters like working methods and dismissals, and take the risk that this will provide industrial action, instead of negotiating beforehand. In many circumstances at present the use of the strike weapon is understandable, and in some cases it is justified.

81. Reform of collective bargaining will remove many of the causes of strikes. Comprehensive and effective company or plant agreements will solve many existing difficulties. Better procedure will resolve disputes before the impatience of those concerned leads to a strike. The need to reduce the numbers of strikes through improved procedures will be an important element in the approach of the C.I.R. Other proposals, such as those on trade-union recognition and negotiating rights (paragraphs 56–59), inter-union disputes (paragraph 60) and unfair dismissal (paragraphs 103–104), will provide remedies for matters which at present give rise to a large number of strikes.

82. In addition to these changes, the Government proposes new developments which will enable it to deploy its services more effectively, and ensure that conciliation is given every chance to work before there is resort to harmful conflict.

118. Before agreeing to a closed shop, employers shall seek to obtain suitable protection for people who refuse to join trade unions on conscientious grounds. Many unions are prepared to accept such people in a closed shop, if they in turn are prepared to show good faith, for example by contributing to charity instead of paying a union subscription. When such employees are dismissed from employment because they will not join a union, the Government proposes that they

should have the right to complain to an Industrial Tribunal as a case of
alleged unfair dismissal.

2) *Equal Pay Act 1970*
1. (1) The provisions of this section shall have effect with a view to
        securing that employers give equal treatment as regards terms
        and conditions of employment to men and to women, that is to
        say that (subject to the provisions of this section and . . .)
   (a) for men and women employed on like work the terms and
        conditions of one sex are not in any respect less favourable than
        those of the other; and
   (b) for men and women employed on work rates as equivalent . . .
        the terms and conditions of one sex are not less favourable than
        those of the other in any respect in which terms and conditions
        of both are determined by the rating of their work . . .

3) *Industrial Relations Act, 1971*
(i)   Industrial Relations Bill: Explanatory and Financial Memoran-
      dum (as brought before the House of Commons 25 March
      1971)
      [This Bill anticipated the creation of an Industrial Relations
      Court, or Industrial Court as it became known, which would
      deal with the problems of trade-union rights, collective bargain-
      ing procedures and the claims of employers]

PART II – RIGHTS OF WORKERS

Clause 5 gives to every worker the right to belong to an
independent trade union, to take part in its activities, and to
seek office in that union. It also gives to the worker the right not
to belong to an independent trade union or other organisation
of workers. Any action by an employer which discriminates
against the worker for exercising these rights will be an unfair
industrial practice except where there is an agency agreement
covering the workers' employment and the worker either
refuses to join the union or to pay the appropriate contribution
to its funds or to charity, or where there is an approved closed
shop agreement covering the workers' employment and he
refuses to join the union. For an employer to encourage a

worker to join a trade union which he recognises for bargaining purposes will not be an unfair industrial practice but to compel him would be.

PART III – COLLECTIVE BARGAINING

Clause 32 creates the presumption that any written collective agreement entered into after the commencement of the Act is intended by the parties to it to be a legally enforceable contract except in so far as it contains an express provision to the contrary.

PART V – OTHER UNFAIR INDUSTRIAL PRACTICES

Clause 92 makes it an unfair industrial practice for a person other than a trade union or employers' association or a person acting within the scope of his authority on behalf of such an organisation in contemplation or furtherance of an industrial dispute to induce or threaten to induce a breach of contract other than an enforceable collective agreement.

Clause 93 makes it an unfair industrial practice to take or threaten industrial action in contemplation or furtherance of an industrial dispute in support of any other unfair industrial practice.

Clause 94 makes it an unfair industrial practice for any person in contemplation or furtherance of an industrial dispute to induce another person to break a contract (other than a contract of employment) or to interfere with the performance of it where that is his purpose or principal purpose and he knows or has reasonable grounds to believe that the commercial contract exists with a party to the dispute and the action is directed at someone who is neither a party to the original dispute nor supporting it.

PART VI – NATIONAL INDUSTRIAL RELATIONS COURT, INDUSTRIAL TRIBUNALS, COMMISSION ON INDUSTRIAL RELATIONS AND INDUSTRIAL ARBITRATION BOARD

Clause 102 enables an aggrieved worker to bring before an industrial tribunal a complaint against an action taken by or on behalf of an employer which constitutes an unfair industrial practice. . . .The tribunal is enabled to make an order determining the rights of the parties and to award compensation against an employer.... Where an employee has been dismissed and a tribunal finds against the employer ... it shall consider and, where practicable, recommend re-engagement. Failing re-engagement it is to award compensation to be paid by the employer.

PART VII – RESTRICTIONS ON
LEGAL PROCEEDINGS

Clause 125 gives the Industrial Court exclusive jurisdiction in proceedings concerning the interpretation or enforcement of collective agreements.

Clause 128 continues in force, and extends certain immunities from actions in tort provided by the Trade Disputes Acts 1906 and 1965 in respect of acts done in contemplation of furtherance of an industrial dispute. In that situation it protects individuals from actions for conspiracy for combining to do something which would not be unlawful if done by a single person, and protects individuals who agree together to break their own contracts of employment or interfere with an employer's trade or business. The clause also affords protection from actions in tort for inducing a breach or interfering with the performance of a contract in contemplation or furtherance of an industrial dispute.

Clause 131 removes the protection formerly given by section 2 of the Trade Disputes Act 1906 in respect of picketing a person's home but provides that peaceful picketing (other than at a person's residence) shall not of itself constitute a criminal offence or a tort.

Clause 132 continues for registered and other organisations the protection against criminal proceedings for being in unlawful restraint of trade provided hitherto by sections 2 and 3 of the Trade Union Act 1871.

PART VIII – EMERGENCY PROCEDURES

Clause 134 enables the Secretary of State to apply to the Industrial Court for an order if he considers that industrial action has begun (or is likely to begin) which is likely to endanger the national economy, national security, public health or public order, and that a discontinuance or deferment of the industrial action would be conducive to a settlement by negotiation, conciliation or arbitration.

Clause 135 empowers the Industrial Court to make an order directing that no person specified in the order shall call or support a strike or lock-out, or threaten to do so, for the period of the order (not exceeding 60 days). It sets out the matters which the Court is to consider before it makes an order, the items to be specified in the order, its scope and the steps to be taken to secure its effective application.

Clause 137 enables the Secretary of State to apply to the Industrial Court for an order requiring a ballot to be taken where either there are emergency circumstances as defined in clause 134 or the livelihood of a substantial number of workers in any particular industry is likely to be seriously affected and there is reasonable doubt as to whether the industrial action has the support of the workers involved.

(ii) *Industrial Relations Bill 1970 (as brought from the House of Commons 25 March 1971)*

PART VI
NATIONAL INDUSTRIAL RELATIONS COURT INDUSTRIAL TRIBUNALS, COMMISSION ON INDUSTRIAL RELATIONS AND INDUSTRIAL ARBITRATION BOARD

95. (1) There shall be established a court to be known as the National Industrial Relations Court (in this Act referred to as 'the Industrial Court')

(2) The Industrial Court shall consist of –

(a) such number of judges as may be nominated from time to time by the Lord Chancellor from among the judges (other than the Lord Chancellor) of the High Court and the Court of Appeal;

(b) at least one judge of the Court of Session nominated from time to time by the Lord President of that Court; and

(c) such number of other members as may be appointed from time to time by Her Majesty.

112. (1) In any proceedings before the Industrial Court on a complaint under this Act where an award of compensation is made by the Court against a trade union (whether such an award is also made against any other

party to the proceedings or not) the compensation awarded against the trade union in those proceedings shall not exceed the appropriate limit.

(2) For the purpose of this section the appropriate limit –

    (a)   in the case of a trade union having a membership of less than 5,000, is £5,000;

    (b)   in the case of a trade union having a membership of 5,000 or more but less than 25,000, is £25,000;

    (c)   in the case of a trade union having a membership of 25,000 or more but less than 100,000, is £50,000; and

    (d)   in the case of a trade union having a membership of 100,000 or more, is £100,000.

4) *The Pentonville Dockers and the failure of the 1971 Act*
(Richard Barber, *Trade Unions and the Tories*, Bow Group, 240 High Holborn, London, p. 2)
[. . .] The second difficulty which the Government faced was amply borne out by the result of imprisoning four dockers for Contempt of Court in failing to lift their picketing of the Midland Cold Storage premises in East London. No sooner were the dockers in Pentonville than the Official Solicitor appeared like a fairy godmother to 'spring' them from jail and in the process deal the Act a mortal blow.

5) *The Miners' Strike, 1972 and the case of the Saltley coke depot, Birmingham*
(Arthur Scargill, *New Left Review*, no. 92, July–August 1975)
They [the police officers] said to us that we could only have twelve people on the picket line, and we said 'no, we're having all the pickets we've got and more besides.' So it was obvious that there was a confrontation in the air. . . . If I tell you we had 180 arrested, it gives you some idea. I was black and blue. They [the police] were punching with their heels into the crowd, they were hitting with elbows. They were in the crowds with plain clothes on, a copy of the *Morning Star* in one pocket and *The Workers Press* in the other shouting: 'Shove the bastards!', and as soon as you did you were arrested. They had telescopic lenses on top of the buildings, filming the incidents all the

time, they had police officers changing their uniforms each day with different numbers on them so you could not identify with them. [. . .] They were marching them down, seventy at a time, and they were changing them every hour. Seventy marching down like stormtroopers, you could see them on both sides. Then they started to bring them down every half-hour to intimidate. I yelled through my megaphone: 'We've got them on the run lads, they can only last half an hour instead of an hour'. . . .

6) *Social Contract, c. 1972 to the mid- and late 1970s*
(i)   *Labour Party intent*
        (Labour Party, *Labour's Programme For Britain*, London, 1972, p. 24)
        [A future Labour government would] separate the policies and machinery concerned with collective bargaining and industrial relations reform, from policies dealing with economic management, inflation and industrial power. . . . Once we have rid the nation of the divisive and irrelevant Tory legislation, we can begin to implement our programme of voluntary industrial relations reform, with the co-operation of trade unions.
(ii)   *TUC and Labour Party*
        (TUC-Labour Party Liaison Committee, *Economic Policy and the Cost of Living*, London, February, 1973, paragraph 20, p.7)
        . . . it will be the first task of that Labour Government [a future Labour government] on taking office, and having due regard to the circumstances at that time, to conclude with the TUC, on the basis of the understanding being reached on the Liaison Committee, a wide-ranging agreement on the policies to be pursued in all these aspects of our economic life and to discuss with them the order of priorities and their fulfilment.
(iii)   (Labour Party, *Britain Will Win with Labour*, London, October 1974, p. 5)
        Naturally the trade unions see their clearest loyalty to their own members. But the Social Contract is their free acknowledgement that they have other loyalties – to the members of other unions too, to pensioners, to the lower paid, to invalids, to the community as a whole.

(iv)   *The Trades Union Congress and the Social Contract*
        (Proceedings of 108th Annual Trades Union Congress, 1976,
        pp. 523–4)
        Lord Allen (Union of Shop and Distributive and Allied
        Workers) moved the following:
        This Congress welcomes the continued reduction in the
        annual rate of inflation which has arisen largely as a result of
        the TUC/Government initiative on prices and incomes. It is
        further encouraged by the response given by the trade union
        Movement to the Social Contract 1976/77, and recognizing
        the sacrifice and restrain shown by all workers during the
        economic crisis of the last 18 months, supports the view that a
        planned return to free collective bargaining should begin to
        take place in 1977. [The motion continued to suggest that a
        free-for-all could be avoided by rewarding skills, raising base
        rates, strengthening the Wage Inspectorate to protect the low
        paid and other arrangements.]
        . . . let me make it clear from the outset that this composite
        motion is not a thumbs down message to the Government.
        That was embodied in Motion 58. It is not an attack, implied
        or implicit, on the Government. It is not a retreat or a run to
        cover from the realities of Britain's economic and social
        problems now or in the immediate years ahead. Contracting
        out of our partnership with the Government is not part or
        parcel of this motion. This Government as Len Murray said in
        his statement – and I make no apology for repeating it – has
        done more for the trade union Movement in the space of a few
        years to advance the rights of working men and women, in
        some cases restoring rights removed by the former reactionary
        Government . . . than any previous administration in the
        United Kingdom. [. . .]

7) *The Trade Union Act, 1974 (1974 c. 52)*
        Repeal of the Industrial Relations Act, 1974
**Repeal of Industrial Relations Act 1971 and re-enactment of
certain provisions**
1–(1) The Industrial Relations Act 1971 is hereby repealed.
        Peaceful Picketing

15–(1) It shall be lawful for a person in contemplation or furtherance of a trade dispute to attend –

(a) at or near his own place of work, or

(b) if he is an official of a trade union, at or near the place of work of a member of that union whom he is accompanying and whom he represents,

for the purpose only of peacefully obtaining or communicating information, or peacefully persuading any person to work or abstain from working.

(2) If a person works or normally works –

(a) otherwise than at any one place, or

(b) at a place the location of which is such that attendance there for a purpose mentioned in subsection (1) above is impracticable,

his place of work form the purpose of that subsection shall be any premises of his employer from which he works or from which his work is administered.

(3) In the case of a worker who is not in employment where (a) his last employment was terminated in connection with a trade dispute or (b) the termination of his employment was one of circumstances giving rise to a trade dispute, subsection (1) above shall in relation to that dispute have effect as if any reference to his place of work were a reference to his former place of work.

8) *Trade Unions and the Tories, 1976*
(Richard Barber, *The Trade Unions and the Tories*, Bow Group, 240 High Holborn, London, 1976, pp. 1, 12)
The biggest single obstacle to the return of a Conservative Government is the . . . widespread belief that through inability to work with the Trade Unions it would be unable to govern. Not surprisingly, the present Labour Government and Trade Union leadership have skilfully sought to perpetrate this belief and they have been assisted by the regular failure of the Conservative Party to formulate a strategy to defend it.

The threat the Trade Unions pose to the Conservative Party has two distinct strands. First there is the threat that a Conservative Government could not pursue a successful economic policy because of its inability to control wage demands. This problem can almost certainly be overcome. Secondly, there is the threat that unless a Conservative Government pursues democratic policies approved by the Trade Unions the latter will begin a fresh round of strikes and industrial unrest of a kind which succeeded in destroying the last Heath administration. [. . .]

The current Conservative policy towards Trade Unions appears to consist of persuading their leaders that they have nothing to fear from a Conservative Government and that their legislative privileges will remain intact. [. . .] The weakness of this policy is that it is more likely to persuade voters that there is little to be gained by a change of Government and that they might just as well support the Party which is unequivocally subservient to Trade Union interests. [. . .]

CONCLUSION

The electoral problem which the Conservative Party faced in relation to Trade Union power is not insoluble. However, the present low key approach is misconceived for it serves to perpetuate the damaging impression that the power of Trade Unions is such that only a Government subservient to their wishes can hope to rule.

Main Points

(1) Force trade unions to face the economic consequences of their action.

(2) New Industrial Relations Act needed.

(3) Closed shop should be outlawed. . . .

(4) Postal ballots should be mandatory for all Trade Unions elections of Officers above a certain level. [. . .]

9) *Grunwick, 1976–77*
(*The Times*, 6 November 1976)

Firm's mail collected after union end ban
by Penny Simon

Staff of Grunwick Processing Laboratories in Willesden, north London, were allowed yesterday to start collecting mail that had piled up in the Post office depot at Cricklewood because of the ban imposed by the Union of Post Office Workers.

The postal workers called off their four days ban on Thursday after the firm, which processes films sent by post, indicated that it would be prepared to discuss the prolonged industrial dispute with the Advisory Conciliation and Arbitration Service. The postmen had taken their action in sympathy with the staff at Grunwick who have been on strike for 11 weeks over pay and conditions.

Mr. Justice Chapman, sitting in chambers at the High Court yesterday, refused to grant an ex-parte injunction against the Post Office and the Union of Post Office Workers. Instead he granted the company leave to give the notice to the Post Office and the union of an inter parte hearing next Tuesday.

The National Association of Freedom, which is backing the firm's action, said that it was seeking protection for the future. [. . .]

The strike began over an argument between a process worker and manager over pay and conditions. Others walked out in sympathy.

The firm pays £28 for a 40-hour week to process workers and £25 for a 35-hour week for those in office jobs. About 85 per cent of the process staff are Asian and 10 per cent West Indian. The strikers do not want to turn the dispute into a racial issue but they cannot help feeling that they are being exploited because they are not certain of their rights.

The strikers have joined the Association of Professional Executive, Clerical and Computer Staff, and are demanding that the union is recognized by the Grunwick management.

10) *The Winter of Discontent, 1978–9*
(*The Times*, 12 January and 22 January 1979)

(i)   The Prime Minister last night failed to prevent the Transport and General Workers' Union from declaring the national lorry drivers strike official.

Within an hour a state of emergency was declared in Ulster where the unofficial tanker strike is continuing and where the lorry drivers action has hit particularly badly [. . .]

Mr. Callaghan's uncharacteristic intervention in the dispute resulted in union officials being called to Downing Street for a meeting with the Premier and Senior Ministers.

He did not specifically ask the general secretary Mr. Moss Evans to abandon plans for making the strike official. But he virtually dared the union leaders to go ahead and face the consequences.

Mr. Callaghan pointed out that other members of the TGWU could be laid off although they were not directly involved in the dispute and that some haulage companies would not recover if the dispute became a drawn-out affair.

(ii)   With 1,500,000 public sector manual workers staging a 24-hour strike today local authority employers are likely to be pressed by the Energy Secretary, Mr. Peter Shore, to agree to terms of references for an inquiry into public service pay comparability.

Unions have made progress in agreeing terms with Ministers. The National Health Service employers – covering ambulancemen and hospital ancillary workers – have also agreed to go along with the general approach favoured by the Government.

But local government employees are holding out on two important issues, unions say. They want the study to be carried out by their own negotiating secretaries and they want to cover all employees – teachers, administrator, and professional, technical and clerical staff.

Even if an inquiry can be set up soon it will not stop the campaign of disruption beginning today. The Government says its results must apply to the next pay round and any award must be staged. Unions insist there must be better settlements for council workers than the 8–9 per cent the Government is currently proposing to allow.

Mrs. Shirley Williams, the Education Secretary, said last night: 'Tomorrow, many children will not be able to attend because of the caretakers strike, coupled with the appalling threat from some NUPE officials that children will be physically stopped from crossing the picket line.

'It is a legitimate action for NUPE members to withdraw their labour, but preventing children from going to school is a wholly unjustified use of the strike weapon.'

11) *The General Council and Wage Claims, 1979*
(General Council, *Guidelines for Negotiators,* 14 November 1978)

The General Council will not 'vet' claims, act as watchdogs . . . or scrutinise settlements. They believe on the contrary that negotiators should themselves accept the specific responsibility both in the

framing of claims and in the process of negotiation, to ensure that
the guidance both in spirit and in letter is fully respected.

12) *The Employment Act, 1980*
(1980 *c.* 42)
An Act to provide payments out of public funds towards trade
unions' expenditure in respect of ballots, for the use of employers'
premises in connection with ballots, and for the issue by the Secretary of State of Codes of Practice for the improvement of industrial
relations; to make provision in respect of exclusion or expulsion from
trade unions and otherwise to amend the law relating to workers,
employers, trade unions and employers' associations; to repeal section 1A of the Trade Union and Labour Relations Act 1974; and for
connected purposes.

[August 1980]

Trade union ballots and Codes of Practice
Payments in respect of secret ballots
1. (1) The Secretary of State may by regulations make a scheme
(below called 'the scheme') providing for payments by the
Certification Officer towards expenditure incurred by independent trade unions in respect of such ballots to which this section
applies as may be prescribed by the scheme.
(2) This section applies to a ballot if the purpose of the question to
be voted upon (or if there is more than one such question, the
purpose of any of them) falls within the purposes mentioned in
subsection (3) below.
(3) The purpose referred to in subsection (2) above are –
(a) obtaining a decision or ascertaining the views of members
of a trade union as to the calling or ending of a strike or other
industrial action;
(b) carrying out an election provided for by the rules of a trade
union;
(c) electing a worker who is a member of a trade union to be
representative of other members also employed by his
employer;
(d) amending the rules of a trade union;
(e) obtaining a decision in accordance with the Trade Union

(Amalgamations, etc.) Act of 1964 on a resolution to approve as instrument of amalgamation and transfer.

Exclusion from trade union membership

Unreasonable exclusion or expulsion from trade union

4–(1) This section applies to employment by an employer with respect to which it is the practice, in accordance with the union membership agreement, for the employee to belong to a specified trade union or one of a number of specified trade unions.

(2) Every person who is, or is seeking to be, in employment to which this section applies shall have the right –

(a) not to have an application for membership of a specified trade union unreasonably refused;

(b) not to be unreasonably expelled from a specified trade union.

Compensation

5–(1) A person who has made a complaint against a trade union under section 4 above which has been declared well founded may make an application in accordance with subsection (2) below for an award of compensation to be paid to him by the union.

Restrictions on Legal Liability

Picketing

15–(1) It shall be lawful for a person in contemplation or furtherance of a trade dispute to attend –

(a) at or near his place of work, or

(b) if he is an official of a trade union, at or near the place of work or a member of that union whom he is accompanying and whom he represents,

for the purpose only of peacefully obtaining or communicating information, or peacefully persuading any person to work or abstain from working.

Secondary action

17–(1) Nothing in section 13 of the 1974 Act shall prevent an act being actionable in tort on a ground specified in ... or (b) of that section in any case where –

(a) the contract concerned is not a contract of employment, and

(b) one of the facts relied upon for the purpose of establishing liability is that there has been secondary action which is not action satisfying the requirements of subsections (3), (4) or (5) below.

(2) For the purposes of this section there is secondary action in relation to a trade dispute when, and only when, a person –

(a)   induces another to break a contract of employment or interferes or induces another to interfere with its performance, or

(b)   threatens that a contract of employment under which he or another is employed will be broken or its performance interfered with, or that he will induce another to break a contract of employment or interfere with its performance, if the employer under the contract of employment is not a party to the trade dispute.

(3) Secondary action satisfies the requirements of this subsection if –

(a)   the purpose or principal purpose of the secondary action was directly to prevent or disrupt the supply during the dispute of goods or services between an employer who is party to the dispute and the employer under the contract of employment to which the secondary action relates; and [Numerous other examples on when secondary action might be regarded as legal – the purpose of which was to prevent secondary action in the form of the flying pickets that descended upon Saltley in 1972.]

13) *Employment Act 1982 (1982 c. 46)*

[Royal assent was given to this bill on 28 October 1982. It affected certain aspects of unfair dismissal and closed shop arrangements. It attempted to weaken the power which closed shop gives the unions by, for instance, increasing compensation to the individual who loses employment due to closed shop regulations but also by preventing any contract stipulating that trade-union or non-trade union labour should carry it out.]

Union membership or recognition requirement in contracts
Prohibition on union membership requirements

12–(1) Any term or condition of a contract for the supply of goods or services is void in so far as it purports –

(a)   to require that the whole, or some part, of the work done for purposes of the contract is to be done only by persons who are not members of trade unions or not members of a particular trade union; or

(b)   to require that the whole, or some part, of such work is to be done only by persons who are members of trade unions or members of a particular trade union.

14) *The National Graphical Association, Eddie Shah and the* Stockport Messenger, *1983*
(*The Times*, 18 November 1983)
The National Graphical Association print union was fined £50,000 for contempt of court – the first time a trade union has been found in contempt for defying the Government's new legislation.

It appears that the union might refuse to pay the fine leaving its assets open to sequestration! NGA policy is to refuse to recognise the employment acts of 1980 and 1982.

Last night the union said that it would seek financial and industrial assistance from the TUC and would also call upon the General Council to reaffirm its support for the NGA dispute with the Messenger Group Newspapers of Stockport. [. . .]

Last month the TUC general council issued a statement supporting the NGA's claim for a closed shop agreement with the Messenger Group but it may be unwilling to support the union further after the mass demonstrations and violent clashes on the picketlines at the Messenger Group's Warrington print works this week.

The NGA has been trying to prevent the distribution of six free newspapers published by the Group, and claim that its chairman Mr. Eddie Shah has reneged on an agreement to conclude a closed shop. Mr. Shah denies this.

At the High Court in Manchester, yesterday, Mr. Justice Eastham ruled that the NGA was deliberately flouting the injunction granted to Mr. Shah on October 14, which restrained the union from deliberately interfering with the Messenger Group's business. [. . .]

There was also evidence that some 600 people had attended outside the Warrington premises in an attempt to disrupt business. The judge said that the group's chairman had said that this threatened the well-being of his workers and interfered with the production of newspapers.

'I am satisfied, whatever the intention of the union, this turned out to be unlawful picketing,' he said.

Under the 1980 Act picketing is only lawful at the picket's current or former place of employment.

'The policy of the union, so I am told by a senior official, is to continue with this sort of conduct whatever the attitude of the courts,' said the judge.

'If there are continued breaches of the injunctions, the time may well come when the union is to be taught to obey the law by having all their assets sequested.'

But the judge did not think this was yet the time to agree the sequestration of all the union's assets. [. . .]

15) *The Miners' Strike, 1984–5*

(i)　(*The Guardian*, 15 March 1984)

Yorkshire picket goes on despite court's injunction

The National Coal Board yesterday secured a High Court injunction instructing Yorkshire miners to call off their flying pickets in the deepening coal crisis, but later miners crossed the border into Nottinghamshire.

More than 150 pickets gathered at the Ollerton Colliery near Worksop but a strong police force of about 300 prevented them forming a cordon across the colliery entrance. [. . .] The NCB said that 22 of 25 Nottinghamshire pits were working normally. . . .

(ii)　(*Proceedings of the 116th Annual Trades Union Congress, 1984*, pp. 399–400, 403 and appendix 5)

Miners' Strike 1984

Mr. A. Scargill (National Union of Mineworkers) moved the following motion:

Congress records its total support for the National Union of Mineworkers and its campaign to save pits, jobs and mining communities . . .

Congress reaffirms its commitment to an integrated energy policy, with an annual coal output target of 200 million tonnes as we move into the next century.

Congress condemns the police-state tactics against striking miners and their families and demands that the Government introduce legislation to render the police democratically accountable to the communities they are employed to serve. The police must never be used again, as at the present time, against unarmed working people exercising traditional trade union rights. Congress, recalling its total opposition to the 1980 and 1982 Employment Acts, as reaffirmed overwhelmingly last year, demands the immediate repeal of all anti-union legislation and agrees that, to that end, all affiliated unions be called upon to join in the mightiest mobilisation of the power and strength of the Movement behind the Wembley Conference [of 1982 when the TUC declared its intent to oppose the Conservative government's trade union legislation] decisions and for the maximum solidarity and support for every section and group of workers in struggles for jobs, defence of working conditions and trade union rights.

[. . .] This dispute has cost the taxpayer £4 billion so far. Lost production amounts to over £2 billion. That is the price that the Government and the coal board are prepared to pay to try to defeat the NUM as a step to inflicting a defeat on the entire trade union and labour Movement.

I warned Congress last year that we could not accept the balance sheet mentality of someone like Ian MacGregor. He talks about investment policy and industry. He talks about the company and the business, but he never talks about human beings, whose greatest investment is with their very lives in the industry. That is what should concern us in the trade union and Labour movement.

I have heard references to violence. I accept that we have had violence. Is it not an act of violence to destroy a man's job or that of his son and daughter? Surely that is an act of violence that should be condemned by every man and woman in the Movement. It is an act of violence to say to the miners at collieries like Polmaise or Cortonwood that the pits have five years or 20 years of life and to transfer miners from other pits on the promise that the pits have a worthwhile life ahead of them, and then to tell them one week later that the pits are closing? Surely that is an act of violence. [. . .]

Mr. E. A. Hammond (Electrical, Electronic Telecommunications and Plumbing Union) [. . .] Hitler would have been proud of you lot. If they [the miners' leaders] would do this, have a national ballot and disavow the political objectives of the strike, I would recommend to my executive that we ballot all our members in coal-fired stations to stop work in the miners' support. But the political objectives could not be abandoned and the miners could not have a national ballot: and the NUM leadership thus denied their members in May the possibility of real support, not empty words or conscience money, but real support. It is hard to say to tens of thousands of decent miners who have been out for six months that their leaders have misled them, that they cannot win Scargill's sort of victory. [. . .]

General Council Statement on
Mining Dispute

The General Council condemn the NCB's efforts abetted by the Government to run down the coal industry and affirm total support for the following:

(i) support for the National Union of Mineworkers' objectives of saving pits, jobs and mining communities;

(ii) a concerted campaign to raise money to alleviate hardship in the coalfields and to maintain the union financially:

(iii) to make the dispute more effective by:

    (a) not moving coal or coke, or oil substituted for coal or coke across NUM official picket lines, or using such materials taken across NUM official picket lines;

    (b) not using oil which is substituted for coal.

The NUM acknowledge that the practical implementation of these points will need detailed discussions with the General Council and agreement with unions who would be directly concerned.

The General Council call for a fresh commitment of all to an expanding coal industry.

The General Council call on the NCB to resume negotiations immediately with the NUM to resolve this damaging and costly dispute in line with the Plan For Coal.

16) *Trade Union Act, 1984 (1984 c. 49)*
PART I
SECRET BALLOTS FOR TRADE UNION ELECTIONS
Duty of trade unions to hold elections for certain positions

1.–(1) Subject to the following provisions of this Part of this Act, it shall be the duty of every trade union (notwithstanding anything in its rules) to secure –

(a)   that every person who is voting member of the principal executive of the union holds that position by virtue of having been elected as such a member at an election in relation to which section 2 of this Act has been satisfied; and

(b)   that no person remains such a member for the period of more than five years without being re-elected at such an election.

PART II
SECRET BALLOTS BEFORE INDUSTRIAL ACTION

10–(1) Nothing in section 13 of the 1974 Act shall prevent an act done by a trade union without the support of a ballot from being actionable (whether or not against a trade union) on the ground that it induced a person to break his contract of employment or to interfere with its performance.

(2) Nothing in section 13 of the 1974 Act shall prevent an act done by a trade union from being actionable in tort (whether or not against the trade union) on the ground that it induced a person to break a commercial contract or to interfere with its performance where –

(a)   one of the facts relied upon for the purpose of establishing liability is that the union induced another person to break his contract of employment or to interfere with its performance; and

(b)   by virtue of subsection (1) above, nothing in section 13 or the 1974 Act would prevent the act of inducement referred to in paragraph (a) above from being actionable in tort.

(3) For the purpose of subsection (1) above, an act shall be taken as having been done with the support of a ballot if, but only if –

(a)   the trade has held a ballot in respect of the strike or other industrial action in the course of which the breach of interference referred to in subsection (1) above occurred;

(b) the majority of those voting in the ballot have answered 'Yes' to the appropriate question;

(c) the first authorisation of any relevant act ... took place after the date of the ballot and before the expiry of the period of four weeks beginning with that date. [. . .]

PART III
POLITICAL FUNDS AND OBJECTS

12.(2) A resolution [to form a political fund] shall, if it has not been previously rescinded, cease to have effect –

(a) on the expiry of the period of ten years beginning with the date (whether before or after the commencement date) of the ballot on which it was passed; or

(b) if a ballot is held before the expiry of that period and the result of the ballot is that a new resolution is not passed, on the expiry of the period of two weeks beginning with the date of the ballot.

(4) Where a trade union holds a ballot at a time when a resolution (the 'old resolution') is in force in respect of that union and the result of the ballot is that a new resolution is passed, the old resolution shall be treated as rescinded on the passing of the new resolution.

17) *News International, Wapping and Rupert Murdoch and the Print Unions, 1986–1987*

(i)   (*The Guardian*, 22 January 1986)

Patrick Wintour reports on manoeuvres that
have led to the
next bout of blood-letting in Fleet Street
Mr. Murdoch's bouquet of barbed wire

The growing concern over Rupert Murdoch's newspaper plant at Wapping has the potential to develop into a trauma for the Labour movement on the scale of the miners' strike. Fundamental issues are involved – the right to strike, the rule of law in the workplace, industrial relations, the authority of the TUC over its affiliates and finally the ability of the trade union movement to survive in the face of rapid technological change.

The immediate reason for the crisis is that for the first time in decades Fleet Street management are in the driving seat and finding life at the wheel quite exhilarating. Correspondingly the print unions are in retreat. In an attempt to prevent a rout the unions are edging towards an attempted shutdown of the Rupert Murdoch press in protest at News International demands for a legally binding no-strike deal as a precondition of the traditional print unions being represented at Wapping.

The difficulties facing the union in any such dispute are daunting. Few employers have prepared so long or so thoroughly for such an eventuality as has Murdoch. His £100 million Wapping plant has been turned from a white elephant left idle due to union opposition since 1983 into a technological time machine capable of seeing Murdoch's emergence from the Fleet Street production unions. [. . .]

The workers on Murdoch's four national newspaper titles know that if they strike Murdoch is set to press his advantages. For instance, it is open to the company to respond to any strike by immediately sacking those in dispute without compensation, on the grounds that they have repudiated their employment contracts. As one Times newspaper executive put it, 'Once these people go out it will be the last time they do, they won't come back, never, never.'

Instead Murdoch will transfer his production to Wapping and its sister plant in Glasgow, relying on TNT hauliers to distribute the papers.

The success of the strategy is critically dependent upon the cooperation of the journalists and the printing capacity of the Wapping premises. The print unions are banking on Wapping being unable to churn out the 4.5 million copies of *The Sun* or *The Times* currently being printed each day. [. . .]

No matter how much either party may wish to avoid it, the Wapping crisis is likely to become increasingly a re-run of the recent clashes between the electricians and the TUC over the constitutional authority of the TUC over its affiliates. But unlike the clash over state money for ballots – which the electricians won – the TUC cannot afford to back down. The issue goes to the heart of the Bridlington procedure to organise Collective bargaining in union's sphere of influence.

The electricians may attempt to avoid outright flouting of the

TUC by holding back from signing an agreement with Murdoch covering Wapping, but the decision to hold separate talks with the company and the very act of electricians printing papers at Wapping, is likely to be seen as sufficient grounds for disciplining the union. [. . .]

(ii)   (*The Proceedings of the 119th Annual TUC, 1987*, p. 39–43)

[In an extensive outline of the dispute and the actions of the General Council in dealing with it the following comments were made. It noted that it had not initially condemned the EEPTU but asked it to fall in line with the TUC support for the print unions, and noted the 'last offer' of News International on 17 September, on terms of compensation for those print workers who would lose their jobs.]

[. . .] The main allegation was that the EETPU had secretly colluded in providing workers to work at Wapping. The NGA challenged the EETPU to deny the allegations and, in the absence of the denial, the NGA called upon the General Council to establish the truth or otherwise of the allegation. [. . .]

On December 17, the General Council's attention was drawn to the arrangement for a demonstration to be held at Wapping and Kinning Park plants on January 24 to coincide with the anniversary of the start of the dispute. [. . .]

[. . .] At this demonstration at Wapping there were violent scenes of confrontation between elements amongst some of the demonstrators and some of the police. The General Secretary condemned the violence and called upon the Home Secretary to establish an independent inquiry into events. [. . .]

End of Dispute

On February 5, SOGAT National Executive Council held a special meeting. The union had been told by News International that it would return to the Courts on February 6 to . . . seek sequestration of the union's assets. In view of this, the SOGAT Executive Council concluded they had no alternative but to end the dispute. The AEU withdrew the same day. . . . The NGA decided to withdraw from the dispute on February 6 . . .

(iii)   (*Proceedings of the 120th Annual Trades Union Congress, 1988,*
        pp. 45, 404–11)
        Letter of censure
        On June 17, the following letter of censure was sent to the
        EETPU.
        'I am writing on behalf of the General Council to confirm
        their decision on 25 May to censure the Union through its
        Executive Council and General Secretary for a breach of the
        second of the TUC directives issued in February 1986. That
        directive was broached by the temporary admission of 20 people
        at Wapping to membership of the EETPU. [. . .]
        Wapping has been termed an "unmitigated disaster" by your
        Executive Council. A number of affiliated unions and several
        thousand workers suffered particularly serious damage. The
        TUC's standing was harmed. The EETPU itself has not been
        unscathed. . . . The Union had been in the wrong originally
        and, as a result had had directives imposed upon it by the TUC
        which it accepted in full.
        It was therefore highly surprising and a matter of great
        concern to the General Council that it should subsequently
        appear that one of the directives had not been complied with
        and that the Union should (on the Union's own internal report
        point out) "sail perilously close to the wind". In respect of
        certain other directives. [. . .]
        [. . .] The General Council have now decided that the censure
        should be included in the Annual Report to the 1988 Congress
        and that I should deliver it publicly to Congress.'
        Mr. E. A Hammond (EETPU)
        [. . .] I said in my statement to the General Council that 'In the
        light of our experience, in the previous eighteen months, we
        now assert (i) that the EETPU is the victim of a plan carried in
        early 1987 by the three unions whose influence is dominant in
        the TUC Councils, (ii) that the plan has presently come to
        fruition in a special review body, but it has already influenced
        dispute committee decisions, (iii) that we have not been treated
        fairly by the disputes committees, and (iv) that the TUC should
        listen to members, to people, and not just to unions. In disputed
        membership situations, the individual concerned should have

the right to choose their union and together with their employer the type of agreement covering their employment.'

18) *Trade Union reactions to the 1988 Employment Act and other issues*
(i) (*Proceedings of the 119th Annual TUC, 1987*, p. 32)
On February 24, the Government published A Green Paper 'Trade Unions and Their Members' which proposed further legislative changes affecting trade unions. Its main proposals included: creating a legal right for union members not to be disciplined for not taking industrial action that has been supported by a majority of the workers concerned in a secret ballot; placing new legal constraints of the application of union funds; making union membership agreements legally enforceable; requiring union executive elections and political fund ballots to be fully postal and independently supervised, extending the 1984 Trade Union Acts's statutory election requirements to cover non-voting executive members, President and General Secretaries. . . .

The TUC issued an immediate statement accusing the Government of rushing out the Green Paper for electoral reasons. [. . .]

(ii) (*Proceedings of the 120th Annual TUC, 1988*, p. 1, extract from the General Council Report to Congress)
During the past year the rate of decline of union membership has slowed significantly and 33 of our unions have actually recorded an increase in membership, providing a good basis on which to build for the future. [. . .]

The defence of the National Health Service features prominently in the General Council's progress of work. Fears that the Service was being undermined by the current Administration were translated into a massive TUC March and Rally in London and pressure was maintained through a series of events leading to the NHS's fortieth birthday on July 5.

A central theme throughout the year was the need to protect working people and their families from a range of damaging legislation such as the Education Reform Bill and the 1988 Employment Act. A campaign designed to highlight the iniquities of the proposed Community Charge got under way and the People's Petition Against the Poll Tax supported by the General Council recorded over half a million signatures.

19) *Trade Union Congress Membership, 1978–1989*

1978	11.8 million	1984	10.0 million
1979	12.1 million	1985	9.8 million
1980	12.1 million	1986	9.5 million
1981	11.6 million	1987	9.2 million
1982	11.0 million	1988	9.1 million
1983	10.5 million	1989	8.6 million

BIBLIOGRAPHY

PRIMARY SOURCES

Amalgamated Society of Engineers, *Abstract Report of the Council's Proceedings from June 1st, 1870, to December 31st 1872*

Amalgamated Society of Engineers, minutes and records of the Halifax branches, Calderdale branch of West Yorkshire Archives

Amalgamated Society of Engineers, rules

Amalgamated Society of Engineers, *To All Classes of Workmen in the Engineering Industry* (1892)

Amalgamated Society of Railway Servants, Misc. collection British Library of Political and Economic Science

Amalgamated Union of Dyers' Collection, Bradford branch of West Yorkshire Archives

Barber, R., *Trade Unions and the Tories* (London, Bow Group, 1976)

Barnsley Chronicle

Beveridge Collection on Munitions, British Library of Political and Economic Science

Board of Trade, *Strikes and Lockouts Report*, various

Bradford Observer

Bradford Trades and Labour Council, Minutes

Bradford Typographical records, J. B. Priestley, University of Bradford

Cabinet Papers, Public Record Office

Citrine, W., *Men and Work* (1964)

Communist Party of Great Britain, circulars, South Yorkshire

Conservative Political Centre, *Industrial Advance* (1966)

Gallacher, W. and Paton, J., *The Collective Contract: Towards Industrial Democracy: A Memorandum on Workers' Control* (Paisley Trades Council, 1917)

Gast, J., *Calumny Defeated: or, A Compleat Vindication of the Conduct of the Working Shipwrights, during the late Dispute with their Employers* (Deptford, 1802)

Glass Bottle Makers of Yorkshire United Trade Protection Society, *National Conference Reports, 1893–5, Vol. 1 (First to Twenty-Third Inclusive)* (1908) and various circulars

Hansard

Home Office records, Public Record Office

Huddersfield Examiner

In Place of Strife: A Policy for Industrial Relations (Cmnd 3888, 1969)

Labour Magazine

Labour Party, *Britain Will Win with Labour* (London, 1974)

Labour Party, *Labour Party Leaflet, no. 49*

Labour Party, *Labour's Programme For Britain* (London, 1972)

Leeds Intelligencer

Leeds Mercury

Leeds Trades and Labour Council, Minutes

Liverpool Council of Action collection

London Trades Council, Annual Reports

Loveless, George, *The Victims of Whiggery being a statement of the Prosecution Experienced by the Dorchester Labourers in 1834*

Mann, Tom, *Tom Mann's Memoirs* (1923)

Mann, Tom, *What a Compulsory Eight-Hour Day Means to the Workers* (1886)

Mann, Tom and Tillett, Ben, *The 'New' Trade Unionism* (1890)

Miners' Federation of Great Britain, Minutes and Correspondence copies in the Miners' Office, Barnsley

Ministry of Munitions records, Public Record Office

Murphy, J. T., *The Workers' Committee* (Sheffield, 1918)

National Association for the Promotion of Social Sciences, 1860

National Review

National Union of Railwaymen's Strike Committee Minute Book, Birmingham 1926

National Union of Textile Workers, records, Kirklees branch of West Yorkshire Archives

New Left Review

Northern Star

O'Keefe, T. J., *Rise and Progress of the National Amalgamated Labourers' Union of G. B. & Ireland* (1891)

Place, Francis, MSS
Read, W. J., *The Clerk's Charter*
Records of the Borough of Nottingham 1800–1835 (1952), VIII
Royal Commission on Labour, reports 1892–1895
Royal Commission on Trade Unions, 1867–9
Royal Commission on Trade Unions and Employers' Association, 1965–1968
Saddleworth Union records
Sheffield Independent
South Wales Miners' Reform Committee. *Miners' Next Step* (1912)
Special Bulletin of the Merseyside Council of Action, 1926
Spencer-Stanhope Collection
Tester, John, 'History of Bradford Contest', MSS
Statutory Laws, *including Combination Acts and others*
St Helens Labour News
Sunday Times
The British Worker
The Clarion
The Crisis
The Guardian
The Illustrated London News
The Industrial Syndicalist
The National Clerks' Association, 1893
The Pioneer
The Potters' Examiner and Workman's Advocate
The Times
The Worker
Thorne, W., *My Life's Battles*
Trades Newspaper
Trades Union Commission: Sheffield, 1867
Trades Union Congress Annual Reports: Proceedings of . . .
TUC, *Report to Congress: Trade Union Structure* (1965)
TUC, *The General Council of the Trades Union Congress; its Powers, Functions and Work* (London, TUC, 1925)
TUC General Council, *Guidelines for Negotiators* (1978)
TUC-Labour Party Liaison Committee, *Economic Policy and the The Cost of Living*

Voice of the West Riding
Webb Collection, British Library of Political and Economic Science
Wiltshire General and Agricultural Workers' Union, *The Report of the Inaugural Meeting held at Swindon, December 12th, 1892; Speeches by Mr. Keir Hardie MP . . .*
Workers' Bulletin
Workers' Chronicle
Workers' Weekly
Worsted Committee records, J.B. Priestley Library, University of Bradford
Yorkshire Factory Times

SECONDARY SOURCES
Anderson, G., *Victorian Clerk* (1976)
Aspinall, A., *The Early English Trade Unions: Documents from the Home Office Records, Public Record Office* (London, Batchworth Press, 1949)
Bagwell, P.S., *The Railwaymen* (1963)
Bain, G.S., *The Growth of White-Collar Unionism* (Oxford, 1970)
Bullock, A., *The Life and Times of Ernest Bevin* Vol. 1 (1960)
Clegg, H.A., *A History of British Trade Unions* Vol. II, 1911–1933 (OUP, 1985)
Clegg, H.A., Fox, A. and Thompson, A.F., *A History of British Trade Unions since 1889*, vol. I (OUP, 1964)
Clements, R.V., 'British Trade Unionism and Popular Political Economy, 1850–1875', *Econ. Hist. Review*, 1961
Coates, K. and Topham, T., *Industrial Democracy in Great Britain* (1968)
Duffy, A.E.P., 'New Unionism: a re-appraisal', *Econ. Hist. Review*, 1961–2
Exell, T., *A Brief History of the Weavers of the County of Gloucestershire* (Stroud, 1838)
Farman, C., *The General Strike May 1926* (London, Rupert Hart-David, 1972)
Fox, A., *A History of the National Union of Boot and Shoe Operatives* (Oxford, 1958)
Hay, D., Linebaugh, P., Thompson, E.P., *Albion's Fatal Tree. Crime and Society in Eighteenth-Century England* (Penguin, 1977)

Hinton, J., *The First Shop Stewards' Movement* (London, George Allen & Unwin, 1973)

Hobsbawm, E.J., *Labouring Men* (London, Weidenfeld & Nicolson, 1964)

Hobsbawm, E.J., *Labour's Turning Point 1880–1900* (Brighton, Harvester Press edition, 1974)

Hobsbawm, E.J., *Worlds of Labour: Further Studies in the History of Labour* (London, Weidenfeld and Nicolson, 1984)

History of the TUC 1868–1968 (London, 1968)

Horn, Pamela, *Joseph Arch* (Kineton, The Roundwood Press, 1971)

Hyman, R., *The Workers' Union* (Oxford, 1971)

James, J., *History of Worsted Manufacture in England* (1857)

Liddington, J. and Norris, J., *One Hand Tied Behind Us* (Virago, 1978)

Lovell, J., *British Trade Unions 1875–1933* (London, Macmillan, 1977)

MacDonald, G.W. and Gospel, H.F., 'The Mond-Turner Talks, 1927–1933: A Study in Industrial Co-operation', *Historical Journal*, xvi. 4 (December 1973)

Milne-Bailey, W., *Trade Union Documents: Compiled and Edited with an Introduction by W. Milne Bailey* (London, Bell, 1929)

More, C., *Skill and the English Working Class* (1980)

Musson, A.E., *British Trade Unions 1800–1875* (London, Macmillan, 1972)

Musson, A.E., *The Typographical Association* (Oxford, 1954)

Pelling, H., *A History of British Trade Unionism* (London, Penguin, 4th edition, 1987)

Pelling, H., *The Origins of the Labour Party 1880–1900* (OUP, 1965 edition)

Phelps Brown, E.H., *The Growth of British Industrial Relations* (London, Macmillan, 1959 and 1965)

Phelps Brown, E.H., *The Origins of Trade Union Power* (OUP, 1986)

Phillips, G.A., *The General Strike: The Politics of Industrial Conflict* (London, Weidenfeld and Nicolson, 1976)

Postgate, R., *Builders' History*

Pribicevic, B., *The Shop Stewards' Movement and Workers' Control, 1910–1922* (Oxford, 1959)

Price, R., *Labour in British Society: An Interpretative History* (London, Croom Helm, 1986)

Prothero, I., *Artisans & Politics in Early Nineteenth-Century London: John Gast and His Times* (Folkestone, Dawson, 1979)

Renshaw, P., *The General Strike* (London, Eyre Methuen, 1975)

Rule, J., (ed.), *British Trade Unionism* (London, Longman, 1988)

Rule, J., *The Experience of Labour in Eighteenth Century Industry* (London, Croom Helm, 1981)

Skelley, J., *1926 The General Strike* (London, Lawrence and Wishart, 1976)

Stedman Jones, G., *Languages of Class: Studies in English working-class history 1832–1982* (Cambridge, 1982)

Taplin, E., *The Dockers' Union: A study of the National Union of Dock Labourers, 1889–1922* (Leicester University Press, 1985)

Tolliday, S. and Zeitlin, J., *Shopfloor Bargaining and the State* (1985)

Turner, H.A., *Trade Union Growth, Structure and Policy* (London, Allen & Unwin, 1962)

Webb, S. & B., *Industrial Democracy (1920 edn)*

Webb, S. & B., *The History of Trade Unionism* (1894)

ACKNOWLEDGEMENTS

The list of those to whom I must express thanks is lengthy. The librarians and archivists of West Yorkshire have given generously of their time and knowledge and, though I cannot mention every name, I must express my thanks to Dr Alan Betteridge, David James, and the library and archive staffs in Leeds, Bradford, Huddersfield and Halifax. In addition, I must thank the staff at the British Library of Economic and Social Science, at the London School of Economics.

Although financial help was limited I did receive some research funds from Professor Mike Page, Dean of Research of Huddersfield Polytechnic, without which it would have been difficult to visit the British Library of Political and Economic Science and the Public Record Office, Kew, London.

My colleagues at Huddersfield were more than helpful (especially Dr David Wright and Peter Wood), as were many other historians who live and work in West Yorkshire. But I must, above all, thank the late Jack Reynolds, who first shaped my thoughts on trade unions and Labour history more than a quarter of a century ago.

I would also like to thank Stephen Bird, the Labour Party's Archivist, for permission to quote from the records of the Labour Party. Crown copyright material in the Public Record Office is reproduced by permission of the Controller of Her Majesty's Stationary Office. I must thank the Trades Union Congress for permission to quote from their annual reports, the British Library of Political and Economic Science for permission to use documents from the Webb Collection, and *The Guardian* and *The Times* for permission to use extracts from their reports on industrial action and trade union matters. The author and the publisher also wish to apologise for any inadvertent infringement of copyright and have sought to keep within the publishers' convention in the use of some recently published secondary sources. In every case, the documents have been fully attributed.